What Your Colleagues Are Saying

Dave Stuart's These 6 Things *is among the most helpful, passionate, practical, and insightful teaching resources I have ever come across. It is brimming with simple, practical—and exceedingly realistic—suggestions and strategies for immediately improving the quality of schooling and student work—starting tomorrow.* These 6 Things *is an impressive and arrestingly written book by a working teacher. I hope it gets a wide reading.*

—Mike Schmoker
Author of *FOCUS: Elevating the Essentials to
Radically Improve Student Learning*

Dave Stuart has an important insight: that a skill kids already know how to do, which is argue, also happens to be a central one in the new standards for college readiness. In Stuart's wonderful book, These 6 Things, *he draws extensively on his own classroom experience to show teachers how to help students use their everyday argument skills to energize the classroom, meet these standards, and achieve success. An extra treat is that Stuart himself writes in a down to earth language refreshingly devoid of Educationese. If you're a teacher or school administrator interested in turning your students onto argument, Dave Stuart is your man!*

—Gerald Graff and Cathy Birkenstein
Authors of *They Say/I Say: The Moves That Matter in Academic Writing*

What I appreciate most about Dave Stuart's book These 6 Things: How to Focus Your Teaching on What Matters Most *is that he is one of us: a classroom teacher sharing with us what works for him in ways that will work for us in our own classrooms with our own students. When I read about the poster on his class wall that says "[In this class] we are all about becoming better thinkers, readers, writers, speakers, and people," I think of the years of hard work I have watched Dave Stuart put into his craft and this book, and how the same statement applies to Dave Stuart himself: He is all about becoming a better thinker, reader, writer, speaker, person—and teacher, and showing us how we can do the same.*

—Jim Burke
Author of *Your Literacy Standards Companion*

T0354156

If you're searching for balance as a teacher of literacy, search no further. Dave Stuart Jr. offers a calming voice for a frenzied profession and provides practical classroom strategies that will help you teach adolescents in the rich and meaningful ways they deserve without becoming overwhelmed. This book is packed with ideas that are research-based, student-centered, and most of all, workable.

This is a book written for classroom teachers by a classroom teacher, one who understands the struggle of teachers to navigate the demands of standards and content and offers an accessible, sensible formula for classroom success. Dave is a guide, a mentor, an advocate, and a fellow traveler on the road to nurturing and educating students through positive, focused instruction.

—Barry Gilmore

Co-author of *Academic Moves and Common Core CPR*

In These 6 Things, *Dave Stuart provides a framework and road map that is of value to educators at all stages of their careers, from novices to veterans. He reminds us all to focus in on the things that are most important and to do them well. Much of the book creates opportunities for the kinds of reflection and self-analysis in which most teachers do not have the opportunity to engage. A great tool for new teachers and seasoned teachers alike to find their "Everest" and pursue it.*

—David T. Conley, PhD

Professor at University of Oregon and
Director for Center for Educational Policy Research

These 6 Things *is a joyful shot in the arm for experienced teachers as well as for novices. Is it possible to consolidate the most important aspects of teaching into one book—complete with relevant, engaging examples that have been tried and proven by teachers in various content areas? I wouldn't have thought so, but Dave has managed to do it, all while affirming, encouraging, and acting as a "guide on the side" for those who may feel unsure about trying out new activities with their students. You'll want to carve out some reading time for this book. The journey will yield wonderful rewards for both teachers and students.*

—ReLeah Cossett Lent

Author of *This Is Disciplinary Literacy: Reading, Writing, Thinking and Doing . . . Content Area by Content Area*

these
6
things

How to
Focus Your
Teaching
on **What
Matters
Most**

To my colleagues near and far
who have read my work
over the years and encouraged me:
this book is for you.

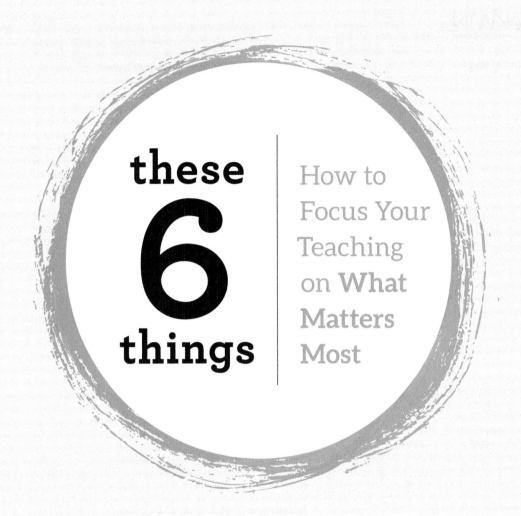

these
6
things

How to Focus Your Teaching on **What Matters Most**

Dave Stuart Jr.

CL CORWIN LITERACY

FOR INFORMATION:

Corwin

A SAGE Company

2455 Teller Road

Thousand Oaks, California 91320

(800) 233-9936

www.corwin.com

SAGE Publications Ltd.

1 Oliver's Yard

55 City Road

London EC1Y 1SP

United Kingdom

SAGE Publications India Pvt. Ltd.

B 1/I 1 Mohan Cooperative Industrial Area

Mathura Road, New Delhi 110 044

India

SAGE Publications Asia-Pacific Pte. Ltd.

3 Church Street

#10-04 Samsung Hub

Singapore 049483

Senior Acquisitions Editor: Tori Bachman

Editorial Development Manager: Julie Nemer

Editorial Assistant: Sharon Wu

Production Editors: Amy Schroller and Laureen Gleason

Copy Editor: Diana Breti

Typesetter: C&M Digitals (P) Ltd.

Proofreader: Wendy Jo Dymond

Indexer: Maria Sosnowski

Cover and Interior Designer: Gail Buschman

Marketing Manager: Brian Grimm

Note: Unless otherwise indicated, photos are by Dave Stuart Jr.

Printed in the United States of America

ISBN 978-1-5063-9103-8

This book is printed on acid-free paper.

18 19 20 21 22 10 9 8 7 6 5 4 3 2 1

Contents

PART III: LITERACY-RICH LEARNING EXPERIENCES   134

Photo by Alyssa Roelofs.

CHAPTER ONE
Teaching Toward Everest

Clarity of purpose . . . consistently predicts how people do their jobs . . . . The fact is, motivation and cooperation deteriorate when there is a lack of purpose. If a team does not have clarity . . . problems will fester and multiply. When there is a lack of clarity, people waste time and energy on the trivial many.

—GREG MCKEOWN (2014, P. 121)

Greatness and nearsightedness are incompatible. Meaningful achievement depends on lifting one's sights and pushing toward the horizon.

—DANIEL PINK (2009, P. 58)

In May 1953, Edmund Hillary and Tenzing Norgay, pictured in Figure 1.1 on the next page, faced a daunting task that no one had yet accomplished: ascending Mount Everest and living to tell the tale. Unlike climbers of Everest today, Hillary and Norgay did not have the benefit of charted territory. They faced the death zone, a place where the body is actively dying. They were climbing at an altitude nearly as high as the airplanes of their day flew. The risks were many, and the reward was glory.

For two important reasons, the work that you and I try to do each year is far more challenging than what those two men faced in 1953. Sure, there's little chance that a day in the classroom will end with frostbite on our noses or our frozen corpses buried by avalanche, but our job is still tougher.

First of all, Norgay and Hillary's task was fairly simple to articulate, and ours isn't. If you were to ask one hundred random people who knew of Norgay and Hillary back in early 1953, "Hey, what are these gentlemen trying to accomplish this year?" most answers would be identical:

"They're trying to climb Mount Everest. Duh."

FIGURE 1.1 • Sir Edmund Hillary and Tenzing Norgay, on May 29, 1953, after completing the first successful ascent of Mount Everest.

But if I were to poll one hundred people in *your* life this year, asking them, "Hey, what is this teacher supposed to accomplish in her job this year?" I'd be shocked if there were even two identical answers, and I wouldn't be surprised if there were some answers that seemed to describe an entirely different profession in a wholly different galaxy. Depending on whether the respondent was your administrator or one of your students or a community member or your state's governor or your school of education professor, I'd be in for a whirlwind of ideas and expectations, wouldn't I? There would be multiple *full-time jobs* represented in those responses.

This incoherence of purpose and its attendant avalanche of expectations is a more insurmountable obstacle than a thousand Everests on top of one another. If this book—or any book—is going to help our teaching practice, then this mountain must be demolished. We can't ignore it. So, let's do something crazy, shall we? Let's place the power of purpose setting in the hands of some people who might know a thing or two: you and me, the people on the ground doing the work alongside our students. Right now, before you do anything else, I'd like you to take half a minute and, without mental editing or revision, answer something in writing:

> *What, in a single sentence, is your Everest this school year? What do you hope that your work will amount to?*

Be as specific as you can be. Ideally, you'd like to know during a given lesson whether or not you have made progress toward your Everest.

My Everest: _____

_____

_____

If you visit my room and sit with my students during a lesson, you'll see, just left of the whiteboard, a simple poster that reads "We are all about becoming better thinkers, readers, writers, speakers, and people" (see Figure 1.2), And on any given day, whether you walk into a world history class or an English class, my students and I know that we had better be working toward one or more of the things on that poster or else we've lost our way. This sentence—more than an impossibly long list of standards, more than the latest list of 28 "priorities" from on high—is what informs my daily, on-the-ground work. There is no sentence that more shapes my classroom, its work, and its culture than this yellowing old anchor chart. Clarity of purpose is necessary for teachers and students alike.

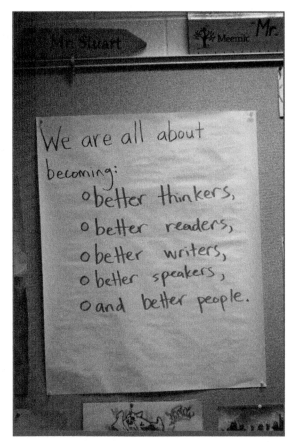

FIGURE 1.2 • "We are all about becoming . . ." Poster in My Classroom

So just do this: put that Everest sentence you just wrote somewhere you'll be forced to revisit for a few days, weeks, or months. Rewrite it from memory the next time you find yourself in a less-than-mission-critical meeting or presentation. And eventually, plaster it on your wall somewhere, introduce it to students, and tell them that this is what we're ultimately after this year— this is what we do. Figure 1.3 shows a sampling of the Everest statements I've collected over the years when doing this exercise with teachers around the United States.

The better, saner teaching life starts with a personally crafted, well-articulated, highest-level objective.

- We are all about planning, producing, and revising our writing; reading to build our knowledge; letting our mistakes guide our growth; and building our future leaders of the Navajo Nation. —Sarah Garcia Nelson, English teacher, Ganado, AZ (Navajo Nation)

- This year, my students will learn how to write and speak with clarity and purpose, develop and explain their reasoning, and understand how the work we do is critical for communicating with the larger world around them. —Bill Curtin, high school English teacher, Carbondale, IL

- As long as students give sincere effort in reading, writing, and thinking on daily basis, I'm confident students will move toward positive long-term academic and personal development. —Tom Dutkowski, tenth-grade American Lit and Language teacher, Powers Catholic High School, Flint, MI

- To instill an invested love of learning, reading, and expressing oneself clearly and passionately. —Jordan H., eighth-grade Language Arts, Tampa, FL

- My Everest is to help students understand and express their own and others' thoughts. —Akahai Lazarus, student teacher, Rexburg, ID

- Every student will be able to produce a decently constructed essay. —Diana Robinson, middle school Language Arts teacher, WI

- I want my students to think and write clearly about texts we read. —Ica Rewitz, English teacher, Orting, WA

- I am preparing students to make effective rhetorical decisions and take effective rhetorical action. —Jennifer Fletcher, professor of English and author of *Teaching Arguments*, Seaside, CA

- We are working to become skilled and independent writers and readers. —Michelle Roy, English teacher/instructional coach, Bunkie, LA

- This year, students will leave seventh grade as confident writers, thinkers, and debaters who can articulate the reasons behind America's historical and current role on the world stage. —Genevieve Gibson, seventh-grade social studies, Centennial, CO

FIGURE 1.3 • Sample of Real Teachers' Everest Statements

Long-Term Flourishing: The Peak of Peaks

We can't stop there, though. If all we do is define our work ourselves, we could easily justify "teach with your door closed," isolationist approaches to our work. Such "Everest Island" approaches concern me. Education has plenty of Lone Rangers and not enough high-functioning teams. Early in my career, my "strategy" was the "Teacher as Savior" approach: be like the guy or girl in whatever Hollywood teacher movie I had recently seen, defy the many forces arrayed against my students and me, and single-handedly produce the glorious, odds-defying results of above-average standardized test scores.

This is a foolish waste of the change potential of our careers.

Our work is only a slice of what schools are for. So what, in a single sentence, is education about? What is its ultimate objective?

The answer is long-term flourishing. Long-term flourishing is broad enough to allow for each of our kids' uniqueness and substantial enough to actually mean something: Rachel may flourish as an auto body technician and car enthusiast, whereas Rashad will flourish as a member of his church and a police officer, while Saylor isn't sure what her future holds except that it's got to include reflective writing and persistent self-improvement (see the Words Matter sidebar).

Let's face it: none of us got into teaching for the impact we can make as measured by an end-of-the-year test; all of us got into it for the tiny contribution we hope our work can make to the life outcomes of our students, twenty years from now. Want to know how this school year is going for me? Ask me in a few decades when I bump into this year's students at the grocery store and find them to be middle-aged, responsible, and contributing professionals or technical workers or parents or spouses or citizens. Did my work contribute to them realizing their potential, albeit in a small, unmeasurable way? Was I 0.01 percent of the reason that things have turned out well for them? Then it was a good year when I taught them; I did good work.

But do you see how painfully immeasurable this long-term view on teaching is? That's the second way that our work is so much more challenging than Hillary and Norgay's was: they *knew* when they were done, and you and I don't. There was no ambiguity to whether or not they had achieved their goal, no room for debate. But for us, there are thirty or more Everests in view during every class period. Long-term flourishing is realized on a life-by-life basis, and it takes a full look of the womb-to-tomb journey for each student before we can know whether it's happened. There's no pretending: measuring the true impact of our work as teachers isn't simple, no matter what the policies or evaluation rubrics say. And please know

Words Matter

Long-Term Flourishing

Long-term flourishing is the first principle of education. Before we espouse our philosophies or techniques or strategies or approaches, we must all agree that what we're after is the long-term flourishing of young people. I say *long-term* because we became educators in hopes that our work might ripple—not just to the end of this school year but also to far beyond the end of what we can see.

And I say *flourishing* because it's clearer, less subjective than *success*. In an era of internet-fueled comparisons, success is an ever-rising bar. There's bound to be someone on Facebook or Instagram who is prettier than me, has more followers than me, lives in a better place than me, or has a cooler job than me. But there's plenty of room for us all to flourish. That's what I want for my students: *long-term flourishing*. It's my job to boost their chances of experiencing that.

that even as I write this paragraph, I, as a practicing teacher in a public high school, also feel the pain of it.

At any rate, with both this universal Everest of long-term flourishing and our personally drafted Everest definitions in view, we now must move into more immediate, but not more practical, realms. The distinction between immediacy and practicality is important. Too often, I find myself falling into believing that if something isn't immediately applicable to my work as a teacher, then it's not practical. But learning how to think is imminently practical. That is what long-term flourishing and defining Everest help us do: they help us think more clearly. In this way, nothing is more practical than the long-term flourishing of young people. When compared to the goal of long-term flourishing, it's standardized tests and grading systems that are impractical. Long-term flourishing isn't merely the A in the ABCs of the teaching profession; it is the entire alphabet.

The long-term flourishing we're after has two aspects: personal and societal.

The personal flourishing we want for our students seems best summarized by Marty Seligman's PERMA framework, which he explores in his appropriately titled *Flourish: A Visionary New Understanding of Happiness and Well-Being* (2012). (It's worth noting here that Seligman is not just some pop-culture self-help author; he's a former president of the American Psychological Association, and he's credited with kickstarting the positive psychology movement.) Here are the five components that Seligman finds indicative of the flourishing life:

- Positive emotion
- Engagement (or flow)
- supportive Relationships
- Meaningful work
- Achievement

Notice how much richer and more durable PERMA is than mere circumstantial happiness. My dad used to tell me, "Dave, I just want you to be happy in life." But in my adult years he and I have talked about how happiness alone isn't what he was talking about. He doesn't just want me walking around smiling with an incessant experience of positive emotion. His desires for me are deeper than that. He wants PERMA.

It used to be that the personal flourishing pieces were all I saw when I conceptualized long-term flourishing. However, I've found that there's a major piece missing. Namely, PERMA doesn't pass the Hitler Test. If Hitler could have experienced Positive emotion, Engagement, supportive Relationships, Meaning, and Achievement in his life, then PERMA isn't a worthy goal all by itself. PERMA, in itself, can't be the sole goal of education; it needs a counterbalance, something beyond the individual.

The societal flourishing component, then, is about a life that *contributes to,* rather than *detracts from,* societal good. This means things like the following:

- Maintaining gainful employment
- Reproducing responsibly
- Maintaining a stable family
- Refraining from criminal activity
- Contributing to civic life (e.g., voting, volunteering)
- Managing personal finances (e.g., using debt responsibly)

There will be times in all our students' lives when some or all of these pieces wax and wane, but what we hope for and teach toward is the increased likelihood that our students will lead lives that ultimately figure as additive to society rather than subtractive.

What I love about aiming our teaching at something like these two components of long-term flourishing is that, even though they will never be buzzy, "flip the project-based twenty-first century student-directed authentic choice-driven classroom" things, they'll always be the true aims of an education. If we could all get on the same page about these ultimate targets, if we could all remind one another that these are what we hoped for when we got into teaching, these are what the parents of our students dreamed of when they first sent their kids to school, these are why society pours treasure into systems of education, then I think we'd take fewer rides on the pendulum of educational fads.

Also, school would make a lot more sense to kids.

I need to admit something: I wrote this book for me. Or rather, for teachers like me who find themselves crushed between two conflicting beliefs. On one hand, we completely believe in the value of teaching. You don't need to convince us that teaching is a noble calling, or that it's worthy of a life's work. We count it a blessing to get to promote the long-term flourishing of kids.

But on the other hand, we've seen the movie *Freedom Writers,* and we're not interested in the whole-life sacrifice depicted in the film. We love that we are called to teach, but we also feel called in other, equally (or more) important directions. For example, I once walked down an aisle and vowed to give all of myself to my wife, Crystal. I've not done this for my students. And then there are these four little Stuart children crawling around my home who have just one father—me—while my ninth-grade students have multiple teachers. I'm all in on teaching during my working hours, but I don't want to be all in outside of them.

In short, I wrote this book for multivocational teachers: we want to be excellent at teaching, but we also want to be excellent at other things.

So here is this book's central argument: there's a way to be both a strong teacher and someone who has a life and interests outside of school. That way starts with knowing why we're here—the long-term flourishing of kids—and it will be fleshed out in the six chapters that follow this one.

I think there are thousands of teachers who, like me, long to be told, "If you and your students are working on this handful of things, repeatedly and with increasing skill, throughout the school year as you move through your curriculum, you're okay. You're not a screw-up."

Those last few words, especially, are important: "You're okay. You're not a screw-up." This might sound really negative to you if you're currently reading this from a good season in your career, but right now I'm talking to the reader who needs to hear that there's a way to focus your work, to major on the majors, and to go home every day without feeling like you're a failure or a fraud or unworthy of your paycheck. Failure marks the road to excellence; feelings of fraudulence are normal for the very public work of the schoolteacher, and you certainly do deserve to be paid for this work. But the work needs to be focused because right now teachers feel expected to do it all, endlessly, and we're hemorrhaging good people from the profession because of it.

THE LEGACY OF ACCOUNTABILITY AND
THE OVER-SCIENCING OF TEACHING

When people subscribe to my free newsletter, I ask them to complete a single, open-ended question: What is the most stressful thing about your job? At the time of this writing, more than 13,000 educators have answered, and they've written nearly four times more words than I've written in this book—more than 250,000.

http://www.davestuartjr .com/newsletter

You, too, can subscribe to my blog via this QR code.

Thirteen thousand educators is not a lot when compared to the total number of educators in the United States, which is about 3.6 million (U.S. Department of Education, National Center for Education Statistics, 2014). I'm not even looking at 1 percent of the teaching pool. Yet it's certainly enough to show clear trends that rise to the surface:

We are highly stressed. It is one thing to read Gallup poll data finding that 57 percent of educators are "not engaged" in their work (Agrawal & Hastings, 2015) or that educators are more stressed in their work than average people (Will, 2017); it is another to read a paragraph about stress and pressure and impossibility written by an earnest human being.

This stress is costly. About a hundred years ago, a couple of scientists created something called the Yerkes–Dodson curve to describe how pressure relates to performance (see Figure 1.4). Optimal amounts of pressure do help increase how

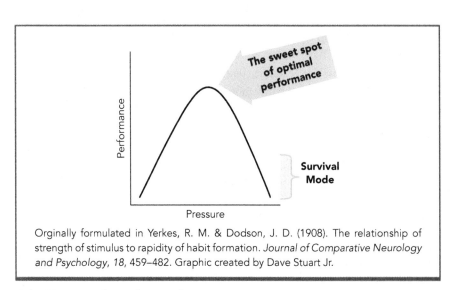

Orginally formulated in Yerkes, R. M. & Dodson, J. D. (1908). The relationship of strength of stimulus to rapidity of habit formation. *Journal of Comparative Neurology and Psychology*, 18, 459–482. Graphic created by Dave Stuart Jr.

FIGURE 1.4 • The Yerkes–Dodson Law

well we do (e.g., I produce more writing when I'm on a deadline than when I'm not), but I don't know of many teachers who work within anything approaching "optimal amounts of pressure." On the curve in Figure 1.4, we tend to live in the "Survival Mode" on the far right end of the curve. This means that our stress is doubly bad: first, it harms our performance in promoting the long-term good of our students, and second, it harms our quality of life.

Much of our stress is from insane expectations. Teachers feel that they are expected to solve all of society's problems, one kid at a time. All of our students are to be well-fed, on grade level, and flourishing by March, no matter what. If the teacher isn't reaching a student, then she must not be using the latest strategy or technique correctly or documenting all of the interventions; it's her fault. If the standardized tests show an unmastered standard, we must, like Boxer in Orwell's *Animal Farm,* say with steadfast resolution, "I will work harder."

Now for some good news: much of that stress is preventable. Mike Schmoker (1999) writes that "our most persistent and unfortunate habit is our tendency to complicate and overload our systems and the people in them" (p. x), yet I think Mike would agree that there are few folks in education who are driven by destructive motives. The majority of teachers, administrators, and coaches live in a perpetual survival mode, which is unhealthy and bad and leads to ill-considered decisions, data for data's sake, hours studying evaluation rubrics, and "Let's learn 1,000 strategies this year" approaches to professional development. We have no sight of Everest; we've given it up long ago, trusting, instead, that data and technique and bureaucracy and technology and programs will somehow take us to the mountaintop.

But it is still possible for teachers, teams, and whole schools and districts to stand firmly on the timeless truth that humans cannot do all things with excellence, and it is therefore wise to focus on a few things. We can say that *because* the stakes are high and *because* the true nature of accountability in this job is so much deeper than policy measures, we will ignore the manifold distractions that assault us and fixate on the few most promising efforts. We cannot singlehandedly correct all deficits, but we can hold to the methods most likely to diminish them.

That is essentially what all of my work is about. I think every teacher should be told, "If you and your students are working on this handful of things, repeatedly and with increasing skill, throughout this school year and during those that follow, you're okay."

The material in this book grew from a desire to give teachers like me permission to simply focus on the work we set out to do when we entered this noble profession. Every one of those survey respondents is an actual person with a story, a flesh-and-blood classroom teacher or administrator, whom we desperately *need*. Professional educators are an endangered species in the United States, yet we throw them away like overused tissues, suffocating them with bloated initiatives and ten dozen "priorities." This is beyond waste; it's unsustainably poor stewardship.

So in this book, we're going to focus on the things most likely to move our students toward long-term flourishing (LTF). LTF is shown in Figure 1.5 as the center of a bull's-eye; it's the heart of our mission as educators, and it's what we want to always keep in focus. We won't *ask* for permission to focus; we will *insist* on focusing, as professionals. For the rest of our time together, I'm

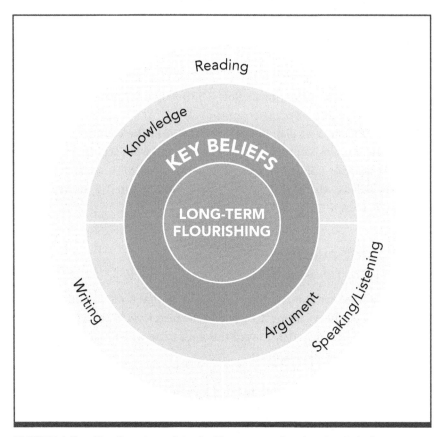

FIGURE 1.5 • The first ring of the bull's-eye contains the Key Beliefs beneath student motivation.

simply going to advocate for six things we ought to go big on, six interwoven areas in which our schools should cultivate excellence in practice. These six things don't necessarily happen as steps or stages, but they all work together to lead to long-term flourishing students—and teachers. Let's work through each briefly.

KEY BELIEFS: START WITH THE HEART

Have you ever tried lifting a car with your bare hands? You're an intelligent person with important things to do, so I'm guessing you haven't. Well, I hadn't either until I wrote that sentence, and so I went outside and I tried it. Here's what I discovered: it doesn't work. I could stand next to my car, lifting with all my might and exerting myself until I died from it, but I still wouldn't lift my 2002 Toyota Corolla off the ground.

But with a lever, I could lift that car with minimal effort. If you sit back and think about it, it is incredible:

- me + every ounce of my effort = not lifting up my 2,500-lb car
- me + car jack + minimal effort = lifting up my 2,500-lb car

The same principle is at play in every classroom in the country, except what we're trying to move is our students as learners, and what act like levers are the beliefs our students hold about us and our classrooms. Most research points us to five Key Beliefs, which we'll explore in Chapter 2. Figure 1.5 shows this next layer of the *These 6 Things* bull's-eye.

KNOWLEDGE BUILDING AND ARGUMENT: MOVE THEM TOWARD MASTERY

Of course, a lever without anything to lift isn't all that useful, so now we come to the start of our heavy lifting. I argue that the next level of our work is helping students master the material. Toward this end, we're wise to target two things: knowledge building and argument.

First, we need kids to learn stuff, to build knowledge. In Chapter 3, I'll demonstrate the special criticality of knowledge: how central knowing things is to learning, thinking, reading, and the flourishing life.

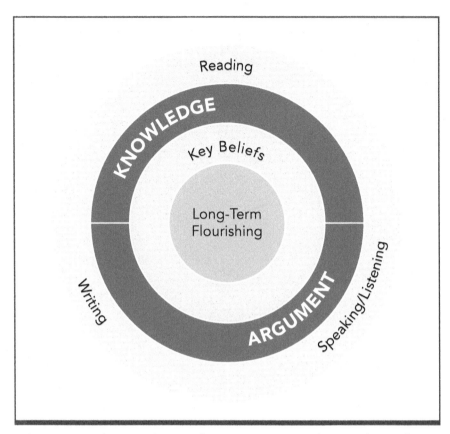

FIGURE 1.6 • The second ring is about our two-pronged approach to making kids smarter: knowledge building and argument.

And second, we need kids to be able to argue—in a winsome, amicable manner—in ways that are appropriate to our disciplines and courses. You'll find me to be far from an argumentative purist; instead, I'm interested in how we can help our students be the kinds of people who are eager to get to the bottom of big questions, willing to roll up their sleeves as they work collaboratively to come to resolutions on tricky issues, and capable of making good decisions. That's what argument ought to aim at throughout the school day: the cultivation of amicable arguers. This is what we'll be exploring in Chapter 4.

Together, knowledge and argument form the next ring of the *These 6 Things* bull's-eye (see Figure 1.6).

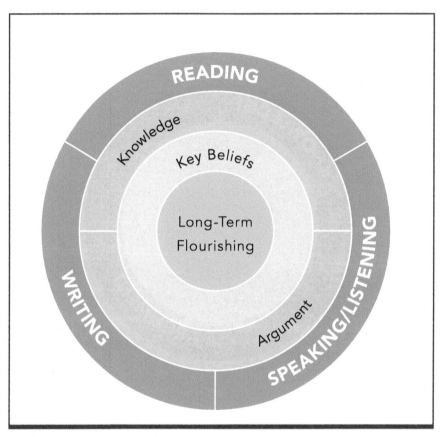

FIGURE 1.7 • The final ring of the bull's-eye involves literacy-rich learning experiences in ways that make sense throughout the school day.

MORE READING, MORE WRITING, MORE SPEAKING AND LISTENING: LITERACY AS A MEANS *AND* AN END

Finally, in this book I'll argue that we ought to target beliefs, knowledge building, and argument work in our classrooms through literacy-rich learning experiences. Specifically, we need to give ourselves space as professionals to get great at incorporating discipline-appropriate reading (Chapter 5), writing (Chapter 6), and speaking and listening (Chapter 7). In all of these areas, we need to consider which reading and writing and speaking/listening exercises are authentic for a given course or discipline and how we might use literacy-rich learning experiences to strengthen mastery throughout the school day.

These three aspects of literacy—reading, writing, and speaking and listening—form the outer ring of the bull's-eye (see Figure 1.7), and that completes our

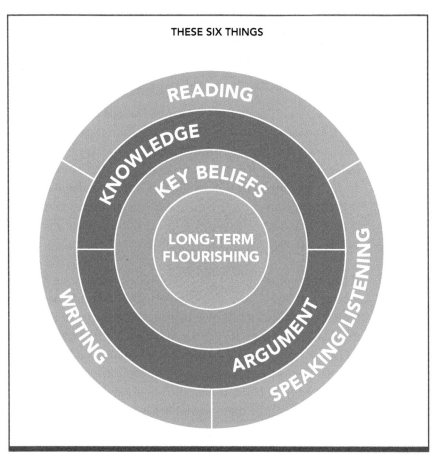

FIGURE 1.8 • Put all together, we have just these six things to focus on for the rest of the book (and perhaps the rest of our careers, too).

picture of where we should target our efforts every school year. These foundational six things (see Figure 1.8) are worth our focus as we strive to guide students toward their long-term flourishing.

Let's Focus on What We Already Know

I need to be forthright with you on a couple of key things before we go further into this book. (I'm really hoping you don't skip this part.) First, there's nothing new here. And second, I'm not naïve enough to think that focusing on six fundamental aspects will remove all our daily stressors and magically solve all teaching and learning challenges. I do hope you'll read on, however, to learn

Even the "nothing new" bent of this book isn't new. For a glimpse at the seminal works in my thinking here, see the following:

- Mike Schmoker's Focus: *Elevating the Essentials to Radically Improve Student Learning* (2011)

- Greg McKeown's *Essentialism: The Disciplined Pursuit of Less* (2014)

- Jim Collins's *Good to Great: Why Some Companies Make the Leap and Others Don't* (2001)

For a full list of the "Dig Deeper" titles mentioned in this book, go to davestuartjr.com/t6t-list.

how focusing on these things we *already know* can be powerful guiding forces in our classrooms.

NOTHING NEW, NOTHING SHINY

Five years of blogging for teachers has helped me discover that I don't write so I can take an old idea and "rebrand" it as my own, but I do try to find the best ideas, attempt them in my classroom, and explain what works (and doesn't work) for me and my students. I'm not an innovator; I'm a reminder and a streamliner. I actually hope that this book does *not* give you a bunch of new things to do. Rather, I hope it gives you fewer things to do so you can do them better.

When we constantly throw new things at teachers, we make it increasingly likely that they won't master anything. If you've been teaching for a while, you're going to see plenty in this book that's familiar—that's sort of my point. I want to show you how we can do great work by limiting ourselves to growing in the six areas laid out in this book. If you're new to teaching, these six items may serve as building blocks as you develop your practice. With a large quantity of work in these areas, I believe you and your students will arrive at quality.

"JUST" THESE SIX THINGS

If you're sensing that these six areas of practice aren't small—that mastering just one of these could take years of deliberate work—then you're getting it. These practice areas are worthy of, and indeed require, years of our earnest efforts toward improvement. I do not mean to reduce the complexity of teaching by saying that we ought to do just these six things; rather, I want to make the complexity of our work manageable, to give it some boundaries, and to make it simple enough to productively discuss. "Reduction and complication," Gerald Graff (2003) writes, "are not opposites, but are both legitimate moments in the process of communication" (p. 139). Yet despite their complexity, what I'm arguing in this book is that these are the six things most worthy of such time investments—more than reworking our grading systems or chasing the next fad.

The truth is, we don't really know what lies ahead for our students; we're preparing many of them for careers that don't even exist yet. If I invest heavily in my ability to promote purposeful and frequent reading in my class, am I likely to find in ten more years that these skills are irrelevant? Will there truly come a day when "Googling it" supplants knowledge building? Is the kind of open-minded, collaborative critical thinking at the heart of argumentation going to lose its value at the family dinner table or the factory floor meeting by 2030?

I don't think so. I don't see that my students today won't be well served by being knowledgeable, literate, strategic thinkers.

I write this book as a colleague, not an expert. So consider this book a colleague's call to focus, year in and year out, on developing our craft in these six key areas. If we do these things, we ought to give ourselves permission to ignore that nagging voice that tells us we're not worthy of this work. When we focus on these six items, keeping long-term flourishing students as the ultimate goal, I think we can confidently say, "Hey, I'm doing the right work. I'm okay."

The Gist

I made this book for teachers like me who are multivocational: we want to be excellent at our jobs for the sake of our students, but we're not willing to sacrifice our entire lives on the altar of teaching success. To start down this path, we need to be clear on our Everests. Our personal Everests matter, and they ought to be posted in our classrooms. Our collective Everest matters, too: the long-term flourishing of kids. This book will show us how six areas of practice are our best bet to be the teachers we always hoped we'd be and stay sane in the process. They are the six areas in which we ought to invest our instructional and professional development time: beliefs, knowledge, argument, reading, writing, and speaking/listening. These are six simple yet robust paths to explore in any given lesson, unit, or school year. Becoming experts in these six pursuits is, unlike the many things expected of teachers, both manageable and exciting.

Better Together

Throughout the book, I'll include examples of ways in which these six areas of practice can be better when experienced and pursued as a group. There have certainly been years in my professional work when I felt as though I was focusing on these areas alone, and I do think that personally applying the material in this book can do much for your sanity, even if no one else around you does the same.

But consider how, even in this first chapter, the work I lay out in the book can be so much richer when done with a team, a professional learning community, a school, or a district:

- As a group, go through the exercise of defining your Everest. I've used the same prompts in this chapter with groups around the country, and the responses are always fascinating. Here's a tip: aim for sentences that point to meaningful, observable academic capacities. As Daphna Oyserman (2015) writes, "pathways to success go through school" (p. xi). We don't want our sentences to neglect the academic components of our job descriptions!

- Work to create a group Everest statement. Many schools that I visit have mission statements on their websites but no actual, functioning mission statement in the hearts of their faculties and staffs. What would it look like to collaboratively create an Everest sentence for your whole team, professional learning community (PLC), or school?

- Start meetings with this Everest prompt: Since our last meeting, how have you worked toward the Everest statement we created last time? Give a specific example. Share these with each other.

Exercises like this help to center us on what it is that we're doing. As you well know, that recentering is critical during the hectic rush that school years always seem to become.

Notes

Start With the Heart

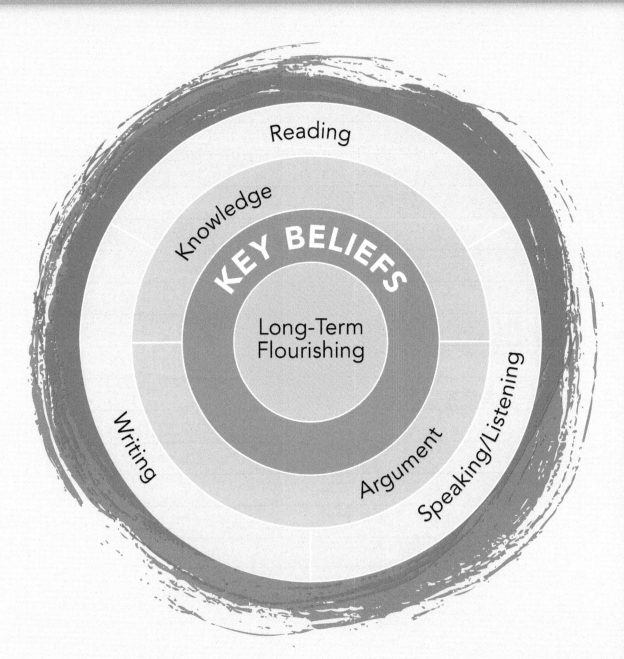

Reading

Knowledge

KEY BELIEFS

Long-Term
Flourishing

Writing

Argument

Speaking/Listening

My grandfather, the mighty Dean Lewis Stuart, used to say that he was successful because he was lazy. The successful part I understood—he never went to college, but he retired as the beloved CEO of a multimillion-dollar organization—but the lazy part confused me. It wasn't until later that I got what he meant: the simplest way to achieve something is the best. Simplicity was beautiful to my grandfather, and over-complexity was his enemy. He attributed his success to this disposition.

Too frequently, I see the opposite of this mentality in myself: I see the hours that I put into teaching as the measure of how successful I am, how much I care. This is absurd, of course. If I spend hours trying to lift my car with my bare hands, does this make me a caring, successful mechanic? Of course not. It makes me an ineffective and sore one.

In this first part of the book, I'd like to argue that all of our work in and out of the classroom ought to be informed by a fundamental, internal layer: the layer of key beliefs. The best kinds of classrooms rely on inside-out learning; they cultivate the right kinds of beliefs in students through the continued use of authentic, meaningful academic work. Because let's face it: if our students don't do the work laid out in the rest of this book, and if they don't do that work with full effort and care, then we're wasting a lot of time. For students to grow, they need to do something—think, read, write, speak, study, ask—and they need to do it with care, attention, effort, and focus (Farrington et al., 2012). So that's what the next chapter will be about: setting the table, as it were, for the feasts of learning we hope to provide our students. Because cultivating key beliefs affects every ounce of work we'll do this school year, it gets its own part.

As you read the rest of this book, consider the five key beliefs laid out in Chapter 2—credibility, belonging, effort, efficacy, and value—and how you can both bring them to bear *and* strengthen them in your students as you have them build knowledge, argue, read, write, and speak and listen.

CHAPTER TWO

Cultivate Key Beliefs

First the heart, then the head.

—MARC TUCKER (2017)

Before you can teach, you have to show that you care.

—DANIEL COYLE (2012, P. 86)

What types of things do you want your students to do? On the lines below, list what you'd love to see all of your students doing.

sample: completing their homework

_____

_____

_____

_____

_____

_____

_____

_____

Here are some of the things I want my students to do:

- Think
- Read
- Write
- Speak
- Listen
- Participate
- Do homework
- Turn things in on time
- Stay organized
- Manage and reduce stress
- Sleep eight hours a night
- Turn their phones off
- Ask
- Engage
- Debate
- Discuss
- Encourage one another
- Be nice
- Strategize
- Pursue goals
- Tell the truth (i.e., don't fake things)
- Lucubrate (look it up— good word)

Of course, there's a spectrum for doing each of these things, isn't there? There's reading by skimming the page, and then there's reading to achieve 100 percent understanding of an author's words. There's the turned-in assignment with illegible scrawling or randomly guessed answers, and there's the turned-in assignment that is careful, thoughtful, and complete. We want our students to *do* these actions, then, but we want them to do them *earnestly*, too. We'd like them engaging, enjoying, questioning, persevering, and focusing on the work. And frankly, I argue that we don't just *want* this kind of effortful work; we *need* it to take place if anything else we attempt within our classrooms is going to have its best effect.

Yet you and I cannot produce those behaviors or that kind of effort in our students. We can't jump into their brains and say, "All right, time to engage." This is a humbling truth about teaching: we are servants, not omnipotent commanders. Another humbling truth about teaching: we actually *do* have an enormous impact on whether or not our students engage in academic behaviors effortfully. The wisest way of instilling effortful engagement that I've found—and the way that a surprising amount of the research corroborates—is by cultivating five simple, robust student beliefs:

1. I believe in my teacher.

2. I belong in this classroom.

3. I can improve through my effort.

4. I can succeed at this.

5. This work has value for me.

These research-based beliefs form the center of the work we do with our students. Learning, in this way, is an inside-out endeavor.

Why Beliefs?

Do me a favor: picture a kid you know who you feel is likely to succeed, to lead a flourishing life. Whose name or face first comes to mind?

(Psst . . . Don't move on before you have a specific kid in mind.)

Are you picturing that student? Now, answer this, in just a word or two: Why did you picture *that* young person? What is it about that child that led your mind to select him or her first?

Write the words or phrases that come to mind in the lines under the image in Figure 2.1.

FIGURE 2.1 • Use this space for the "picture a kid" exercise explained above.

As of this writing, I've asked several thousand educators from around the United States to conduct this simple thought experiment, and the results are fascinating. Guess what percentage of folks answer my question with an intellectual skill—something like "excellent reader," "great at math," "scientifically brilliant," or "smart"? Fewer than 1 percent. And we're talking about trained, experienced educators here, thousands of them, collectively representing *millions* of hours teaching and studying and coaching learners toward success.

Overwhelmingly, this group of practitioners, given no time to formulate anything but a gut reaction to the prompt, cites attributes that won't be on the end of the year test. They use descriptors like these:

- Enthusiastic
- Grateful
- Kind
- Good with people
- Self-starting
- Motivated

- Organized
- Confident
- Resilient
- Persistent
- Always questioning
- Curious

- Driven
- Thoughtful
- Optimistic
- Energetic
- Hard working

At the broadest level, we find in these responses an overwhelming consensus that no matter how much we believe in the power of being a lifelong reader or an authentic writer or a scientific thinker, cognitive factors like the things we measure on standardized tests aren't as predictive of long-term flourishing outcomes as what researchers call "noncognitive factors." In an age where diverse, nation-spanning groups of people can't seem to agree on anything, this consensus is refreshing, and it explains why every single one of us works at cultivating these attributes in our students.

The challenge is that at the more granular level of our approaches to cultivating these abilities in our students, the consensus breaks down. We have all kinds of lists of traits, strengths, habits, and practices. In the schools I've visited across the United States, I've found these lists hanging on our classroom walls or from our hallway ceilings; I've heard them condensed into slogans, hidden in motivational quotations, demonstrated in read-aloud biographies, or unpacked in YouTube videos or TED talks. The list is diverse, and frankly, I like this at an aesthetic level. I like all of these diverse ways of approaching the important stuff.

But at the practical level, this degree of idiosyncrasy is not helpful. As we work in our silos on these noncognitive factors,

Words Matter

Noncognitive Factors

The term *noncognitive*, used in much of the research, should not be taken literally. Clearly, being persistent or enthusiastic or grateful involve a great deal of cognition. The literature alternatively refers to *social-emotional learning*, *character*, *character strengths*, or *virtues*.

too many of us are reinventing the wheel. We're already overly stressed and pressed for time; we need straightforward answers to three simple questions:

- Which one of these factors matter most to long-term flourishing or academic performance?
- How do these noncognitive attributes work together?
- Which, if any, can be taught?

Several years ago, I became a bit obsessed by these questions, so I started reading about them. (In the sidebar, you'll find a sampling of the works I read.) Here's what it boils down to: When our students believe five particular things about our classes, they're far more likely to do the work and to do it with care. And, beautifully, these beliefs are malleable. You and I *do* have the ability to greatly affect them in our classrooms and in our schools.

Four of the five beliefs come from the "Academic Mindsets" chapter of Camille Farrington et al.'s (2012) freely available *Teaching Adolescents to Become Learners*, a critical review of more than 400 studies and resources on noncognitive factors. The fifth belief, which you'll see as first on my list of five, comes from John Hattie's *Visible Learning for Teachers* (2012), which describes an ongoing meta-analysis project that, at the time of this writing, incorporates 80,000 individual studies and 300 million students (Fisher, Frey, and Hattie, 2016b, p. 4; Visible Learning Partnership, 2017). For the truest treatment of these beliefs, then, refer to those works. But to save time, read on to learn how I've come to conceptualize them and bring them to bear in my classroom—and how you can, too.

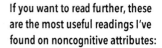
DIG DEEPER

If you want to read further, these are the most useful readings I've found on noncognitive attributes:

- Camille Farrington et al., *Teaching Adolescents to Become Learners. The Role of Noncognitive Factors in Shaping School Performance: A Critical Literature Review* (2012)
- K. Anders Ericsson and Robert Pool, *Peak: Secrets From the New Science of Expertise* (2016)
- Angela Duckworth, *Grit: The Power of Passion and Perseverance* (2016)
- Paul Tough, *How Children Succeed: Grit, Curiosity, and the Hidden Power of Character* (2013)
- James Heckman, John Humphries, and Tim Kautz, *The Myth of Achievement Tests: The GED and the Role of Character in American Life* (2014)

For a full list of the "Dig Deeper" titles mentioned in this book, go to davestuartjr.com/t6t-list.

The Five Research-Based Beliefs That Drive Student Learning Behaviors (and How to Cultivate Them)

With the preliminaries out of the way, let's look again at the list of five key beliefs:

1. Credibility: I believe in my teacher.
2. Belonging: I belong in this classroom.
3. Effort: I can improve through my effort.

4. Efficacy: I can succeed at this.

5. Value: This work has value for me.

In the sections that follow, I'm going to explain each belief and then share some practical ways to go about cultivating them as you have students learn, argue, read, write, and speak in your classroom. Some of those practical ideas will be mine, and the rest will be those demonstrated in the research of wiser colleagues near and far.

Words Matter

Mindsets versus Beliefs

Researchers tend to say *mindsets* rather than *beliefs*. For me, the term belief is more useful. Belief gets to the center of a person—what do you hold to be true, at the deepest level? That's why I like the term *belief*. But by calling these attributes beliefs, I'm stepping into some labeling territory that's not found as frequently in the research.

Throughout the rest of this chapter, I'll include a "How to cultivate it" section for each belief. I chose "cultivate" carefully. The Latin *cultivat* means "prepared for crops." When something is cultivated, it's not guaranteed to achieve results, but it's ready to. Cultivation is never-ending; gardens, I'm told, need constant tending. So, too, with the beliefs. Very few of the practical recommendations I'll make in these "How to cultivate it" sections are "set it and forget it." We're trying to become teachers who earnestly persist in creating lessons and classrooms that make this chapter's key beliefs easier for our students to believe.

BELIEF 1: TEACHER CREDIBILITY

It sounds pretty hokey to suggest that if our students believe in us they'll do better in our classes, but the concept of teacher credibility is validated by the

TEACHER CREDIBILITY

I believe in my teacher.

SYNONYMS	ANTONYMS
This teacher is good at her job.	My teacher is bad at her job.
This teacher can get me to the next level.	I'm not going to learn much in this class.
This teacher can make a difference in my life.	This teacher can't help me.
I trust this teacher.	This teacher isn't fair.

aforementioned, ever-growing Visible Learning study. With an effect size more than twice that of Hattie's "hinge point" bar of acceptability, teacher credibility ranks in the top ten of teacher-affected factors in his list of more than 250 different influences. In short, this is a powerful belief, and it's "always at play" in our classrooms (Fisher et al., 2016b, p. 10).

The tricky thing about teacher credibility is that, unlike the other key beliefs, it can't be targeted directly—you don't strive to convince your students, "Yes, I *am* an awesome teacher!" in the same way you might try to convince them, "Yes, you *can* succeed at this challenge!" Instead, students are most likely to believe in you if they see that you demonstrate three key qualities: caring, competence, and passion (Killian, 2017). Figure 2.2 shows how these three qualities relate.

Let's break each down.

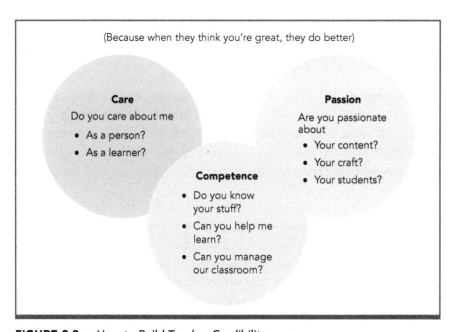

FIGURE 2.2 • How to Build Teacher Credibility

Care

Our students need to believe that we genuinely care about them, and they tend to see this through two different lenses. First, they want to know that we care

davestuartjr.com/dean

Note: I've written more extensively on how I communicate care in "'I Love You and I'm Proud of You' – What Dean L. Stuart Taught Me About Teaching." Use the QR code above, or type the link into your browser.

about them as individuals—that their current and future well-being is important to us. And second, they want to know that we care about them as learners—that it is actually important to us that they master our material. Dirk shares with me that he's currently not getting along with his grandfather and things have been rough lately because he has sensed that I care about him as a person. He also comes to ask me a genuine question about how to make his analytical writing clearer because he has figured out that I care about him as a student. Here are some ways to cultivate credibility through care.

Make eye contact. A simple goal would be to make eye contact with every kid, during every instructional segment, every day. (Band teachers, with your 9 million kids per class, don't throw things at me.)

Communicate care. Although we don't want to be disingenuous with our students, it is appropriate for us to express that we care about their welfare. If you, like me, want to provide the level of education for your students that you would want your own children to receive, then you teach from a place of loving them as if they were your own. This isn't immaterial and should be communicated regularly.

Tell your students the truth about their performance, even when it is a hard truth. "Ellie, those grades aren't acceptable." "Johan, the low quality of your writing this week really surprised me. What happened?" My students seem magnetically attracted to adults who love them enough to speak the truth to them, even when the truth is unpleasant.

Seek, and track, moments of genuine connection. At the start of the school year, I get all of my kids' names on a single piece of paper, clip it to my clipboard, and keep track of moments of genuine connection. I don't always write down what the moment was or what we connected on, but I always at least make a mark (e.g., a green dot) next to the names of kids with whom I've connected at least once. I'm going to share some examples of the types of things that get said during these "moments of genuine connection" because I think that's the clearest way of communicating what I mean.

- A student who succeeded after setbacks: "Henry, I know you joined this class late, and I want you to know that I realize the challenges that come with that. When you scored so well on our most recent quiz, that spoke to me of your determination to improve, and that's exactly what I'm after in you this year. Keep it up, young man."

- A student who I know is shy and anxious: "Jessica, the last thing I was expecting today for our first Pop-Up Debate was for you to stand up first, boldly making your point. Even now with class over, I'm blown away by that, Jessica, just blown away."

- A former student in the hallway: "Noah, I heard you saying that you had a sophomore slump, but listen to me: it sounds like you've recognized that as a problem and that you've set your sights on doing better in your junior year. Doing better happens one day at a time, Noah. Improve one day at a time. If you need anything, I'm here."

- A former student who stopped by after school: "Paige, you came here overwhelmed by how badly you're doing in school this year, and yet when you shared with me your grades and classes, I was shocked. You are actually doing amazing, and I can't describe how proud I am of you. You and I have something in common: we are critical of ourselves. This can be a strength; it can make us get better all the time. But it can also be a weakness; it can drive us crazy and make us think that nothing less than perfection is acceptable. Any time you need help keeping that strength from becoming a weakness, you let me know, Paige. Keep it up, young lady."

- A student who seemed goofy at the start of the school year but showed a real aptitude with one of our recurring tasks: "Kylie, when we did the dates warm-up the other day, I noticed that you're really sharp at it—when other students were 50 percent done, you were closer to 90 percent. That's amazing! Keep up the good work, young lady!"

- A student who I don't know that well yet: "Austin, I just wanted to say that I'm glad you're in my class. If you work hard this year, I know you will set yourself up for a successful high school experience. It will be my job to teach you how to do that while we also learn world history."

- A twin who's fairly quiet: "Maddie, What's it like being in the same class as Cliff? . . . I am fortunate to get to teach you both."

- An eleventh-grade student who gave a flippant answer when I asked, "What's your plan after graduation?": "Bobby, by the end of this year I want you to be able to tell me, without any joking or shame, what your plan is after graduation. You are an enjoyable young man who deserves a life of providing for himself; whether the plan is working right after high school or community college or whatever else, I want you to be able to quickly state it when I ask you to. Let me know if I can help talk it through with you."

Although these are unique examples, they have things in common.

First, *they're not moments of genuine connection if they're not genuine.* Duplicity is the enemy of teacher credibility. I can't dislike my kids behind their backs and genuinely connect with them while they're with me. The integrated life is what we're after—that's what will make us saner in life and better at teaching, all at the same time.

Words Matter

The Integrated Life

An integer is a whole number, and a teacher living an integrated life is a whole person: someone who's not switching his or her identity, behavior, or thinking at various times in the day. I would argue that the integrated life is a less stressful one. You don't have to "pretend" that you love your students; you work toward genuinely loving them. That, to me, is the simpler, smarter approach to cultivating teacher credibility.

Second, regardless of the situation or the kid, *I'm trying to communicate, each time, "Hey, I see you, and I see you as one of us. I'm glad I get to be around you this year. I see potential in you."* I am speaking to my students' sense of self and arguing for that identity to include a shard about being a part of my class. This is an example of targeting two key beliefs at once: I'm working on being more credible to the students by demonstrating my care for them, but I'm also working on helping them to develop the belief that they belong in my classroom (which is the second belief, Belonging).

Third, when I looked through my list and chose the above examples to share with you, I didn't edit them. Despite that, when I look back at my notes, I see that *I say the kid's name, every time.* Early in my career, I had a mentor named Trent Gladstone who always used my name when he spoke to me—probably as often as once a minute. I don't have any research to back this up, but there seems to be something powerful about the use of a person's name.

Here's why I think it's important to not just seek moments of genuine connection but also to track them. Once or twice during the school day, I'll go through my list and add any "moments of genuine connection" that I've had with kids, marking them and moving on to other work. I jokingly refer to this as my "high-tech" clipboard, but this really is a key component of the effort. If I don't keep track of these moments of genuine connection on the clipboard, guess what happens? I forget kids. Had I not kept track this year, I wouldn't have known that Isaac, Aden, and Easton needed a minute of my time, either in the hallway or during class.

Search within yourself for feelings of animosity or apathy about your students. If those feelings are there (and oh, how like weeds they can grow, even in the best of hearts), your students are savvy enough to at least catch a whiff of them. In this case, roll up your sleeves and work at genuinely caring about your kids—even the ones who have hurt or offended you. This is intense internal work that all great teachers are acquainted with. Start with questions like these:

- Which students am I struggling to like right now?
- Do I have any students who make me anxious? Angry?
- Do I have any students I complain about when they're not around?
- What "no-strings-attached" act of kindness might I perform for a student I'm struggling with?

Competence

Are your students confident that you can help them succeed? Do they see that, most of the time, you deliver information accurately? Would they say that you appear prepared? Do they get a sense that you're in command of the classroom, whatever that looks like in your setting? If so, you've got the competence part of credibility down pat. If not, here are a few tips for cultivating credibility through competence.

Especially in the early years of your career, give yourself time for robust lesson planning. Early in my career, I had to learn that the design of my bulletin boards and handouts wasn't nearly as important as the design of my lessons. With this in mind, I started to work on clearly thinking through the learning experiences I had planned for students. Here are some questions to ponder prior to each lesson to make you a more competent planner:

- What do you want students to learn?
- How will you know that they've learned it?
- How will you hook students into the lesson?
- What concepts, skills, or obstacles are students likely to get hung up on, and how will you assist students with them?

And here are some questions for post-lesson reflection:

- What went well, in terms of student learning?
- What could have gone better?
- What did I learn about what *doesn't* work? What did I learn about what *does*?
- What surprised me?

Aim for the shortest path in lesson planning. I like the way Doug Lemov (2014) explains this in *Teach Like a Champion 2.0*:

> The goal in teaching is to take the shortest path from A (lack of knowledge and understanding) to B (durable long-term knowledge and understanding), so the primary criterion for evaluating a lesson should be "How quickly does it get me there?" Sometimes, alternative criteria—how clever, how artfully designed, how inclusive of various philosophies, even how enjoyable to teach a given lesson might be—can distract us from choosing the methods and lesson designs that get students most quickly and effectively to the goal. So it's important to strive to keep in check the part of us that wants to evaluate lessons on how self-actualizing they were to teach or how well they demonstrated some theory or how smart they make us look. (p. 147)

A bad example of "shortest path" thinking would be to take longer to introduce an article than it takes the students to read it. (Not that I've done that or anything . . .) When our kids experience efficient, effective lessons in our classes, they know we've got our stuff together.

Words Matter

Erik Palmer's PVLEGS

In an effort to make clear to his students the elements of effective speech delivery, teacher Erik Palmer (2011) developed the acronym PVLEGS, which stands for the following:

Poise: Avoid distracting behaviors; appear calm and confident.

Voice: Make every word heard.

Life: Express passion and emotions in your voice.

Eye contact: Connect visually with each audience member.

Gestures: Use hands, body, and face purposefully.

Speed: Use pauses for effect and emphasis; otherwise, speak at a good clip.

We'll take a closer look at PVLEGS in Chapters 4 and 7.

Film yourself delivering instruction, and focus on your poise. In Chapter 7, we'll explore in more depth Erik Palmer's (2011) PVLEGS acronym for speech delivery, but for convenience I'm including it in the margin here as well. When students see us speak with poise, they sense we are competent. I've found that the best way for me to check myself for poise is to periodically film myself, even for just five to ten minutes, and then to review the film for distracting behaviors (fidgeting is a problem of mine) or speaking tics (like, you know, um).

Have something ready for kids to do right when the bell rings. If students are aimlessly waiting for you to take roll every day, something's amiss. (Also, wasting one minute per day all school year long means three wasted hours by the end of the school year. We've got to be better than that.) There are plenty of times when I'm writing the warm-up on the screen *as the kids walk in the door,* but by the time the bell rings that warm-up is there. That's the key. In a perfect world, I'd have my warm-ups planned out a week in advance; I don't live in that world yet. Typically, my warm-ups are writing prompts, and I ask my students to produce at least one hundred words in response (I give them five minutes). Sometimes, I'll incorporate knowledge review, reading, or speaking and listening into the warm-up. This cultivates credibility, and once we teach the routines involved—for my students, this is sitting down, opening their spiral notebooks, starting a new entry, reading the writing prompt on the board, and writing quickly and quietly—it's an easy, effective way to get lessons off to a solid start.

Tell personal stories relevant to what you're teaching. Stories can communicate our experiential knowledge of a topic or just our habit of challenging ourselves and overcoming obstacles. I struggled with where to place this one because stories can build trust, they can demonstrate competence, and they can communicate passion. Just be a bit picky here, as there's a line between purposeful storytelling and wasting our students' valuable class time. A good rule of thumb would be that your stories are a rare, useful treat for students rather than a constant, autobiographical onslaught. The stories we tell should be for our students; the students don't come to our classroom for our stories!

TRY THIS

Have a warm-up ready when the bell rings.

Passion

Can students detect your genuine passion for a topic? How about your passion for the challenge of teaching them to attain excellence? If we are genuinely excited about the material we're teaching and our students achieving mastery, we increase the likelihood that our students will be, too. Let's look at some ideas for cultivating credibility through passion.

Don't fake it. Instead, if you come upon a topic or unit you don't enjoy, work at finding a passion point somewhere within it. I'll share two personal examples:

- I don't enjoy Ray Bradbury's *Fahrenheit 451*, but it's part of our English 9 curriculum, so I'm not going to be so arrogant as to disregard it. That decision is above my pay grade. After all, some people really enjoy *Fahrenheit*, and it's a book that will challenge my kids and give us some fodder for comparisons between the world of the novel and the world we live in. Wait . . . I just found two things that I can be passionate about when teaching *Fahrenheit*: the fact that it's challenging (and I'm passionate about my students getting access to challenge) and that it's relevant for analyzing contemporary society. Added bonus:

I can build some trust with students by sharing with them at the start of the unit that, indeed, I don't really like this novel but we're going to work hard at it anyway.

- When my blog *DaveStuartJr.com* started, it was primarily about the Common Core State Standards (CCSS) and written by a guy who is far from a standards lover. But the CCSS was a pressing issue, it was affecting a lot of teachers and kids, and I was passionate about finding a way to wrangle all of this into something positive. I just pictured all of the kids sitting bored or confused in classes where teachers didn't understand how to feel ownership of the CCSS and make these standards make sense to their students—and that's where I found my passion for the topic. I started approaching it from the angle of "This is going to be bad unless enough of us do something about it," and I started to care about the CCSS.

That's how we attack teaching situations where we might not be immediately passionate. Rather than fake it, we find areas of passion within these situations and capitalize on them.

Film yourself teaching, and analyze for passion. Communicating passion isn't synonymous with raising the pitch of your voice and getting squealy. I've noticed that, when I get passionate, my voice often gets lower, and my facial expression can become stern—and I've only noticed this from periodically filming my instruction, as described earlier. When analyzing for passion, look for the Life and Gestures components of Palmer's PVLEGS.

You're Incredible! And You're Credible, Too

Do you see ways in which you demonstrate care, competence, and passion already? Do you see how you can help make your passion for what you're teaching detectable and how you can break down barriers between you and your students? If you're putting thought into how you demonstrate these things, then you are way ahead of the pack, and all those worries about "not being expert enough" can dissolve away. In fact, any lack of expertise you see in yourself may be an asset—you'll have an easier time feeling the pain your students feel and genuinely wanting to assuage it.

In short, there are two key takeaways here, and they are not delivered with demoralization or arrogance. Write your thinking on the following lines so you have an anchor.

- First, reflect on how you are already credible. Right now, write down a sentence explaining why that's true and why one or more of the earlier components is a reason that your students can believe in you.

- Second, brainstorm the areas in which you can become more credible. Write down a sentence explaining one way in which you intend to work on your teacher credibility this school year.

COMMON TEACHER HANG-UP

How We Unintentionally Undermine Our Credibility

It can be helpful to examine teacher credibility from a negative angle, too. What are the ways in which we might undermine our students' belief in us and our ability to help them flourish long term? How might we diminish their perceptions of our care, competence, or passion? I have personal experience with many of these, so if you feel "condemned" by anything in the following list, know that you are in good company, friend. We are never finished becoming the teachers we hoped we'd be when we first set out.

Here are some ways that I've done it wrong:

1. **Don't trust students.** After all, once a kid stole your stapler, right? (Care)

2. **Manage your classroom unfairly.** The sweet and innocent kids are allowed to misbehave once in a while, but those rowdy ones, or the ones that really know how to push your buttons—they can't be given an inch! (Care, Competence)

3. **Have no plan for the first and last minutes of class.** After all, kids need time to get settled and time to unwind, don't they? (Competence)

(Continued)

(Continued)

4. **Accept that, sometimes, in-class debates or discussions just get loud and obnoxious and rude, and there's nothing you can do about it.** That just means they're engaged, right? No. When we don't manage discussions well, and when we don't teach through the hard parts, it gives our kids the impression that the wheels have fallen off. (Competence)

5. **Filibuster.** This is when you kill class time with life stories or tangential conversations. So easy to do. And it kills urgency. Tangents and story time should not be daily occurrences if our goal is for students to *master* as much as possible while they're with us. (Passion, Competence)

6. **Be nice to your students when they are around, but speak ill of them after class.** Kids are smart, and they can tell when we don't like them. Also, our brains and our hearts aren't as good at compartmentalizing as we want to think sometimes. When we speak ill of our kids, we are going to have a harder time really connecting with them. (Care, Passion)

7. **Never share anything about yourself with your students.** While #5 describes a classic oversharing problem, if we don't share anything about ourselves with our kids, then we make ourselves unrelatable. This is a fine line to walk, I know. (Care, Competence)

8. **Pay no mind to your distracting speaking tics.** Alternatively, don't film yourself teaching. Watching myself teach is the most useful (and most painful) way for me to see that I could be speaking better or more clearly. It's the only way to detect my PVLEGS glitches. (Competence, Passion)

9. **Don't commit to hard-and-fast unit end dates.** When we commit to summative assessment dates or due dates, and we share those dates with kids, it shows them that we have a plan and we're going to see it through. An additional benefit here is that setting (and struggling with) unit end dates is the only way we become good at figuring out how long stuff really takes. (Competence)

10. **When students fail, don't reflect about how you could have done things differently.** Even if 99 percent of a student's failure seems to be her fault or her choice or her problem to overcome, there's still the 1 percent that I affected. (Care, Competence, Passion)

Again, I've learned all of these from personal experience. If you feel like one of those is aimed straight at you, then you're in good company.

BELONGING

People like me belong in academic communities like this.

SYNONYMS	ANTONYMS
People like me read.	None of my friends read because we're just not into that sort of thing.
I'm a science kid.	I don't get science.
I'm not a poser in here; these are my people, and I'm theirs.	People who care about school are posers or try-hards. I'm not like them.
It's not weird that I'm writing right now because people like me write.	I'm not a writer.
I'm shy, but I still stand up for Pop-Up Debates because plenty of people in our class are shy, and we challenge ourselves through public speaking.	I'm too shy to participate.
My contributions and abilities are valued by this community.	People think I don't have what it takes to be in here.
The things I struggle with are normal for people in this community.	I'm the only one having a hard time in here.

This belief is about creating a fit between who our students see themselves as and the kind of work that we'll do in our setting. If our students don't think of themselves as the kinds of people who read things for school, then they probably won't. James Clear (2015) summarizes behavior change into three areas: results (the things we want to achieve), actions (what it takes to achieve those things), and identity (the beliefs we have about ourselves). Importantly, Clear argues that identity is what comes first (see Figure 2.3).

Because Clear's (2015) audience is made up of adults who want to change their behaviors, he treats the problem differently than you and I need to; after all, we are adults who want to help our students change or improve *their* behaviors. In other words, the results we want for our students are found in those Everest sentences we wrote in Chapter 1. On a more immediate timeframe, the result we're after is that our students will master the material of our class, be it art history

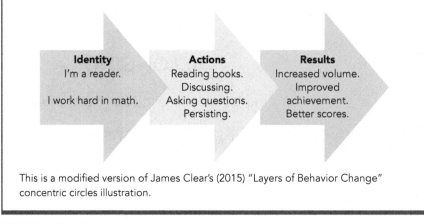

Identity
I'm a reader.

I work hard in math.

Actions
Reading books.
Discussing.
Asking questions.
Persisting.

Results
Increased volume.
Improved
achievement.
Better scores.

This is a modified version of James Clear's (2015) "Layers of Behavior Change" concentric circles illustration.

FIGURE 2.3 • The Important Role of Identity in Behavior

or health or computer programming or world geography. To achieve that result, we need our students to engage in certain behaviors. The ones I focus on in this book are those that involve knowledge building, reading, writing, speaking, listening, or arguing. But for these behaviors to really add up to the result we're working toward, we need our students to see themselves as the kinds of people who do those kinds of things.

Let's look at a few ways to cultivate this belief in our own settings.

davestuartjr.com/Walton

Use this link or the QR code to access the full Walton interview.

Use an attributional retraining intervention. That label is wonky as all get out, but all it's getting at is that, when things go poorly, we sometimes attribute it to something that's uniquely wrong with us, when really the negative situation may just be something that's normal. Terminology aside, this is the most scientifically validated (and experimentally replicated) idea I'll share around this belief, so take note. As Greg Walton (2012) describes in *Encouraging a Sense of Belonging*, students in a challenging transition year (e.g., first year of college, first year of high school, first year of middle school) are shown videos or given narratives from upperclassmen, and these upperclassmen describe how they initially worried about their belonging during their transition year, but they found it to be just a normal part of the transition. These narratives include examples (e.g., "I didn't get invited to the party," or "I did poorly on a test everyone else seemed to do well on") showing how these events are a normal part of everyone's experience.

Participants in the interventions were then directed to write to future students about what they had learned from the videos or narratives and why it's important to keep these lessons in mind. This brief writing assignment is important, explains Walton (2012), because it's "not remedial"; in other words, participants feel that they are acting as part of the solution to this problem by writing to future students.

Amazingly, this simple intervention has predicted long-term improvements in academic outcomes. This makes sense: those first transition years are critical to achievement in later years (see, e.g., Easton, Johnson, & Sartain, 2017). But what's incredible is that all it takes is a 30-minute, two-part exercise to produce these results. Also, this intervention is especially powerful for students who experience what psychologists call "stereotype threat"—when people are in a work or school environment where they are a minority and they fear that their performance might confirm negative stereotypes about their group. For example, African American males often experience stereotype threat during their first year if they attend a college with a minority African American population. Another example is female engineering students, who often experience stereotype threat if they are pursuing an engineering major in a school with a small percentage of female students. You can view a student video I use for conducting this type of intervention early in the school year by scanning the QR code in the margin.

davestuartjr.com/att1

To see an example of student video used for attributional retraining intervention, use the QR code above, or type the link into your browser.

Communicate with parents and guardians. Whether through text messages, email, or phone, actionable communication from teachers to parents increases the odds that parents will speak to their children about school, improves the quality of these conversations, and improves student outcomes (Kraft & Rogers, 2014). Such efforts, which can be as simple as sending a reminder text to parents once a week about something their child can improve upon (e.g., attendance, focus, missing assignments, studying), reinforce the school–home connection, and this, in turn, seems likely to increase the degree to which students identify with school.

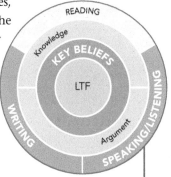

Positive identity index cards. I like having a deck of index cards for each of my classes. Throughout the year, I use them to facilitate calling on students at random during the Share portion of Think–Pair–Share (see Chapter 7). At the start of the year, however, these index cards give me a chance to get to know my students, and they give my students a chance to reflect on who they'd like to become.

For several years, I had students create index cards for me by grabbing a seat and an index card on the first day of class, then writing their name on one side of the card, nice and large. On the other side, I'd ask them to write adjectives or phrases that described them. In my head this made sense—I was getting to know

TRY THIS

Have students write on index cards statements about the kinds of people they want to be, then share what they wrote with a partner.

them, and with the activity I was telling them that I cared about who they are. And, indeed, I did and I do.

But there was a problem with this activity: I'd often have my fourteen-year-old students writing things like "Loud" or "Lazy" to describe themselves. Comments like this hurt me—especially that latter adjective—because I was giving them an assignment that was inadvertently encouraging them to identify with bad habits. Loudness isn't inherently bad, but the way my kids mean it usually implies a lack of self-control or a lack of consideration for others. And then laziness—whoa, that's just straight up Bad Habit Central. I don't want that as a part of the identity of anyone I love. I build my class on the idea that we do hard things, and doing hard things is a part of who we are. And yet here I was, accidentally encouraging kids to begin their year identifying with descriptors I hoped to help them weed out from the gardens of their hearts.

Eventually, inspiration struck, and I made an important change to this assignment. With a big smile on my face, I now introduce the index card like this:

> *Family and team, I am excited for you today because today is a new start. As of right now, the things you've not done well at in the past can only help you to answer two questions: What did I learn? and What can I do better for next time? That's it. Any kind of thoughts like "I'm dumb" or "School's not for me" won't help; if you let your failures tell you those things, you are doing failure wrong. Picture yourself literally plucking those kinds of ideas from your heart right now and chucking them into the sun.*

> *Here's what we're going to do: brand new semester, brand new index cards. On one side, I want you to write your name, nice and large. On the other side, I want you to describe the person you want to be some day. I'm not looking for that person's job description; I'm looking for the way that person's friends and family members will talk about her when she's not around. What kind of impact do you want to create while you've still got air in your lungs? What kind of person do you want to be remembered as? That's what I want you to write on the other side of that index card.*

Here are the kinds of things kids write:

- "I want to be a dependable friend, a kid my parents can be proud of, not the one people think is dumb."

- "I hope to be generous."

- "I want to be a hard worker."

- "I don't want my life to be a waste."

- "I want to be someone who my parents can be proud of and that they'll want to show off."

- "I don't want to just be known as the quiet one."

- "I want to be known as someone who dominated life."

- "I want my mom to be able to see I can make it without her."

In this exercise, students are defining a positive possible identity, or a positive "future self," as the psychological research often calls it. Although it's true that "just because the future self can matter does mean that it always will" (Oyserman, 2015, p. 5), connecting positive future selves to our classrooms is necessary work in the cultivation of the Belonging belief.

Regularly move the seating chart. For the first few weeks of the school year, I change the seating daily. The kids become accustomed to this; every time they enter the class, I've laid their class set of index cards out in a new arrangement. (Well, it's mostly new, but since I only have a minute or so to create each day's new chart, most often it's left up to chance.) My goal is that "everyone in the room gets to know each other, not by reputation or history, but by working directly together, here and now" (Daniels & Steineke, 2014). Inevitably, they ask why I do this, and I tell them that one of my goals for the year is for them to see that we, as a class, are a family and a team. (This language targets a sense of belonging.) Everyone's necessary; there's no "optional" person in the classroom. There's *no* big reward for competition—I don't grade on a curve or anything like that—and *only* big rewards for cooperation (namely, joy and a sense of camaraderie).

davestuartjr.com/care

The QR code or the link above will take you to my blog article "CARE: Four Underlying Principles of Classroom Management."

Master classroom management. As it turns out, classrooms with clear management routines and structures don't just support Teacher Credibility, they protect Belonging, too. I have to have a clearly communicated, consistently executed plan in place for dealing with comments or behaviors that are not conducive to feelings of belonging. For example, side conversations while other people are talking are not, in my experience, conducive to every child feeling like he or she belongs. Cross talk during Pop-Up Debates or discussions (see Chapter 4) has the same negative effect. My classroom management policies support a safe environment.

Value introversion and extroversion explicitly and by creating mandatory learning experiences. Our introverted students will tend to prefer learning through independent work, whereas our extroverted students will tend to prefer learning through collaborative work (Cain, 2013; Cain, Mone, & Moroz, 2017). Speaking to the value that both of these personality styles and learning preferences have is one way to create a sense of belonging for students along the introversion–extroversion spectrum; facilitating experiences in which all students write to learn (see Chapter 6) and all students participate in small-group Conversation Challenges (see Chapter 7) or whole-class Pop-Up Debates (see Chapter 4) is another.

BELIEF 3: EFFORT

davestuartjr.com/
perfectionism

The QR code or link above will take you to my blog article "Perfectionism Behind, Improvementism Ahead." Teachers struggle with this just as much as students do!

EFFORT

I can improve through my effort.

SYNONYMS	ANTONYMS
I'm an improvementist.	I'm a perfectionist.
I'm a hard worker.	I'm smart.
I push myself in math.	I'm good at math.
I like challenges.	I like things I know I'll succeed at.
Failure is my best teacher.	I hate it when I fail.
If I'm to get better at this, it's up to me.	I can't get better at this.

A big part of the Effort Belief has been popularized by Carol Dweck's (2007) writings on growth mindset, but it's also about what students attribute their successes or failures to. When we believe that some people are just born good at school and others aren't—when that's our highest internal principle for how school works—then there's not much incentive to work hard. "If I'm to get better, then it's up to me"—that's the spirit we're after. As one particularly effective TEDx speaker puts it (Briceno, 2012), at the core of the Effort Belief is the realization that I'm not "special"; just like anyone else, excellence for me will take hard work and persistence. There are a number of ways to cultivate effort in your classroom:

Praise the process, not the person. In the early years of my career, I was really quick with this piece of praise: "Wow, you are really smart!" According to the literature on growth mindset, that's what *not* to do. More common in education is communicating the idea that everyone is a genius—"Hey class, look at those tests! How smart are we?"

Instead of this, we want to target our praise at the specific processes by which learning and mastery come about, not the people who successfully engage in these processes. In the table shown in Figure 2.4, we see some examples drawn from the helpful website MindsetKit.org (2015).

DON'T DO THIS (PRAISING THE PERSON)	DO THIS (PRAISING THE PROCESS)
Awesome! You must be smart at science.	Awesome! You must have worked hard and smart. What strategies did you use?
Look at that document-based question score—see, you really are smart at world history!	You've really been working at your DBQ skills, and your improvement on this part of the rubric shows it. Congratulations.
Yes, that's correct—I told you you're great at math!	That's right, and I appreciate how many methods you used to try to solve that problem.
You're such a great student!	You do the things it takes to learn successfully, like taking good notes, quizzing yourself, and using effective study groups. Keep that up.

FIGURE 2.4 • The Difference Between Praising the Person and Praising the Process

Notice the specificity of each process-oriented compliment in Figure 2.4—that's important, as recent research indicates that vague praise of effort can actually estrange adolescents (Gross-Loh, 2016; Sparks, 2018).

Create a culture of improvementism. The Effort Belief is hugely influenced by the classroom cultures we create. If my students are to flourish long term, I need to help them see the impossible standards that "perfect" social media personas create for us. I'm relentless about creating classroom cultures where improvementism is normal and perfectionism is weird, illogical, and even harmful.

Doug Lemov (2014) outlines this idea well when he describes what he calls "cultures of error" in *Teach Like a Champion 2.0*. Such classroom cultures, Lemov argues, have multiple benefits. Students are more resilient when error-making is a normalized part of the learning process; they are also more likely to share their hang-ups, making it easier to teach them. Here are some methods for building this kind of culture in our classrooms:

- Praise risk taking. I had a student, "Jeremy," who was great at asking questions when he wasn't clear on something—a big risk for ninth graders—yet who almost always preceded his questions with, "This is probably a dumb question, but . . ." Over time, I was able to disabuse Jeremy of this self-denigrating habit by simply praising him for asking questions in the face of confusion. To help draw questions like Jeremy's out, we can ask students to nominate "things they would like to review" (Lemov, 2014, p. 65) after a challenging set of problems, concepts, or readings.

- Mind your tone. When our students struggle or demonstrate misunderstandings, everyone in the classroom listens to our tone of voice. In these situations, we must strive to maintain a tone of voice that is "calm, steady, nonjudgmental" (Lemov, 2014, p. 65). Use language like "Thank you for putting that idea forward. There are some inaccuracies in what you said, and those inaccuracies are actually pretty common, I've found. Let's unpack what's going on."

- Expect and welcome error. Consider a situation in which a student volunteers an answer to a question, and his answer is incorrect. What is the difference between responding with "I'm so glad you made that mistake; it's going to help me help you" and with "Listen, we can't keep making this mistake"? Obviously, the former response cultivates a culture in which error is normal and even helpful, whereas the latter communicates to students that there's a limit to how often they can be wrong. So then, why don't I always respond in the right way? I, too, frequently *don't expect* students to make mistakes. By adjusting my expectations and beliefs about mistakes, I can improve my ability to respond to student mistakes productively.

- Teach effective learning techniques. If we don't equip our students with effective learning techniques, they will likely put in bursts of effort only to find the goal of that effort frustrated. I want my students to work hard *and* smart, so I teach students to develop "new strategies to tackle difficult problems, rather than [use] sheer effort" (Blad, 2016). Early on in the school year, then, I like to introduce my students to techniques for note taking, focusing, active reading, and self-quizzing.

EFFICACY

I can succeed at this.

SYNONYMS	ANTONYMS
I can write 100 words in response to a quick-write prompt.	There's no way I can write that much.
I can master World History this year.	I've never been good at history.
I can learn Physics.	I'm going to fail Physics.
I can get better at drawing this year in Art class.	I can't draw.
Chemistry doesn't make sense right now, but it will.	I just don't get Chemistry.
I can turn my work in on time. I can stay organized.	I always turn things in late. Whenever I try getting organized, I always end up getting messy again. The same thing is going to happen this time.

When's the last time you were highly motivated to do something for which you felt there was zero chance of success? I'm not talking about golf, where (at least for me) there's always that 1 percent chance of success during my annual-or-so game. I'm talking about guaranteed failure. It kills your mojo, right? When our students think that they can engage with and enjoy *To Kill a Mockingbird*, when they think that they might be able to master the concepts of physics, the Efficacy Belief begins to activate.

At the core of this belief is optimism, resilience, and confidence that we can succeed. We can cultivate self-efficacy in our students through a number of common-sense and research-informed practices, like these:

Define success wisely and cultivate the inner scorecard. In Alice Schroeder's (2009) fascinating biography of Warren Buffett, she shares the following Buffettism: "The big question about how people behave is whether they've got an Inner Scorecard or an Outer Scorecard. It helps if you can be satisfied with an Inner Scorecard. I always pose it this way. I say: 'Lookit. Would you rather be the world's greatest lover, but have everyone think you're the world's worst lover? Or would you rather be the world's worst lover but have everyone think you're the world's greatest lover?'" While I'm not ready to have my students consider Warren's question on what kind of lover they'd like to be, I do resonate with what he's getting at. For my students, the question could be put like this:

- Would you rather be the world's greatest friend, but have everyone think you're the world's worst friend, or be the world's worst friend, but have everyone think you're the best?

- Would you rather be the world's greatest psychology student, but have everyone think you're the world's worst, or be the world's worst psychology student, but have everyone think you're the best?

Externalism, I've found, is one of the most difficult belief orientations to counteract in my students. Grades, scores on tests, how many Snapchat streaks they have going—all of these things define success as something externally sourced and therefore something that's outside of their total control and fraught with anxiety. As Dr. Peter Gray (2010) writes, "it is reasonable to suggest that the rise of Externality (and decline of Internality) is causally related to the rise in anxiety and depression." This is an academic issue as well as a mental health issue.

I've yet to solve this problem, but I work toward its solution by building a culture in my classroom of inner scorecards rather than outer ones. I have students set goals (see the next recommendation) targeting improvement on measures under our control (e.g., I will study for 25 minutes per night using my flashcards) instead of measures outside of our control (I will get 100 percent on my Spanish exam).

Facilitate goal-setting, -striving, and -attaining with mental contrasting and implementation intentions. To increase the odds of my students doing the work required to succeed on a given task or unit of instruction, I use a tool called WOOP (Oettingen, 2014), which stands for Wish, Outcome, Obstacles, Plan:

- The Wish is just the goal, and it should be meaningful to the student. Make sure that it's got some time frame attached to it—a day, a month, or longer—and a memorable three- to six-word summary.

- The Outcome involves students visualizing what it will be like to achieve the goal. This can be done through writing or through closed-eye imagining, but I tend to go for the written approach as my freshmen are more apt to engage with it. What we want here is for our students to really imagine what it will be like to achieve this outcome.

- Next, students visualize the Obstacles that are likely to get in the way. If this is a homework-related goal, what things are bound to make homework completion challenging? If it's a performance-related goal, why will performing at that level be hard? Again, this can be done through closed-eye imagining or written reflection, just as long as they engage in mentally contrasting the outcome and the obstacles.

- Finally, students create a simple if–then Plan: "If [insert specific obstacle], then [insert actions that will take place to overcome the obstacle and do the work needed to achieve the goal]."

There are two processes at play in WOOP that draw upon replicated studies. The first is mental contrasting: this is the Outcomes and Obstacles part, during which participants visualize both the goal achievement condition *and* the present obstacles in their life most likely to stand in the way of achieving that goal. The second is forming an implementation intention: a simple, yet specific if–then Plan for what participants will do when their obstacle arises. In one student, participants who used mental contrasting and implementation intentions ate fewer unhealthy snacks (Adriaanse et al., 2010). In another, results suggest that mental contrasting works particularly well in helping participants energize for particularly stressful tasks (Oettingen et al., 2009). In a study quite relevant to the work you and I do, high school students who used mental contrasting and implementation intentions completed 60 percent more practice questions than students who did not (Duckworth, Grant, Loew, Oettingen, & Gollwitzer, 2011). How can our students flourish long term without tools for setting and working toward goals? Activities like WOOP shouldn't be left to study skills courses; they should happen throughout the school day.

https://www.characterlab .org/WOOP

The best treatment of WOOP is the "Playbook" created by Character Lab found at https://www.characterlab .org/WOOP.

Be a role model of success. Perhaps the most enjoyable means by which teachers can help shape their students' conceptions of success is representing well-rounded success for our students (Wilcox, 2017). Although I'm cautious about over-personalizing my instruction, I do periodically give my students examples from my own life of pursuing mastery and excellence rather than externalized goals:

- As a father, I try to reflect on where I am falling short and challenge myself to improve in measurable ways (e.g., more one-on-one conversations with each of my children).

- As a husband, I try to surprise my wife at least once per month. This has led me to give her gifts I wouldn't have thought of before, perform small acts of life-giving spontaneity, and even take spur-of-the-moment trips to places within a short drive of our home.

- As a teacher, I share with my students some of my professional goals, such as my desire to have each year's students outperform preceding years' groups in end-of-the-year Pop-Up Debates.

- As a shy and introverted person, I share with my students how I seek opportunities to speak to groups of teachers. They know that I do this to push myself to face fears and overcome internal obstacles.

In short, I want my students to see success as John Wooden (Carty & Wooden, 2005) perceived it: "Peace of mind which is a direct result of self-satisfaction in knowing you did your best to become the best that you are capable of becoming." When our students begin measuring success by the pursuit of their potential versus the achievement of a certain grade on a test, it becomes much easier for them to resiliently believe that they can succeed in our classes.

Scaffold carefully. Perhaps the most important building block for confidence is succeeding at a challenging task. Our aim as teachers, then, should be to create learning experiences that are both challenging *and* achievable for our students. Self-efficacy is built through a string of successful experiences happening right in our zone of proximal development (Vygotsky, 1978) or, to use a more recent term, the "sweet spot" (Coyle, 2012). As Daniel Coyle describes it, the kind of practice that makes us get better the fastest takes place in the sweet spot, where our success rate is only 50 percent to 80 percent. The better our curricula move from concrete to abstract, less difficult to more difficult, and so on, the more likely our students will be to develop a resilient belief in their ability to succeed in our class. I think I will be working toward mastering the art of scaffolding for my whole career. It's a difficult but worthy task to try to create "sweet spot" learning experiences in classes of more than thirty secondary students.

VALUE

This work has value for me.

SYNONYMS	ANTONYMS
Band is important.	Band is dumb.
Spanish is going to make me better at life.	Spanish won't help me in life.
Reading makes me happy.	Reading is boring.
Writing is a skill I can use in almost any profession.	Writing is useless.
Sociology is challenging and intriguing.	Sociology is annoying.

Any group of students may give dozens of reasons why the work I ask them to do is valuable. Caleb may value my class because he enjoys world history or English, while Alexis values it because the literacy skills she's developing will be useful in the future, and Martín buys into the idea that hard work is valuable simply because it's hard. As teachers, we cultivate the value belief all the time—when we seek to make kids more curious, when we teach a love for learning, when we incorporate real-world action projects into our curricula—and we can cultivate value in the following important ways, as well.

Use Chris Hulleman's "Build Connections" exercise. Several years ago, I came across a fascinating article called "I could be changing the world right now, but instead I'm solving for X" (Hulleman, 2015). In it, researcher Chris Hulleman lays out the expectancy-value theory of motivation. He represents it as a math equation:

(The Expectation That I Can Make It) x (The Value Of The Goal) = Motivation

In other words, expectancy-value theory focuses on the latter two beliefs that we've been discussing in this chapter.

The reason this article matters for us is that Hulleman didn't just lay out a theory; he highlighted some studies he had conducted with science students (e.g., Hulleman & Harackiewicz, 2009) in which a simple writing assignment targeting the value belief increased students' perceived value of the task, particularly those who identified little expectancy prior to the intervention.

The intervention, which Hulleman and several collaborators at Character Lab turned into an evidence-based, teacher-friendly playbook for CharacterLab.org, involves three simple steps, as demonstrated in Figure 2.5:

1. Students list the interests, people, hobbies, and goals that are important in their lives.

2. Next, students list and describe the topics they are studying in class right now.

3. Finally, students choose one item from the first list and one from the second list that have a connection, and they write about the connection between those two things, including a specific example of how that connection might apply to their life.

What I love about Build Connections is that it tackles several things I care about: I want my students to value the work we do in my class, I want them to understand that ownership is an internal job, and I want them to review things they've learned and write about them. All of those objectives are met in this brief, once-per-unit exercise.

Have students argue about which of a group of classes is the best. At least once per year, I like to have my students do a Pop-Up Debate (see Chapter 4) in response to this question: Which of the following subject areas—math, science, social studies, English, or world language—is the best? I can add or delete classes from this list, but my unstated goal in this debate is for my students to hear all kinds of student-created, value-based arguments about school. To encourage them to argue across the list, I keep a tally of how many arguments have been put forth in favor of each subject. This is typically a lively, enjoyable argument, and the students produce some surprisingly eloquent ideas in support of classes that you would not have expected them to speak for.

INTERESTS, PEOPLE, HOBBIES, GOALS IMPORTANT TO MY LIFE	TOPICS STUDIED IN CLASS RIGHT NOW	CONNECTION
Video games	Linear functions	Video games and linear functions **are connected because** I can use the function to decide if I should rent a video game (linear function) or buy it (fixed cost) based on how much I will use it. Linear functions **could be important in my life.** I can use them to determine the exact usage over time that would make buying something cheaper than renting it.
Technology	Expansion of interregional trade routes in the post-classical era	Technology and the expansion of interregional trade routes **are connected, and here's why:** as human beings become more connected through trade, technology tends to improve at a faster rate. In our earlier unit, we saw humans very slowly developing from bronze to iron metal working. As trade routes developed through the classical era, technological improvements increased as different regions began sharing ideas. The same pattern continued in the post-classical era, and it continues to this day with the crazy connectedness brought about by the internet. **This is important to my life** because I love technology and it's interesting to me to see that we live in a time of never-before-seen global connectedness.
My friends	The novel *A Separate Peace*, by John Knowles	My friends and Knowles's novel **are connected because** in the novel, the characters have some twisted parts of their friendships. For example, Gene is secretly jealous of Finny, who is successful at a lot of things, and the novel has helped me see that I, too, am sometimes jealous of my friends who are less socially awkward than me or more athletic than me. This kind of jealousy can eat away at friendships, and in the case of Gene they might have even caused him to hurt Finny. Seeing **this could help my life** because I can do something about the jealousy before it consumes me.

FIGURE 2.5 • Example of a "Build Connections" Exercise

Prior to the debate, I teach a target skill (e.g., the Paraphrase Plus set of discussion moves described in Chapter 4), and I give whole-class feedback and coaching on that skill throughout the debate. So on the surface, students experience this as yet another situation in which we are practicing argumentation, speaking, and listening skills. But much more important is that, in addition to those stated

davestuartjr.com/expectancy-
value-pop-up-debate

For in-depth treatment
of this debate, see
"An Expectancy-Value
Pop-Up Debate."

objectives, my students are hearing a few dozen reasons why the classes they experience each day are worth more than suffering through. They are having the value belief modeled for them by their peers.

Enjoy the creative potential of communicating value. This is one of my favorite challenges in teaching. I know that when I explain the value of working hard at the six things to my students, I'm not going to hit the heart of every kid in the room— probably not even most of them. This is why my strategy is to communicate value persistently and creatively, gently and forcefully, day in and day out.

Many great teachers do this. Remember Edmund Hillary and Tenzing Norgay from Chapter 1? One of their predecessors, George Mallory, is said to have been asked, "Why do you want to go and climb Mount Everest?" His response is legend: "Because it's there." I once met a math teacher in Dearborn, Michigan, who uses this as one of his favorite ways of explaining to his math students why they need to master the quadratic formula: "Because it's there," he says, "and because it's beautiful that it's there." Again, I'm sure this doesn't work for all of his students, but I bet it strikes a few of them.

Communicate the utility of an education. I don't want my students to get the impression that education is only valuable from a utilitarian perspective—it prepares you to compete in the workforce—but I do want them to understand the utilitarian reasons for applying oneself to school. This is why one of the first texts we'll closely read as a class is the most recent "Unemployment Rates and Earnings by Educational Attainment" chart from the U.S. Bureau of Labor Statistics (see Figure 2.6).

I like to ask my students basic questions about this at first:

- What is the chart about? What do the bars on the right and left represent?
- What trends do you see?
- Challenge question: How much will a median bachelor's degree recipient earn in his or her lifetime, assuming a retirement age of 63, compared to a median high school diploma holder?

At first, they quietly read the chart and write responses to one or more of the preceding questions. After five minutes or so, I have them talk with a partner about what they wrote, and afterward we share out. My goal is to quickly move

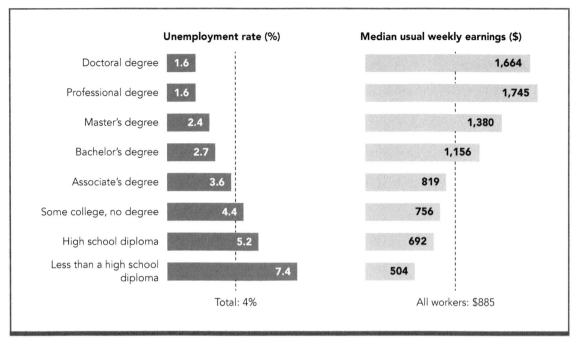

FIGURE 2.6 • Unemployment Rates and Earnings by Educational Attainment, 2016

Source: U.S. Bureau of Labor Statistics. October 24, 2017. Retrieved from https://www.bls.gov/emp/ep_chart_001.htm.

Note: Data are for persons age 25 and over. Earnings are for full-time wage and salary workers.

the discussion from comprehension (What's the chart saying about educational attainment?) to application (What does this mean for my life?). I'm careful to explain to students what a median is, and I want to be clear that the chart isn't wrong because Bill Gates dropped out of college and is now a billionaire or because Uncle Jimmy dropped out of high school and now owns some really sweet muscle cars. The point of this reading, writing, and speaking exercise is to help my students see that educational attainment tends to have economic utility. That's far from the only reason why it's important, but it's certainly one of the reasons.

Communicate the academic foundations required by careers, too. I like doing a similarly brief, targeted close reading activity with David Conley's (2014, pp. 47–49) readiness spectrum (see Figure 2.7). College obviously requires academic preparation, but many of my students are surprised to learn that careers do, too. Conley (2012) classifies careers as post-secondary pathways that require pathway-oriented training or certification in addition to high school coursework. Important for a good percentage of my students each year, this includes military and technical pathways.

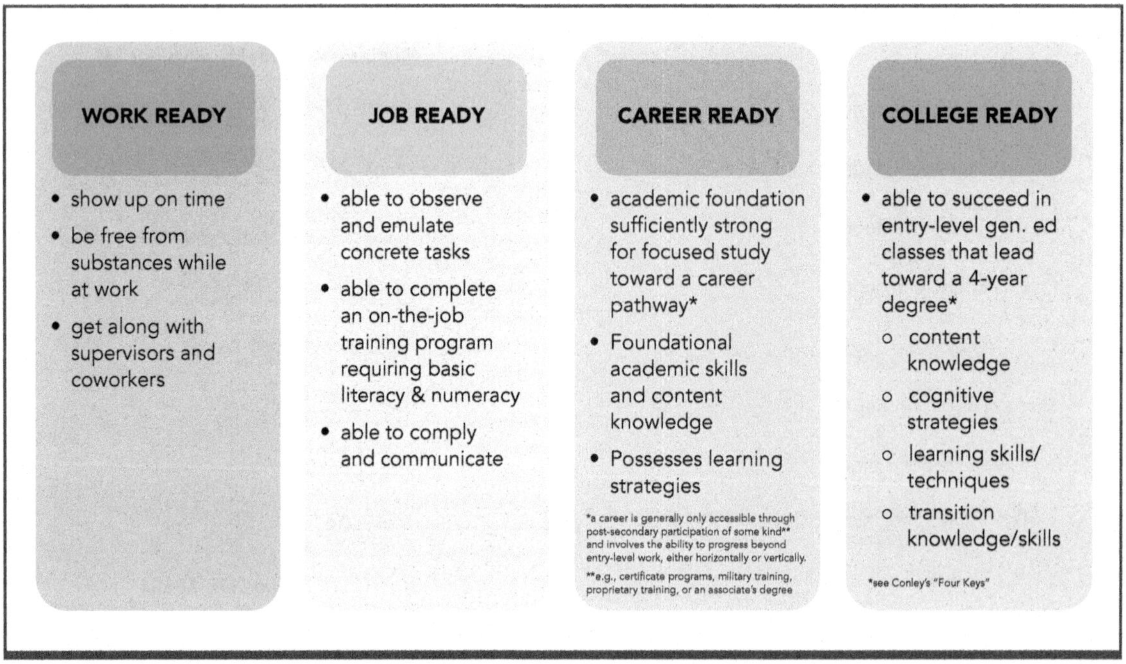

FIGURE 2.7 • Conley's Readiness Spectrum

Source: From David Conley's Getting Ready for College, Careers, and the Common Core (2014); image by Dave Stuart Jr. of DaveStuartJr.com.

For secondary teachers, this is especially important to establish. When we emphasize college alone, we needlessly estrange some students from dreaming about flourishing postsecondary pathways. Using Conley's research, however, we can help our students see that academic preparation is a wise investment even for career pathways.

Communicate the value of their interests. When possible, I think it's wise to incorporate our students' interests into our course material, if only to explain things in a way they'll be most likely to understand. For example, I sometimes tell my students that becoming college- and career-ready is akin to becoming a Navy SEAL of life. If you meet me in person, you'll note that I'm not exactly Navy SEAL material, but I've read enough about the process of becoming a SEAL to know that when a soldier first earns the right to wear the trident, that soldier isn't trained for the specific missions he'll face; rather, he's only demonstrated a readiness to successfully complete such further specialized trainings. He's ready to be a SEAL and to do the work required to prepare for any number of future challenges. The college- and career-ready student is similar: she's not trained to be a radiologist or an accountant or a call center manager, but she's cognitively and physically prepared to do what it takes to get to those destinations.

Establish a "Do Hard Things" ethos. On the opposite end of utilitarianism, there's the Do Hard Things mantra that I picked up from a book of the same name (Harris & Harris, 2008). Written by two teenagers, *Do Hard Things* is the fascinating story of two teenage boys who, primarily through blogging, created a movement of teens "rebelling against low expectations." While the book's strong Christian themes preclude me from assigning it to my public school students, the authors' argument resonates with my freshmen: teens ought to be insulted that a "good teenager" is often seen as someone who doesn't do drugs or doesn't get pregnant, someone who turns in her homework and makes her bed. The Harris boys argue that this is preposterous and that teens should rebel against low expectations by pushing themselves to be the kind of people who do challenging things.

Angela Duckworth, the MacArthur grant–winning psychologist who co-founded Character Lab and popularized the term *grit,* actually riffs on this theme within her own family. In the Duckworth household, there's a "Hard Thing Rule": everyone needs to be engaged in doing something challenging. Specifically, Duckworth explains,

> The Hard Thing Rule . . . has three parts. The first is that everyone— including Mom and Dad—has to do a hard thing. A hard thing is something that requires daily deliberate practice. I've told my kids that psychological research is my hard thing, but I also practice yoga. Dad tries to get better and better at being a real estate developer; he does the same with running. (2016, p. 241)

Duckworth (2016) goes on to explain that the second part of the Hard Thing Rule is that you can quit, but not until a natural stopping point (e.g., the season is over), and the third part of the rule is that each person picks his or her own hard thing. "Nobody picks it for you," she says, "because, after all, it would make no sense to do a hard thing you're not even vaguely interested in" (p. 241). Here, of course, my classes are different from the hard things Duckworth refers to—whether students are interested in world history or English 9 or not, they're required by state law to receive credit for those courses. But still, I find that my students rally around this idea of being people who do hard things. I teach every day beneath a sign on the wall that shows this mantra in big, bold type (see Figure 2.8). This group identity is something that my students find compelling, and I hope it cultivates in them a value proposition that can travel outside my room: the work I do in school is valuable *especially* when it's hard because I'm the kind of person who does hard things.

FIGURE 2.8 • Every day, I teach beneath a reminder of our classroom's Do Hard Things ethos.

Source: Photo by Alyssa Roelofs.

Give them choice. Shared knowledge building is too important to me to provide students with a choice-only learning environment, but that doesn't mean choice has no role in my classroom. For example, after we complete our first Burning Questions of the Year (BQY) article series (see Chapter 3), I ask students to brainstorm questions that they'd like to explore. My students ask questions that cohere around big, burning questions like "What could end the world?" and "What can we do to make the world better?" Their questions, then, drive the future weekly articles I'll give them as we seek to build knowledge beyond the curriculum. Because my choice of articles is directed, in part, by the things they are curious about, it's easier for my students to find personal value in this work.

The ideas in this chapter can be a bit overwhelming, and it only gets worse once you start diving deeper into the research (see Dig Deeper sidebar on page 27). I find it helpful and clarifying to organize belief-supporting efforts by time of year. Here you'll find an example based on the contents of this chapter.

COMMON TEACHER HANG-UP

I want to cultivate key beliefs, but I don't know when to do what.

WHEN	WHAT	WHAT BELIEF IS BEING TARGETED	HELPFUL HINTS
First week of school	Introduce and begin implementing classroom management policy	Teacher Credibility (competence) + Belonging (making a safe space for students)	Use Michael Linsin's approach, explained at www.smartclassroom management.com
	Positive identity index cards	Belonging	See pp. 41–43
First month of school	Attributional retraining exercise	Belonging	See pp. 40–41
	Utility value of education	Value	See p. 54
	Comparing career and college readiness	Value	See pp. 55–56
	Teach students effective learning techniques and study skills	Effort	Use Erica Beaton's tips, explained at www .davstuartjr.com/beaton
Monthly	Low-effort parent contact	Credibility (care) + Belonging	See p. 41
	Hulleman's Build Connections exercise	Value	See pp. 51–-53 or CharacterLab.org
	WOOP goal-setting exercise	Efficacy	See pp. 48–49 or CharacterLab.org
	Rearrange classroom seating chart	Belonging	See p. 43
Around mid-year	Pop-up debate about which subject is the best	Value	See pp. 52–54 for description of activity and pp. 114–116 for how to hold Pop-Up Debates

At the end of the day, we want to create an abundance of "messages" about credibility, belonging, effort, efficacy, and value ("both one's own intrinsic value and the value of one's education"), being mindful that messages are both the "intended and unintended, [the] explicit and implicit," as these "are at the core of building students' academic mindsets" (Farrington et al., 2012, p. 34). This is why I call them Key Beliefs; they are critical and complex. As I've worked (and revised my practice) over the years to instill these Key Beliefs in my students, I've learned a few things about dynamics at play in this kind of inside-out work beneath the lessons we teach our students.

BEYOND THE HEAD AND INTO THE HEART

If we succeed at getting our students to intellectually assent to the idea that our course material is valuable to their lives, or that they are the kinds of kids who think like scientists, that's only a start. These beliefs move our students to learning behaviors when they are held at the operational level—when they've worked themselves in deeply. This is why our goal for this area of the *These 6 Things* bull's-eye isn't to create a few belief-supporting lessons; rather, our goal is to undergird all that happens in our classrooms with these five Key Beliefs, aiming at the creation of classrooms in which these beliefs are as natural as the presence of water is to a fish.

When these beliefs are operational, they help our students to filter effectively the many stimuli they'll receive in a given school day:

- "Man, this assignment is hard," a student might think. "Yes, it is hard, but Mr. Stuart said it would be hard; so once again, Mr. Stuart was right." (teacher credibility)

- "I keep getting this problem set wrong, but that just means there's some kind of error in my process. I'll go back through it more slowly; I can figure this out." (effort, efficacy)

- "I really want to play my Xbox right now, but that will only be fun today. Studying for that health exam, on the other hand, will give me pleasure in the future." (value)

- "I'm so nervous about tomorrow's Pop-Up Debate. I'm terrible at speaking in front of the class! But I know that other people in

the class are nervous, too—actually, most are. I won't be alone."
(belonging)

Our students constantly face potentially demotivating internal and external messages, and when the beliefs become ingrained, they act as a filtering mechanism (EL Education, 2015). Our kids see and interpret their world through what they believe—just like you and I do.

NAVIGATIONAL AIDS AND ANALYTICAL TOOLS RATHER THAN MAGIC PILLS OR WEAPONS OF JUDGMENT

The beliefs do not magically remedy skill deficits, and every day I teach many students who are multiple years behind where they should be as thinkers, readers, writers, and speakers. Believing the things that we've laid out in this chapter won't magically catch them up—I don't ever want to give that impression. All that the beliefs do is serve as levers for the knowledge-rich, thoughtful, literacy-drenched learning experiences I'll provide my students with all year long. For our students who are years behind their peers, only years of belief-infused, scaffolded work will get them caught up.

It is important to reconcile our high aim—the creation of classrooms where these beliefs are constantly reinforced—with our real jobs—teaching in a complex, distracting world with students who don't view us as the focal points of their lives. So we use these Key Beliefs as navigational stars to guide our efforts over the course of the year, keeping them in view as we make our way toward long-term flourishing. We use them as analytical tools, as well, when issues of student motivation arise. I've not written this chapter to provide teachers with another label to place on students—"Well, Suzanne just doesn't value mathematics, and that's that." Rather, I see these beliefs as a means for digging deeper into what's going on with Suzanne: *"Why* doesn't she value mathematics? What's getting in her way?"

CONTEXTUAL, NOT UNIVERSAL

It is common enough to hear in the news that some religious leader has forsaken his vows and done something far outside the bounds of his belief system. Sure enough, the pundits weigh in that this person must never have really believed what he claimed to believe, another classic example of a hypocrite who acts one way during worship and another during the week.

But if we slow down a bit, we see that this is just how belief works. In fact, Camille Farrington and her colleagues have demonstrated what we've all seen too often: in first hour, a student might strongly value the work she's asked to do and might demonstrate a robust growth mindset, but in second hour, the student is quick to quit (EL Education, 2015). With the fallen religious leader example, we see the same process at play: some contexts (e.g., church on a Sunday morning, or Biology class for the student who has always loved studying living things) make beliefs easier to act upon than others. This is why it's critical for us to know our students so that we might better determine who needs extra support in developing or maintaining tentative beliefs.

IT STARTS WITH US

Key Beliefs List for Easy Reference

1. Credibility: I believe in my teacher.
2. Belonging: I belong in this academic community.
3. Effort: I can improve through my effort.
4. Efficacy: I can succeed at this.
5. Value: This work has value for me.

Before we close, join me in an important exercise. Let's look at the list in the sidebar one last time, and ask ourselves the following:

- Do *I* believe that these statements are true for each of my students?

- Do *I* think all of my students belong here? Are there kids I want out of my class?

- Do *I* think that all of my students can get better through effort? Or do I think some of them are lost causes?

- Do *I* think all of my students can succeed?

- Do *I* think that the work we do this year has value for all students? Am I working to help them see how what we do in this class is aimed at their long-term good?

I find that I need to ask myself these questions periodically throughout a school year as the many challenges of this work inevitably erode the beliefs I want to hold about all of my students. The internal work of teaching is critical in the cultivation of key beliefs in our students.

The Gist

Much has been studied and written about character, soft skills, noncognitive factors, social-emotional learning, and whatever else you'd like to call this constellation of life-critical attributes that don't appear on standardized tests. I've tried many of the approaches in the literature but have found none as coherent and manageable as the Five Key Beliefs suggested by two big works of research: John Hattie's (2012) teacher credibility, and Camille Farrington et al.'s (2012) belonging, effort, success, and value beliefs. I can target these through all of my actions as a teacher.

These beliefs aren't magical, and they certainly don't autocorrect for skill deficits or at-risk home lives. Yet they are critical levers for the rest of the work we'll tackle in this book. When our students believe these things as they experience our lessons targeting knowledge building, argument, reading, writing, speaking, or listening, they engage with the work *and* they do it. That's not a silver bullet, but it's certainly a great start.

Better Together

When the beliefs of this chapter are cultivated across the entire school, students find themselves truly immersed in belief-supporting contexts. Much of what this chapter laid out is powerful in a single classroom, but it's truly transformative when the work is done in unison with a whole school's worth of professionals.

Here are some ways to do this work together:

- There is a lot of research that supports these key beliefs, so it's not a bad idea to make an all-year staff reading project of some of the work mentioned in this chapter. If I were coordinating something like this at my own school, my first priority would be to have teachers read and discuss the first couple chapters of *Teaching Adolescents to Become Learners* (Farrington et. al., 2012), up to the end of the chapter on academic mindsets. Developing a baseline knowledge about these concepts is the first step to thinking critically about them.

- Then, I would have teachers brainstorm practices they already use to develop each of the five key beliefs in this chapter. We've all intuited some or all of the beliefs I've laid out, and so we've all been working at building them in our students. As a team, department, PLC, or school, create lists of practices that work in helping develop the credibility, belonging, effort, efficacy, and value beliefs.

- Enroll some or all of your staff in my all-online, schedule-friendly Student Motivation Course. Using 35 brief, on-demand video lessons, the SMC allows me to lead teachers around the world into a robust understanding of how to cultivate the five key beliefs in all kids. Participants in the course have called it among the most powerful professional learning experiences of their careers. Learn more at davestuartjr.com/smc.

Belief cultivation is a lot of work, and it pays greater dividends when we spread the work across a team or staff.

Notes

PART II

Making Mastery

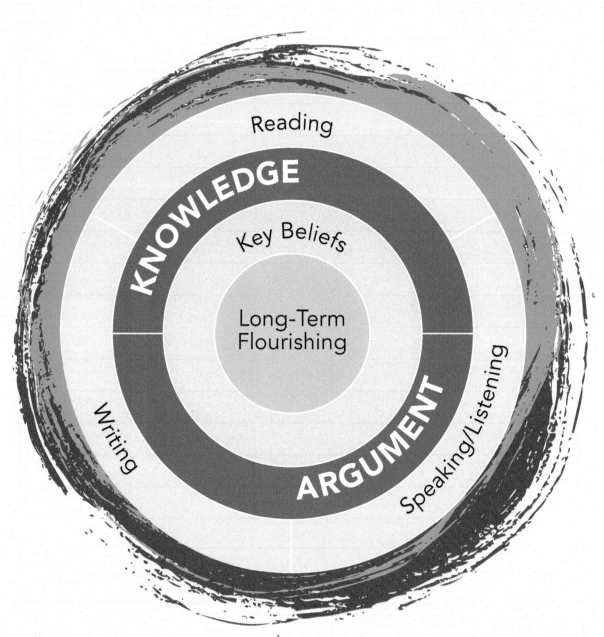

Reading

KNOWLEDGE

Key Beliefs

Long-Term
Flourishing

Writing

ARGUMENT

Speaking/Listening

Skills and knowledge are not separate, however, but intertwined.

— ANDREW J. ROTHERHAM AND DANIEL T. WILLINGHAM (2009, P. 17)

Perhaps the greatest false contrast in American education is that between skills and knowledge. "Why teach facts when they can be looked up? Teach skill instead." This is a common enough refrain. But until the day when computers attach to our brains, the person who knows things is always going to be quicker and more adept at critically thinking about those things. As Daniel Willingham (2017) said in an op-ed for the *New York Times*, "You still need your brain."

And yet, skills and knowledge are inseparable. Who will have the best argument about whether or not the Xbox is the greatest gaming console—the teachers in my hallway, none of whom play video games, or the group of ninth-grade boys in my world history course for whom study sessions often devolve into gamer talk? The teachers have decades of argumentative experience beyond those of the ninth-grade boys—they've graduated academia; they've participated in departmental debates over curricula and strategy—but, of course, the ninth-grade boys will have the better argument about gaming consoles, firing off quips about MMORPGs and TwitchTV and graphics cards and the like. Knowledge is inseparable from the critical thought that argument requires. Yet, at the same time, knowledge all by its lonesome doesn't automatically engender argument. That takes classrooms and schools where argument is normal, argument is compelling, and argumentative quality is pursued. Knowledge without argument makes you a trivia master; argument without knowledge makes you a bag of hot air.

So in Part I, we examined the lever-like beliefs that undergird all the work that happens in our classes. For the rest of the book, these beliefs inform our work. If at any point we're noticing that kids are checked out or apathetic (in my own classroom, this is an all-too-frequent recurrence), then we return to the beliefs to help us identify the apathy's root. In Part II, however, we'll explore how knowledge and argument work together and separately to make our students smarter about the world and more adept in our disciplines. Along the way, we'll examine practical means for getting better in these areas.

And as we go, we keep reflecting on how the six areas of practice work together:

- How can I provide students with opportunities to build their knowledge through reading and listening and to refine that knowledge through writing and speaking?
- How can I give students the chance to read, write, speak, and listen to arguments?
- How can the quality of arguments in my classroom be improved by helping my students build their background knowledge on the topic under debate?
- How can arguments motivate my students in their knowledge-building efforts?

In other words, we're always looking for the connections among the various rings of the bull's-eye. What follows is meant to provide threads that will be interwoven and layered throughout instruction and student learning.

CHAPTER THREE

Build Knowledge Purposefully and Often

Content knowledge is the foundation.

— DR. JUDITH L. IRVIN
(2017, P. 4)

What do the following have in common?

A middle school student, whose reading scores on college placement exams label him as college ready, sits down to read the following passage by Eamonn Brennan (2017):

> SMU, a No. 6 seed experiencing its first tournament breakthrough of the Larry Brown restoration, led its first-round opponent—13-loss, 11-seed UCLA—by two with 22 seconds remaining. The Bruins inbounded from the sideline. By design, guard Norman Powell circled right and drove to the baseline, while Bryce Alford used a backscreen on the opposite wing. By the time Powell's pass hit Alford in the short corner, however, SMU's rangy defenders had closed in. Alford retreated, circled back around another screen, and then—despite having 12 seconds left, despite Markus Kennedy's towering contest—flung an inexplicable fadeaway prayer from 23 feet.

Afterward, he is asked to explain what is happening in the passage. In his explanation, he demonstrates minimal comprehension of the text. He is then asked to read the passage aloud, and he does this flawlessly and fluently.

Reading

KNOWLEDGE

Key Beliefs

Long-Term
Flourishing

Writing

Argument

Speaking/Listening

A high school biology student, whose experiments demonstrating the variables that affect plant growth wins a regional science prize, is asked to explain why, in a physics experiment, one rocket flew better than another rocket. Though the student has demonstrated adept scientific thinking and exceptional argumentative skill in her prize-winning biology work, she makes frustratingly little progress in explaining the variables at work in the rocket experiment.

An air-traffic controller is given a cognitively demanding test of his situational awareness, a skill he uses every day on the job. Situational awareness is critical thinking on steroids; as one study describes it, it is "the continuous extraction of environmental information [and the] integration of this information with prior knowledge to form a coherent mental picture [and then] use that picture in anticipating future events" like, you know, whether or not planes will all have a runway to land on without crashing into each other (Hendrick, 2016; cf Dominguez, McMillan, Vidulich, & Vogel, 1994). On this situational awareness test, which asks the controller to use situational awareness with colors and shapes moving around a screen rather than airplanes and vectors, the air-traffic controller earns a score no different from the average test-taker.

So what gives in these three scenarios? In a word, knowledge. The middle school reader, perhaps never having taken an interest in basketball or the annual NCAA March Madness tournament, cannot comprehend a passage that a fourth-grader who watches Sports Center every morning easily can. She can read it aloud just fine; she just can't understand it. The biology student, achieving above her regional peers in a familiar discipline, is frustrated in a discipline that she's not yet studied. The air-traffic controller has achieved situational awareness in his field but not with colors and shapes, of which he has no meaningful experiential knowledge.

The Criticality of Knowledge

In short, knowledge must be a part of our bull's-eye because it is integral to high levels of thinking, reading, writing, speaking, and listening. We can't teach with anything less than a desire for our students to learn as much as possible while they are with us. This chapter's old-fashioned message is that the flourishing life is a knowledgeable one. Google doesn't change that. It's pretty cool that I can ask my smartphone to define a new word or show me the news, but it's the data that I've accumulated in my head over several decades of my life that makes any new information interesting and more likely to stick. The technology of our day ought to help us build knowledge and do creative things with it, not pretend that somehow we don't need to know things.

Let's look at a few examples of what I'm talking about.

READING IS NOT A SKILL

Few would argue that reading comprehension doesn't belong in a list of skills critical to the flourishing life, so it's worth camping out for a minute on this particularly misunderstood "skill" and its relationship to knowledge. There is one problem: it's not a skill at all. "The mainspring of comprehension is prior knowledge," cognitive scientist Daniel Willingham (2009) writes, "the stuff readers know that enables them to create understanding as they read." Without knowledge of a subject, the spring of understanding a text runs dry, even for the best readers.

In the summer of 2017, I heard Willingham give a talk on this topic, and he said that if we conceive of a skill as something that transfers broadly, then reading can't be a skill. For example, if I tell you that I'm a skilled piano player, then you wouldn't be crazy to expect that I could sit down at a piano and play a random sheet of piano music. I might need a minute to acquaint myself with the piece, but that should be it. But if I tell you that I'm a good reader who has scored a perfect 1700+ on the Scholastic Reading Inventory test, and then you hand me an article from *The Astrophysical Journal*, you will find that, although I could probably decode the text well enough, I would not be able to make much sense of it even if you gave me an hour. Decoding, then, is a skill, but the reading that we're after at the secondary levels is comprehension, not decoding. And that, it turns out, isn't a skill at all.

And this is no small deal, as Willingham (2009) argues that "the mistaken idea that reading is a skill—learn to crack the code, practice comprehension strategies, and you can read anything—*may be the single biggest factor holding back reading achievement in the country*. Students will not reach standards that way. The knowledge base problem must be solved" (emphasis added). Comprehending diverse reading materials, I would argue, is a core component of the flourishing life. Knowledge building, then, isn't optional in our quest to promote the long-term flourishing of kids.

HIDDEN RIGHT IN FRONT OF US

Experts have been weaving this into their writing on teaching for a long time. In *Readicide*, teacher-writer Kelly Gallagher (2009) warns that "if we are serious about building strong readers, we need to be serious about building strong knowledge foundations in our students" (p. 38). In other words, teachers are reading teachers not because they teach students reading strategies but because they teach students facts. Yet reading isn't all that's to be gained from knowledge-rich learning experiences: E. D. Hirsch (2016) argues that literacy as a whole is what's at stake: "Competence in language is gained by knowledge of things. The best way to learn lots of words is to systematically and coherently learn lots of things" (p. 171). Prolific teacher-researchers Douglas Fisher, Nancy Frey, and John Hattie (2016b) add to the case for knowledge, arguing that it stands as a gateway to deeper, transferable learning:

> Like a swimmer entering the water, the initial steps require breaking the surface. . . . A reader's ability to engage in interpretive and critical thinking can be inhibited if she hasn't had the opportunity to acquire and consolidate the knowledge and skills she will need. (p. 36)

ISN'T ARGUMENTATIVE SKILL TRANSFERABLE, THOUGH?

I once gave my students an article on North Korea's latest unsanctioned missile test. After having them read, annotate, and write in response to the article, I asked students to participate in a Pop-Up Debate on how the world ought to respond to this growing problem. (We'll discuss Pop-Up Debates more in Chapter 4.) At this point in the school year, my students were well versed on the pop-up format, had learned to overcome their public speaking fears, and had received intentional scaffolding and feedback on their speaking. (We'll unpack this in Chapter 7.) Despite all this, their performance on the North Korea question was superficial in the best moments and incoherent in the worst. The most popular proposal was that we "oughta nuke 'em." Ten minutes into the debate, I realized my error and ended it, using the rest of our class time on some other activity. My students didn't need a lecture on why nuking was bad or how they needed to try harder. They just needed to build more background knowledge on the issue.

Later in this chapter, we'll come back to this story. For now, suffice it to say that critical thinking and argumentative ability are not transferable skills, in the same way that reading comprehension isn't. Ask me to debate a student who is a death metal fan on the relative merits of Morbid Angel and Napalm Death, and you will witness my destruction. I've got far more formal experience than the student at argumentation—just as you do—but there's a fatal knowledge disadvantage. In the words of one journalist, "students need to be given real and significant things from the world to think with and about"—they need knowledge—"if teachers are going to influence how they do that thinking" (Hendrick, 2016). There's no sense trying to teach argument if we don't provide ample opportunity to build knowledge on a topic beforehand.

Words Matter

Pop-Up Debate

In a Pop-Up Debate, every student in the class is expected to speak at least once; typically, the teacher also places a maximum on the number of speeches per student, to keep the debate from taking too long. To speak, students simply stand–or pop–up and start speaking. Whoever speaks first has the floor, and the teacher models and enforces cordial behavior throughout.

I discuss this in depth in Chapter 4.

TYPES OF KNOWLEDGE: DISENTANGLING ROTE FROM INFLEXIBLE

I used to avoid knowledge building for fear of getting a bunch of kids wasting their precious time memorizing information by rote. However, not all knowledge is created equally. To illustrate the following types of knowledge, I'll use two examples from the content areas that I teach:

- In world history, I require my students to memorize when Islam was founded: 622 CE.

- In English, I require my students to memorize the seven situations in which commas ought to be used, including to separate items in a series.

Let's look at the types of knowledge in light of these examples, going from least to most useful, as represented in Figure 3.1.

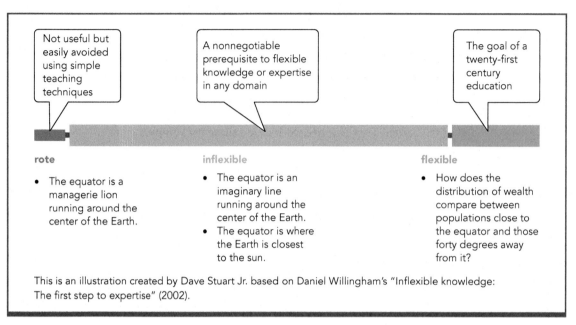

This is an illustration created by Dave Stuart Jr. based on Daniel Willingham's "Inflexible knowledge: The first step to expertise" (2002).

FIGURE 3.1 • The Three Types of Knowledge

First, there's *rote knowledge,* which is what we get when we memorize something that makes no sense to us. If a student had memorized the date above as only rote knowledge, he might mistakenly say that someone found Islam (rather than founded it) in 622. In this case, he doesn't understand the meaning of *founded*, so he doesn't understand much of what happened in 622. A similar error with the comma rule might be that a student tells a friend that commas are to be used any time a movie or book series is mentioned. Again, misunderstanding *series* leads to a misunderstanding of the whole rule.

If you're reading those examples above with any degree of skepticism, however, you realize that *these cases would be quite rare in the case of even a mediocre teacher.* In teaching about the founding of Islam, a teacher would surely share the story of Muhammad and the angel Gabriel, and this would likely lend enough context to the verb *founded* to make it sensical for the child. Similarly, in teaching the rule about setting off items in a series with commas, sample sentences would be an obvious teaching tool, and these would diminish misunderstandings about the meaning of the word *series*. In other words, rote knowledge is certainly undesirable and something to avoid in our classrooms, but it is totally avoidable through the use of simple teaching techniques (e.g., direct instruction, using concrete examples, modeling) and checks for understanding.

The simplicity of these strategies is why rote knowledge is much rarer than critics of knowledge building let on. Frequently, the kind of knowledge building we're uncomfortable with is the building of *inflexible knowledge*, a term coined by Daniel T. Willingham (2002). In this case, our discomfort is unfortunate because inflexible knowledge is "absolutely vital to a student's education . . . [and is] the unavoidable foundation of expertise" (p. 32). Before a student can use commas with mechanical accuracy, the student needs to know rules for comma usage (see Stark, 2017, for one list) and basic examples of these rules in practice. Initially, placing commas around items in a series may be limited to simple sentences with obvious lists (e.g., "I like apples, oranges, and bananas") versus sentences with more complex lists (e.g., "I went to the store, saw my friend Tony, shook his hand, and then asked, 'How do you do?'").

Once students are able to correctly use commas in a sentence containing any kind of series, they have acquired *flexible knowledge* of this particular kind of comma usage. Flexible knowledge, of course, is what we want for our students. We want them to deeply understand how commas work, or how the introduction of Islam in 622 marks a turning point in the history of post-classical Afroeurasia that echoes still today. Unfortunately for us and our silver-bullet-seeking tendencies, there doesn't seem to be a shortcut from inflexible to flexible knowledge. One simply needs to build knowledge on an incident-by-incident basis. In other words, you need to know a little about a lot of things to achieve broad literacy. It's that or staying confined to one's echo chamber.

ARE YOU A PROBLEM SOLVER, OR AREN'T YOU?

I mentioned earlier that I once heard Daniel Willingham give a talk on how reading is not a skill and that he has written emphatically that "the knowledge problem must be solved." After his talk, I did something that I normally don't do: I made my way up to the front of the room so that I could corner—I mean, talk to—him. I didn't record the conversation, but the gist of what I asked him was this: Dr. Willingham, the logic and science behind your arguments seem unassailable to me. I'm with you; the knowledge problem must be solved. So, how do we solve it, particularly at the secondary level where students arrive with such huge variations in prior knowledge?

COMMON TEACHER HANG-UP

Which Knowledge?

Once we understand that inflexible knowledge paves the road to mastery, we're faced with a major, daunting task: identifying and organizing the broad array of inflexible knowledge in our disciplines. This immediately presents us with a problem: we don't have much time. American teachers have more contact hours with students and fewer noninstructional hours on average than international peers (Walker, 2016). This often means that they have inadequate opportunities to collaborate vertically or horizontally. When this lack of time combines with inadequate access to high-quality, guaranteed, and viable curricula (Marzano, 2003), we wonder, "How can I make my room one where useful, meaningful knowledge building is the norm?" We'll either ignore it (which is negligence), or we'll let it drive us crazy (which is insanity), or we'll fix our eyes on the long-term flourishing of our kids. Toward that worthy peak, we aim to create classes where students master material and where that mastery includes knowledge building. Clearly, our secondary students, despite their often poor preparation in knowledge building, deserve to enter adult life fully literate. So we must work at knowledge building, and that starts with choosing *which* knowledge.

My principal, Anne Kostus, often asks the social studies department, "How do we make it so our students can answer the types of questions Jay Leno would ask during his Jaywalking segments?" In other words, what type of knowledge would we be mortified to see our students answer incorrectly? The subject area with perhaps the easiest answer to this question might be social studies. The U.S. Citizenship and Immigration Services (2017) *Civics (History and Government) Questions for the Naturalization Test* contains one hundred questions that prospective citizens of the United States need to be able to answer. What if this list of one hundred questions—rather than the often bloated standards that allegedly govern social studies courses— became the backbone of knowledge throughout a secondary social studies course progression? What if students routinely encountered and explored this information in history, government, economics, and English courses, and what if this information was routinely assessed over the years so as to aid long-term retention?

Not all subjects, of course, can benefit from the one hundred questions on the citizenship test, so here are two freely available, substantive resources you can use to help identify key knowledge. Just remember that you'll probably need to do some work to fit the actual confines of your school, its schedule, and its kids.

- **E. D. Hirsch's *Core Knowledge Sequence* (2013).** This is freely available and covers all subjects in grades PK–8. At 285 pages, it is significantly beefier than the one hundred questions on the aforementioned naturalization test, and it does a comprehensive job of treating the specific knowledge that "general audiences" are assumed to possess. Here, you'll find ample ground for course-, grade-, department-, or school-level explorations of the knowledge each of our courses should endeavor to teach. Also, this is useful for my high school colleagues, too: many of my ninth graders lack the knowledge laid out in Hirsch's standards for some of the earliest grades (e.g., Hirsch calls for studying the spread of Islam and early and medieval African kingdoms—topics that we study in my ninth-grade world history courses—in *fourth grade*.)

- **The College Board's Advanced Placement Course and Exam Descriptions.** These are freely accessible through a simple Google search by content area (e.g., search "AP Biology CED" and you will find it). Even if you don't teach advanced courses, studying the CED most appropriate to the course you teach can help you to prioritize the key knowledge in our disciplines.

American education has for years operated on the premise that knowledge building is the equivalent of giving a person a fish, whereas skill building is teaching the person to fish. In fact, knowledge building and skill building are inseparable; they're both fishing. Though it's a big project to select and organize content knowledge as we hone and focus our curricula, it's a worthwhile one in our efforts to increase the long-term flourishing odds of all our students.

His response was this: "The problem is huge and requires a systemic, curricular movement to truly be solved. One or even two years with a knowledge-rich curriculum won't solve the knowledge problem for student X. But we can make progress, and we can move the student ahead of where he or she is now." His belief is that we must first clearly conceive of the problem before we can hope to do something about it (personal communication, July 13, 2017).

I was reminded of my grandfather, Dean Lewis Stuart, who used to say that "there are two kinds of people in the world: problem solvers and everyone

FIGURE 3.2 • The author's grandfather, Dean Lewis Stuart. This guy was a problem solver.

else" (see Figure 3.2). The first step to solving a problem is clearly understanding it. Up to this point, this chapter has been all about understanding why knowledge is important, why not knowing things is a problem, and what this problem looks like in terms of the everyday experiences we have as teachers. So basically, we've established that in order for students of ours to have a shot at climbing Everest, one thing we owe them in our classes is the opportunity to learn content—languages and the scientific method and mathematical principles and geography.

But how do we do this in a way that won't kill our students with boredom or leave our struggling students behind? Let's get practical. In the second half of this chapter, I'd like to explore what effective, student-centered knowledge building looks like, including multiple examples from real-life classrooms.

Promising Practices Toward *Meaningful* Knowledge Building

One of the troubles with targeting knowledge building in the secondary grades is that older students tend to be less curious than younger ones. As former elementary principal Mike Duffy commented, "In first grade, everyone's going to be the president or an astronaut, and as long as you use age-appropriate pedagogy, they're pumped to learn about everything and anything. But by fourth grade, they know who the 'smart kids' are and their enthusiasm for learning has gone from a raging fire to a smoldering coal" (personal communication, 2017).

While this may be depressing, I've found it pretty accurate. At the time of this writing, my children Haddie, Laura, Marlena, and Dean are seven, five, three, and one, and these kids are eager to learn just about anything I can think of. The limiting factor is not their motivation to learn things about the natural world or how numbers work or the stories of history—the limiting factor is their dad! But for my ninth-grade students, that curiosity isn't as stoked. When I try convincing my students that yes, in the age of the smartphone, it's important to learn things—to actually have them imprinted into your brain and accessible at will—I tend to run into resistance.

Unless, that is, the knowledge is meaningful. We must obsess over making this so. Here's the good news: there are as many ways to make knowledge building meaningful as there are stars in the sky. While one student likes memorizing must-know dates because it's fun, another does it because she wants to understand her world history readings better, and another does it because she wants to impress her parents. As we discussed in Chapter 2, ideas of value are beautifully individualized. This variance between students can either stress us out or make us delight in the job—let's choose the latter.

One way that we can make knowledge building meaningful is to minimize the gap between effective knowledge-building practices (e.g., retrieval practice—we'll discuss this and other practices in the next section) and real-world applications. For example, a world languages teacher might teach five conversational sentence stems and ten useful vocabulary words, telling students that tomorrow they will be conversing with one another in a marketplace simulation. As homework, students might be assigned fifteen minutes of quizzing themselves using flashcards or a Quizlet study pack. In this situation, students are just memorizing sentence stems and vocabulary words, but they are doing so in a meaningful context—tomorrow, they'll be simulating a marketplace with their peers, and they'll need this memorized information to succeed in the simulation.

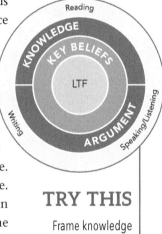

TRY THIS

Frame knowledge argumentatively.

My own go-to approach for fusing knowledge building with meaningfulness is to frame the things we're going to learn along argumentative lines. And, when time permits, I have students engage in argumentative conversations or whole-class discussions using their newly gained knowledge. I'll discuss this in further depth in our next chapter, but here's an example. In our first unit in world history, my students are learning about how human interaction with the environment shaped ancient world history up to the year 600 BCE. To be able to explain this process, my students need to learn all sorts of academic vocabulary (e.g., Paleolithic, Neolithic, foraging societies, pastoral societies, sedentarism, deforestation, domestication), geographic locations (e.g., the Nile River Valley, Tigris, Euphrates, Huang He, Harappa, Mohenjo-Daro), and ancient civilizations (e.g., the Chavín, Olmec, Hebrews, Phoenicians, Sumerians). There is a large amount of knowledge building that needs to take place, and that fits my bias: always, always, always, I want to help my students learn as much as possible. I also introduce them to key concepts (e.g., diffusion, egalitarian, patriarchy) and detailed knowledge (e.g., specific monumental structure types, such as the Olmec heads, the Egyptian and Nubian pyramids, and the Sumerian ziggurats) beyond just what's listed in our school's curriculum. And what I find is that large amounts of inflexible knowledge yield the deeper thinking we're after. (I'm trying to create topic immersion, a practice we'll examine in just a few pages.)

And the way that I approach this is by framing the lessons argumentatively. As we compare the ancient civilizations, our driving question is, Was the advent of civilization positive or negative? As we compare paleolithic societies, our question is, Were foraging and pastoral societies mostly similar or mostly different? These arguments aren't the kinds of things that kids debate outside of my room, but the fact that my students do enjoy debates brings a level of meaningfulness to knowledge-building work that doesn't exist otherwise.

Let's now examine actual classroom examples of research-based practices for knowledge building. Here we've arrived at the *work* of knowledge building with our students. What follows are descriptions of various best practices in knowledge building, with each best practice illustrated with a helpful case study.

INCIDENTAL LEARNING

Not all knowledge ought to be directly taught. Daniel Willingham (2006a) elaborates:

> Students can learn facts incidentally. Incidental learning refers to learning that occurs when you are not specifically trying to learn. Much of what you know stuck in your memory not as a result of your consciously trying to remember it, but as a byproduct of thinking about it, such as when you reflect on a novel word that someone used in conversation or are fascinated by a new fact. When schools use a content-rich curriculum, students have many incidental learning opportunities as they are immersed in meaningful, connected facts throughout the day.

In other words, when we seek to teach everything we know, every day, constantly, we make incidental learning possible. A well-known example of this is high school English teacher Kelly Gallagher's (2009, 2015) article of the week (AoW) assignment.

Years ago, Kelly Gallagher became concerned with his students' lack of knowledge about the world, so he began assigning a one- or two-page article every Monday.

The assignment was meant to be manageable, so you will notice that it's very simple:

- For fifteen minutes, Gallagher helps guide students into the article, providing motivational hooks, modeling purposeful annotation, and allowing students to get started on the reading. (We'll examine these moves in Chapter 5.)

- As homework, students are expected to read, annotate, and write a one-page reflection on the article. To help with the writing piece, Gallagher provides response options, too. The work is due on Friday, and Gallagher puts as little time as possible into grading them. (After all, the purpose of the assignment is knowledge building for students, not grading time for teachers. For more explanation on this, visit www .davestuartjr.com/grading.)

TRY THIS

Assign an article of the week and model for students how to purposefully annotate and respond.

Grading should be as minimal as possible; many teachers give a simple score out of ten based on a quick scan of the student's work. The purpose of this assignment is knowledge building, not grading!

Teachers around the country, including me, have adapted this assignment for use in their own classrooms. For my slight tweaks on the assignment with my own students, see Figure 3.3. By doing this activity regularly, students receive roughly forty opportunities for incidental knowledge building each school year (one per week). Such simplified approaches to knowledge building throughout the school drastically increase the incidental learning opportunities our students experience as well as the number of opportunities they get to read and write.

TOPIC IMMERSION

Earlier in this chapter, I shared my students' initially weak Pop-Up Debate performance on how the world ought to respond to the North Korean crisis. After that debate, I took any spare minute I could find to immerse my students in the issue (mainly, I gave them multiple articles of the week on the same topic, plus the occasional short video or radio clip as a class warm-up). After several weeks of this knowledge building, I had my students engage in the same Pop-Up Debate. The difference in the two performances was dramatic.

Instructionally, I didn't add much. I did not create any quizzes, design any interleaved practice (which we'll discuss in a minute), or plan any lessons. Instead,

HR:3

How the FCC's move on net neutrality could impact consumers
By Kaitlyn Schallhorn for *Fox News*

The Federal Communications Commission took a step toward dismantling the Obama-era net neutrality regulations Tuesday.

The current rules impose utility-style regulations on Internet service providers (ISPs) that prevent them from favoring their own services or certain customers over that of competitors.

[handwritten: The government wants to end net neutrality.]

But Ajit Pai, the Trump-appointed Federal Communications Commission chairman, said Tuesday that he plans to "repeal the heavy-handed Internet regulations" and "return to the light-touch framework under which the Internet developed and thrived before 2015."

The move sparked renewed debate between those who applaud President Donald Trump's efforts to scale back on regulations as well as consumer groups and Internet companies. Here's a look at what net neutrality is and how Pai's plans could impact consumers nationwide.

So what even is net neutrality?
Net neutrality is the idea that ISPs must treat all legal Internet data the same — regardless of where it comes from or who it is going to.

[handwritten: Net neutrality is the idea that all internet data should be treated as equal.]

A vote by the Federal Communications Commission on December 14, 2017 will decide the fate of net neutrality. But what is it?Video
What is net neutrality?

Page 1

FIGURE 3.3 • Sample Article of the Week

Note: For a slew of ready-to-use articles of the week, Google the phrase "article of the week."

Harold Feld, senior vice president with the Washington, D.C.-based nonprofit Public Knowledge, compared net neutrality to "an on-ramp to the Internet," meaning ISPs are "not allowed to interfere with what the subscriber wants to do or where the subscriber wants to go."

Under net neutrality regulations, ISPs are not allowed to block or throttle — meaning slow down — websites or applications.

What does the FCC's chairman plan to do?

Pai's plan to repeal net neutrality regulations will be put to a vote by the FCC commissioners on Dec. 14.

Net neutrality benefits only some peoples not most.

Pai, 44, said that he believes the net neutrality rules adopted during the Obama administration discourage the ISPs from making investments in their network that would provide even better and faster online access.

"Under my proposal, the federal government will stop micromanaging the internet," Pai said in a statement.

How could this impact consumers?

Repealing net neutrality regulations means consumers could start paying more for their Internet services, criticis said. Consumers could also see ISPs start to "bundle" services — such as certain websites or applications — and charge more depending on what a person wants access to, experts said.

"Right now, the FCC has designated [the Internet] as a telecommunications service — like a phone service which includes all of the rules that apply to prevent [a company] from blocking or throttling or favoring one company over another," Feld told Fox News. "The real question, to some degree, is: is the Internet going to work like the old telephone where you get to decide who you called and what you do or is it going to become more like cable?"

Net neutrality would make consumers pay more.

"If it's one thing that cable companies have proven to be good at over the years, it's more ways to get money out of consumers and into their own pockets," he continued. "Primary broadband providers will take advantage of this to find new ways to charge customers if they want to get high quality service."

Julian Sanchez, a senior fellow at the libertarian think tank Cato Institute, said broadband providers would "presumably ... try some things consumers don't like and others that prove to be popular." But he dismissed the notion of predicting just what exactly providers would do should the regulations be scaled back.

"There's plenty of scaremongering around steps broadband providers could take in the absence of neutrality regulation — blocking off certain sites, or charging extra fees to access certain services — but not a ton of reason to think they would do these things, which would antagonize customers, be technically tricky to enforce against sophisticated users, and invite the re-imposition of regulations," Sanchez told Fox News.

"What's more realistic is the introduction of plans that provide higher speeds for specific bandwidth-intensive services," he said, pointing to streaming high-definition Netflix videos as an example of such a service. "Or, similarly, content providers might end up subsidizing higher-speed access to their services for subscribers who've only paid for slower all-purpose Internet access."

Response Options:

- First, summarize the idea of net neutrality and why it is making news right now.
- Then, paraphrase the main points made by the people interviewed for this article. What do **they say?**
- Finally, what do you think? Should net neutrality be protected, or should it be removed according to FCC chairman Ajit Pai's plans?

Page 2

COMMON TEACHER HANG-UP

I Don't Have Time for AoW!

I find it unfortunate that the AoW idea was popularized by an English teacher and is therefore most commonly found practiced in ELA classrooms around the country. ELA teachers already feel loaded down with bolt-on initiatives—a few minutes for choice reading here, a few for mechanics instruction there, plus the word of the day, Latin word chunks, writer's notebook, mentor text study, and on and on . . . AoW can start to seem, to both teachers and students, like just one more thing.

This is why I advocate for AoW initiatives to begin *outside* the ELA classroom. Doesn't a weekly article on a current event lend itself nicely to any social studies class? How about a weekly graph in science class? Or a weekly health-related article in health class? Grading them needs to be speedy and simple, not extensive or elaborate, and their roll-out can cost as little as fifteen instructional minutes per week.

I created the conditions for what E. D. Hirsch (2006a) calls "topic immersion": I just let my students and myself soak in one compelling question for a number of weeks.

I started to see this as something significantly different from how I had been using Gallagher's article of the week approach in my classroom. I was still using the basic structure—an article each week, fifteen minutes on Monday, one page of writing—but it had become less about "what's current" and more about "what's important." I started calling it Burning Questions of the Year, or BQYs ("Boo-keys"), but you could also call it Pressing Question of the Month, or whatever you need to make it fit within your timeframe. What's important about this approach is that it allows students "to learn new material about the world and connect it to prior knowledge" (Willingham, 2006a), which in turn increases their ability to remember and think deeply about learned material.

I had started to notice that too many students don't engage with AoWs because their lack of prior knowledge makes the articles too difficult. Because they lack so much prior knowledge, they don't build as much knowledge through the article work. BQYs, on the other hand, let students focus on key questions.

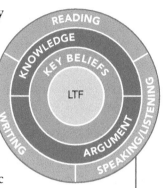

The BQY concept has been a huge *Aha!*, but providing full detail of its evolution goes beyond the scope of this chapter. Here's the gist:

Using the same time constraints as Gallagher's article of the week—fifteen minutes to get into the text on a Monday, drawing exclusively during this fifteen minutes from the before- and during-reading moves in the nine moves for teaching with texts (see Chapter 5)—and the same basic assignment requirements—one or two mature, purposeful annotations per page and a 250-word written response—I really only changed two things: I gave students a chance to stick with one burning question each month, and we held a Pop-Up Debate on the question at the end of that month's readings.

TRY THIS

Burning Questions of the Year combine articles of the week with a set of driving, debatable questions—perfect fodder for Pop-Up Debates.

Just like articles of the week, BQY assignments aim at incidental learning, and they are extracurricular in the sense that my department does not require me to use them. Unlike articles of the week, BQYs aim at maximizing knowledge gains using topical immersion and maximizing student engagement by organizing articles around compelling, debatable issues. In Figure 3.4, you'll find two sample BQY series.

Before we move on, it's important to note that I've been especially excited to see BQY modified for use in staff professional development settings. At the end of this chapter, I share one example of this from Wisconsin.

www.davestuartjr.com/bqy

I encourage you to take a more detailed look at how I roll out BQY on my website.

RETRIEVAL PRACTICE

When we attempt to retrieve something from memory, two things take place: first, we quickly realize whether we truly know the information, and second, we're more likely to retain that information in the future. This second point refers to the "testing effect": things on which we're tested are more likely to be remembered down the road (Brown, Roediger, & McDaniel, 2014, pp. 19–20). To increase the degree to which their learning sticks, our students need regular opportunities to retrieve learned information.

This doesn't mean we quiz them on everything—as I've said, our students can build much of their knowledge incidentally, through topic immersion in

BURNING QUESTIONS	ARTICLES, VIDEOS, GRAPHS
What life skills does every young adult need? Note: During the summative Pop-Up Debate on this burning question, I had a student keep track of the life skills suggested by classmates, and we then transferred this list of life skills onto an anchor chart that I keep in the classroom. I frequently refer to this chart, saying things like, "All right, today we're going to be doing some challenging reading and writing, so I want you to recall some of the life skills you mentioned several months ago during our BQY Pop-Up Debate."	**Academic Mindsets:** "Struggle for Smarts," by Alix Spiegel for NPR **Sleep:** "Teachers, Students, and Sleep," by Dave Stuart Jr. for DaveStuartJr.com **Study skills:** "Study Smarter," by Joe Stromberg for *Vox* **Financial literacy vs. reading, writing, and arithmetic:** "Pro/Con: Should All Students Take Personal Finance Classes?" by K. Alexander Ashe and Wayne Madsen for *Tribune News*, adapted by *Newsela* staff **Managing the urge to procrastinate:** "Procrastination: Is Your Future Self Getting a Bad Deal?" by Timothy Pychyl for *Psychology Today* "Inside the Mind of a Master Procrastinator," by Tim Urban for TED (video) **Managing technology/mental health:** "How Smartphones Are Making Kids Unhappy," by Audie Cornish for NPR **Writing Skills:** "The Writing Is on the Wall," by Esther Cepeda "Writing: Ticket to Work or a Ticket Out," by The College Board
How should the world respond to the North Korea crisis?	**Intro:** "Nine Questions About North Korea," by Alex Ward for *Vox* **Complexity:** "Why the Sudden Collapse of North Korea Would Be Hell on Earth," by Harry Kazianis for The Week **Human rights abuses:** "Surviving a North Korean Prison Camp," by Catherine Garcia for *The Week* **American vulnerability:** "Can America Protect Itself From North Korean Missiles?" by *The Week* staff **Creative approach:** "What if North Korea Were in America?" by Maxwell Anderson for *The Weekend Reader*

FIGURE 3.4 • Sample BQYs

Note: For a current list of BQY, as well as PDFs of the actual articles I use in my classroom and a detailed description of how I roll out the BQY assignment with students, visit www.davestuartjr.com/bqy.

content-rich curricula—but there *are* certain facts that we want to ensure all of our students memorize. For example, in world history, I'm content to allow incidental learning do its work through content-rich units, but I do take care to ensure that students memorize a list of key dates and geographic locations for each unit. This means lots of retrieval, which can take many forms, as our next classroom snapshot demonstrates.

COMMON STUDENT HANG-UP

I Heard It on the Fake News

An additional benefit of the BQY approach to Article of the Week is that it gives students experience with one of the best methods for determining source quality: lateral reading. As McGrew, Ortega, Breakstone, and Wineburg (2017) explain in their accessible "The Challenge That's Bigger Than Fake News," much of the internet's sources "defy labels like 'fake' or 'real,'" and a landmark study conducted by Wineburg, McGrew, Breakstone, and Ortega (2016) demonstrated that "young people's ability to reason about the information on the Internet can be summed up in one word: *bleak*." One of the proposed solutions to this problem is what the authors call "lateral reading": reading sources other than a target source to identify the degree to which the target source ought to be trusted.

In Amy Holmes's Spanish classes, students are expected to build knowledge weekly, particularly in the form of grammar and vocabulary. To strengthen how well her students commit each week's new material to memory, Holmes has them engage in a variety of low-stakes retrieval practice activities:

Partner quizzing: Students partner up and exchange their current vocabulary lists. On these lists, Holmes has her students highlight words they don't know, and she actually has students highlight based on their level of knowledge. One partner reads the words on the list that the other partner can recognize in Spanish, and the person being quizzed responds with the word in English. Then the partner reads in English the words on the list that the other partner is able to produce, and the person being quizzed responds in Spanish. Typically, Holmes gives no more than five minutes for this activity.

Conjuguemos: At Conjuguemos.com, students are able to select a packet of information (e.g., present tense regular verbs), and they receive a variety of conjugation prompts. Holmes's favorite thing about Conjuguemos.com is that, when students are signed in, they can send their performance on these mini-quizzes to her so that she can use that information for ongoing support. Similar functionality exists on Quizlet.com.

Words Matter

Retrieval Practice

Retrieval practice is the act of pulling something from memory so as to strengthen our ability to retrieve that information. Retrieval practice is sometimes referred to as "recall practice" or "self-quizzing."

The concept of retrieval practice is well-treated in these resources:

- Brown, Roediger, and McDaniel's *Make It Stick: The Science of Successful Learning* (2014)

- Barbara Oakley's *A Mind for Numbers: How to Excel at Math and Science (Even If You Flunked Algebra)* (2014)

- Benedict Carey's *How We Learn: The Surprising Truth About When, Where, and Why It Happens* (2015)

For a full list of the "Dig Deeper" titles mentioned in this book, go to davestuartjr.com/t6t-list.

TRY THIS

Partner Quizzing. Students pair up and use a list of required knowledge to quiz each other.

Cold call questioning: When Holmes asks a question of the whole class (e.g., "What is the present tense *usted* form of *estar*?") she'll ask students to put their thumbs up if they know it. Sometimes, she'll cold call on students who don't have their thumbs up in this situation, and sometimes she'll call on students who do.

Daily warm-ups: When students walk in the room, Holmes has a warm-up exercise on the board that they complete during the several minutes it takes her to take attendance and handle other housekeeping matters. This warm-up doesn't just serve a classroom management purpose, however; it always asks students to retrieve and use knowledge they've learned in the past.

It's important to note here that frequent opportunities for retrieval practice need not mean multiplying the number of assignments we need to grade. Grades don't aid in knowledge building; retrieval practice does.

INTERLEAVED PRACTICE

Knowledge is also strengthened when we vary how we practice retrieving and using it. When we switch between modes of knowledge use and types of knowledge during an exercise or a study session, it strengthens our command of this knowledge. I know no better example of this than the means by which high school English teacher Doug Stark helps his students master knowledge of English grammar.

Stark teaches students the mechanics of language by organizing this work into a series of warm-ups that he then embeds during his standard curricular units (e.g., writing a research paper or reading Orwell's *1984*). He has organized his mechanics warm-ups in the popular *Mechanics Instruction That Sticks* series of eBooks (Stark, 2017), and to demonstrate what interleaving looks like, I'll use a few snippets from those warm-ups here. Before we go further, it's critical to note that these exercises are *not* used by Doug as a set of worksheets. He calls them warm-ups for a reason, and he uses them to scaffold knowledge building in the manner that follows.

At the start of each unit, Doug introduces the unit's core knowledge in a brief interactive lecture. During this lecture, Doug and his students annotate a dense unit starter page (see Figure 3.6).

(Text continues on page 92)

COMMON STUDENT HANG-UP

"But I Studied!"

Student: "I don't get it—I read the selected textbook passages, took notes, and then re-read my notes, but I still did poorly on the test. I could've sworn I learned this stuff!"

We can probably all relate to the above scenario. In such cases, the student is confused about the difference between learning and familiarity.

If something is learned, it can be produced (or, in the case of skill, executed) by the learner, without any aid. Successful learning ends with "I can do it myself."

Familiarity, on the other hand, is what happens after we experience an initial lesson on a topic, or after we read something, or take notes, or re-read those notes, or re-read the textbook. The tricky thing is that the more times we do familiarity-producing things like those that I just listed, the more we experience the "illusion of competence" (Bjork & Koriat, 2005)—it feels like we've built knowledge, but we haven't.

Let's pick an example from my classroom.

In the spring, I teach a lesson on the process of African decolonization from 1945 to 1995. The lesson involves listening, speaking, reading, and writing, and my objective is for students to build knowledge of five nation-state case studies of decolonization in Africa. From a long-term flourishing perspective, I want kids to understand decolonization so that they can think critically about the African continent and its many stories today.

After students read and discuss these case studies, I have them take a short-answer quiz (see Figure 3.5.). Here we see the elements of the *These 6 Things* bull's-eye in action: knowledge building (through reading, note taking, and discussion) leads to argumentative writing.

When I taught this last spring, students struggled with the quizzes, not because they hadn't participated in a lesson in which the material was taught but because the material had not been fully learned. Most students were *familiar* with the material, but they hadn't learned it.

(Continued)

(Continued)

SHORT-ANSWER QUESTION

1. Some historians have argued that African decolonization resulted in decades of instability primarily because of the actions of European powers.

    a. Identify and explain TWO examples during the period 1945–2017 that support the historians' assertion. Examples must be from at least two modern African nations.

    b. Identify and explain ONE example in the period that refutes the historians' assertion. Example must be from a country not used in Part a.

STUDENT NAME: _____

PLEASE DON'T WRITE ON THE RUBRIC. YOUR TEACHER WILL USE THIS.

CATEGORY (EACH = 1 POINT)	SCORE	COMMENTS
Identifies & explains 1 supporting example		
Identifies & explains another supporting example (from a different nation than those used above)		
Identifies & explains another refuting example (from a different nation than those used above).		

FIGURE 3.5 • Short-Answer Quiz

To help kids overcome the familiarity-to-learning gap, we can start by

- **Empowering them to learn** by explaining the difference between learning and familiarity and giving them basic self-quizzing strategies that they can use at home (e.g., flash cards).

- **Quizzing them ourselves**, using things like Think–Pair–Shares with no notes in front of them; frequent, efficient, and low-stakes quizzes that involve fill-in-the-blank, matching, one-word answer, or multiple choice; or short-answer quizzes in which students either earn a point or don't earn a point for their response to one to three questions.

Both are important: lessons with built-in, efficient quizzing, and teaching the kids to own their learning with simple, effective learning strategies. We'll explore these more in the next section.

Clauses and Phrases—Unit 2

An **independent clause** is a clause containing a subject, a verb, and a complete thought. An independent clause can stand alone as a sentence.

INDEPENDENT CLAUSE by itself: *Steve excels in the classroom.*

INDEPENDENT CLAUSE as part of a sentence:

Because he studies regularly, *Steve excels in the classroom.*

TWO INDEPENDENT CLAUSES joined in a compound sentence:

Steve is not a great athlete, but he excels in the classroom.

A *dependent clause* contains a subject and a verb but does not express a complete thought. It cannot stand alone as a sentence.

DEPENDENT CLAUSE as part of a sentence:

Because he studies regularly, Steve excels in the classroom.

Steve excels in the classroom *because he studies regularly.*

AAAWWUBBIS is an acronym to help you remember the basic subordinating conjunctions. An AAAWWUBBIS turns a sentence/independent clause into a dependent clause.

After **A**lthough **A**s **W**hen/Whenever **W**hile **U**ntil/Unless **B**ecause **B**efore **I**f **S**ince

---

SENTENCE: I studied for the test.

DEPENDENT CLAUSE/FRAGMENT: Although I studied for the test.

CORRECT: Although I studied for the test, I still did poorly.

(Continued)

(Continued)

> A **phrase** is a group of words that does not contain its own subject or verb. It cannot stand alone as a sentence. For the sake of brevity, we will focus on a few types of phrases that are generally set off by commas: **participial phrases, absolute phrases,** and **appositive phrases**.
>
> **Participial phrases** consist of a verb form ending in –en, –ed, or –ing that functions as an adjective. Participial phrases should always be placed next to the word or words that they are modifying.
>
> **Ex.** *Shaken and disturbed,* Aaron turned off the television.

FIGURE 3.6 • Unit Starter Page

Source: Worksheet created by Doug Stark. Used with permission.

At the end of this introduction, Doug checks for initial understanding using a simple identification activity. Notice that this is a kind of retrieval practice (see Figure 3.7).

After Doug quickly goes over those answers with students, he has them practice the new information in a slightly more challenging manner, having them mark independent and dependent clauses in example sentences without the aid of any boldfaced type. Calling on students randomly, Doug quickly completes the activating background knowledge and identification work on his own sheet, correcting misunderstandings as they arise. Students then move on to constructing sentences with their newly acquired knowledge. Notice how this is a different kind of practice: instead of identifying, they are creating (see Figure 3.8).

When these are completed, Doug invites students to share sentences with a partner, and then he calls on a few students at random to share their sentences. This is typically a fun exercise, as students enjoy sharing sentences that showcase their unique tastes and personalities.

The warm-ups Doug uses proceed in this fashion, with him mixing up—interleaving—the ways in which students practice using and retrieving the unit's knowledge. Sometimes, they revise incorrect sentences. At other times, students complete multiple-choice exercises (see Figures 3.9 and 3.10).

All of this work is situated in the context of whatever writing Doug's English students are currently working on, as well, so these "warm-ups" provide efficient direct instruction and retrieval practice to increase how well his students

Identify the Boldfaced Portion

DIRECTIONS: Identify the boldfaced portion as either an independent clause (IC), a dependent clause (DC), or a phrase (P).

1. ***Until you learn how to play defense***, you will have to sit on the bench. _____

2. ***Embarrassed and emotionally drained***, Ron locked himself in his room. _____

3. ***The students worked on their tests*** while the teacher graded papers. _____

4. Most of the students, ***even the ones with failing grades***, respected the teacher. _____

5. Until you learn how to play defense, ***you will have to sit on the bench.*** _____

6. Embarrassed and emotionally drained, ***Ron locked himself in his room.*** _____

7. The students worked on their tests ***while the teacher graded papers.*** _____

8. Most of the students, even the ones struggling to pass the class, ***respected the teacher.*** _____

FIGURE 3.7 • Identification Activity

Source: Worksheet created by Doug Stark. Used with permission.

learn this basic language knowledge. As students complete writing assignments throughout the school year in Stark's classes, he persistently references the knowledge that students learn in each of his mechanics warm-ups units, but this knowledge is virtually always brought to bear on actual things they are writing for his class. Knowledge building isn't silo-ized for Stark; it's ingrained into developing competent writers.

SPACED PRACTICE

To help knowledge stick long term, we want to distribute retrieval practice over time. For older concepts to remain retrievable, they must be occasionally retrieved. We may cover what is a subject and verb early in our mechanics work, but we want to require students to retrieve this knowledge and put it into practice repeatedly over the course of a year if we hope for it to stick long term. In the best scenarios, key knowledge is treated across multiple grade levels

SENTENCE CONSTRUCTION: Use the visual and written models below to help you craft your own sentences.

If a sentence starts with an **AAAWWUBBIS**, it will create a **dependent clause** or a phrase. A phrase or dependent clause cannot stand alone, but it can be used as an **"opener."**

Dependent clause opener,	independent clause.

Model Sentence: Until Doug apologizes to the athletic director, he will not see the court.

1.   **Your**   **Sentence:**
_____

If the **dependent clause comes second** in the sentence, a comma is generally not needed. In other words, if you were to take the model sentence above and flip the order, you wouldn't need to use a comma between the two clauses.

Model Sentence: Doug will not see the court until he apologizes to the athletic director.

2.   **Your**   **Sentence:**
_____

FIGURE 3.8 • Sentence Construction

Source: Worksheet created by Doug Stark. Used with permission.

DIRECTIONS: One of these examples is correct. Each of the other examples contains one error. Identify which sentence is correct and explain why. Be prepared to explain why the other examples won't work.

   A. Although he is still furious with you, Joe will except your apology.
   B. Although Joe is still furious with your. He will accept your apology.
   C. Putting aside his anger. Joe will accept your apology.
   D. Joe accepting your apology in spite of his anger.
   E. Although Joe is still furious with your, he will accept your apology.
   F. Although Joe is still furious with you, he will accept you're apology.

The best answer is _____ because _____
_____
_____

FIGURE 3.9 • Clauses and Phrases

Source: Worksheet created by Doug Stark. Used with permission.

DIRECTIONS: Examine the underlined portions. Plug in each possible answer. Choose the best answer.

5 6	5. A. no change	7. A. no change
Having no other place to <u>go. Andrea</u> headed to her <u>mothers</u> house. The two of them	B. go Andrea	B. too
	C. go, Andrea	C. two
7 8	D. go and Andrea	D. and
would have to find some way <u>to</u> get along with each <u>other. If</u> they were going to survive.	6. A. no change	8. A. no change
	B. mother's	B. other, if
	C. mother's	C. other so
	D. mother's	D. other if

FIGURE 3.10 • Multiple-Choice Exercise

Source: Worksheet created by Doug Stark. Used with permission.

at ever-increasing depth and complexity, thus "spiraling" content over years (Brunner, 1960; Johnston, 2012).

In Erica Beaton's U.S. history course, students are taught and quizzed throughout the year using a large, grid-like tool she's built called the Big Picture Guide (BPG; see Figure 3.11). The columns of the BPG contain the four themes Beaton wants her students to attend to, and the rows are the United States presidents from Lincoln to Trump. Within each grid, Erica teaches her students key facts, and over the course of the year she quizzes her students on the cumulative material they've learned, including information from units finished in previous months.

As Erica and her students move through the year, she asks students to add to the BPG notes. This extra attention to the major events students need to know helps reinforce students' preparation for end-of-unit assessments—but what's most important to note about the BPG is that they *never* drop their retrieval practice of all the earlier presidents. Students are expected to retain all the BPG facts throughout the entire year, and hopefully beyond, to support their long-term flourishing.

Erica uses cognitive science strategies to create challenging, spaced retrieval practice to make sure this retention actually happens. She starts by introducing

BIG PICTURE QUIZ #1 (Presidents #16-19)

NAME Write the first initial and last name of each US President in order.	SOCIAL Write the name of the era or time period. Mark the major social activities.	POLITICAL Mark the major amendments and political actions. Briefly explain each.	ECONOMIC Mark the major economic events, policies, or belief systems	MILITARY Mark the major US wars and battles.
16. A. L _____	President was _____	E _____ P _____ which freed the slaves in the rebel states		Secession and _____ War
17. A. J _____	President was _____	Amendment # _____, which abolished slavery Amendment # _____, which guaranteed citizenship to those born in the USA		
18. U. S. G _____		Amendment # _____, which gave all men the right to vote		Battle of _____ which _____ was the last Native American victory against USA troops
19. R. B. H _____		_____ of 1877, which pulled federal troops out of the South and ended the Reconstruction Era		

FIGURE 3.11 • Erica Beaton's Big Picture Guide

Source: Worksheet created by Erica Beaton. Used with permission.

only four or five presidents at a time; this number generally matches the eras of the unit studies. During that time, she focuses on three to five must-know social, political, economic, or military events/policies from each of those presidential terms.

As new knowledge sets are added unit after unit, it's essential to both space out the practice to allow time for forgetting to set in and to do frequent quizzing that increases in difficulty over time. For example, in the Civil War & Reconstruction Era Unit, Erica introduces the must-know facts associated with Presidents Lincoln, Johnson, Grant, and Hayes. The earliest quizzes, as exemplified in Figure 3.11, are set on "level easy" because students only need to recall the presidents' last names and the title of the each big picture event or policy.

In time, after her class moves on to a new unit and students are quizzed again, she increases the difficulty. So, in Erica's example, the first set of U.S. presidents moves from simple recall to "level medium," where students recall and describe the major events. Ultimately, because she keeps coming back to this same must-know content week after week, unit after unit, students not only solidify their understanding of content today in class, but they can confidently access the information twenty years from now. "They won't become informed global citizens if the content spills out of them and remains left behind on a Scantron bubble sheet. I want my students to be fluent in the language of history, the way bilingual speakers can switch languages with each breath," Erica explains (personal communication, 2017).

PLAY

Retrieval practice need not neglect fun and games. In fact, games engage students in a way that boosts students' recall. Robert Marzano (2009) states it best: "Games not only add a bit of fun to the teaching and learning process, but also provide an opportunity to review the terms in a nonthreatening way." In other words, knowledge-based games are both fun *and* effective for knowledge building.

http://www.ericaleebeaton
.com/five-steps

To read more about Erica's approach to spaced practice in her U.S. history classroom, visit her blog article on the topic.

Some of us are old enough to remember the Jaywalking segment Jay Leno repeated on his late-night show from time to time. He'd go around asking random pedestrians questions from the United States Naturalized Citizenship test— and we'd all not only laugh at the responses but also cringe at the lack of basic knowledge most people showed. I've adapted this and turned it into a game

I call The Citizenship Test. Certainly, this is the kind of challenge a social studies department could easily equip its students to handle, and it could be done in a fun, playful manner using freely available Quizlet study packs. The following activity would require a 1:1 setting; when I do things like this in my classroom, I allow students to use their personal devices or a Chromebook from one of our hallway's carts. I do think it's possible to do something like this without technology; for example, I could hold up flashcards for my students as they kept track of their answers in a notebook, and we could tally at the end. It would certainly take a bit more elbow grease, but one could still weave "play" into classrooms without access to internet-connected devices.

Step 1: Without any warning, I ask my students one Friday if they've ever heard about the citizenship test. We discuss, and I make sure students understand that the test requires prospective citizens to memorize one hundred questions and answers, and then on the test day they are asked ten random questions and expected to answer six or more correctly. I ask my students if they think it would be fair for a U.S. high school graduate to be expected to answer eleven questions correctly. They agree.

Step 2: I have students get on a device, and I create a Quizlet Live game using a one-hundred-card Quizlet citizenship test pack. Students navigate to the Quizlet.live link that the software creates for me, and they input their name. We wait until all students are registered. (Quizlet tutorials are available online. These packs are searchable and copyable on Quizlet, but make sure you edit the questions that are unique to your geographic location, e.g., Who is your state's governor?).

Step 3: The software then sorts students into teams, and I allow them to relocate in the room with their team. This is going to be important in a minute.

Step 4: I click "Start Game," and the student teams are then presented on their screens with identical questions. The game encourages collaboration, however, because for a given question (e.g., Who is the vice president of the United States?), only one student in the group has the correct card.

Step 5: The game ends when the first team gets twelve consecutive answers correct.

Step 6: I discuss with students how they think it went. What surprised them? Did they know as many as they thought they would?

Step 7: Now I introduce the challenge I want them to master this school year. I want *all* teams to get to eleven correct answers within 1.5 minutes. This means that we can't have one strong team winning all the rounds—we need to have every team getting to eleven correct answers before we end the game.

Step 8: I allow students to take up this challenge every week or so for ten minutes. Typically, I would save this for a Friday, or for natural places where my lessons might allow a spare ten minutes (e.g., after end-of-unit tests).

Step 9: If my students achieve the goal, I will then present them with the ultimate challenge. Still using Quizlet Live, I want them to again get all teams to eleven correct responses within 1.5 minutes, but this time, no talking is allowed, and they're not to sit with their groups. This forces *every* student to know the Citizenship Test. Earlier in my career, I might have attached some kind of treat to meeting these challenges. When I do this today, I simply tell my students that the challenges are worth doing because they're challenging. After all, in this class, we're the kind of people who do hard things.

The Gist

There's no such thing as creating literate students who don't know a lot of things. Abilities that we prize in the twenty-first century, including the ability to learn, to read, and to think critically, are not transferrable to domains in which we have little knowledge. Because of this, it is difficult to conceive of a school that values literacy and mastery but does not give the ample time and attention required to identify key knowledge per course and develop best practices for helping students build this knowledge over time. The only way teachers will be able to climb this particular path on the mountain will be if they are given time and permission to focus their efforts and attention. Although this can all be overwhelming, we approach the mountain with a one-step-at-a-time, practical mentality. We won't perfect our knowledge-building efforts this year, but it's reasonable to expect that we can make them a little bit better—and add to our efforts *and* our students' knowledge base each year.

Better Together

Like the other five things in this book, knowledge building is both easier *and* more effective when the load is shared across grade levels, departments, professional learning communities, or school buildings. Here are some ways to make knowledge building better together:

- Reading specialist and literacy coach Patty Sankey's principal was in the habit of giving the staff weekly articles to read for professional development—an excellent practice. Patty brought the idea of cohering a month's worth of articles around a burning question that was relevant to their school: *What instructional strategies are most impactful and will help us work toward closing the achievement gap for the following student categories: gender, special education, and socioeconomic status?* Teachers read related articles for a month, and then at their next professional development meeting they sat at tables of mixed disciplines and discussed the burning question, using the articles for support. Each group had to list two or three strategies that the staff could use to close the gap, and teachers ended by individually reflecting on one change they could make to close the gap for at least one student. As Patty described, "This method of PD was SUPER successful. By reading research, all the staff had background knowledge. Instead of paying thousands for an 'expert,' we all became our own experts. The conversations were focused, professional, *and* we came up with strategies to use that we could 'buy into.' In March, we are going to use a 1/2 day in-service to work on our next steps, which will involve everything from grant writing, to summer proposals, to committee work, to data analysis. We are *actually excited* to work on this. It's real. It's do-able. It's good stuff" (personal communication, 2017). Apparently, the BQY approach isn't only useful for our kids; it's useful for teachers, too!

- Identifying key knowledge for a course or discipline is a daunting task, and in this chapter's Common Teacher Hang-Up we explored two resources to help with that task: Hirsch's *Core Knowledge Sequence* and the College Board's *Course and Exam*

Descriptions. With your colleagues, familiarize yourselves with these documents and then examine the portions that are relevant to your curriculum. Afterward, come together and discuss (or Pop-Up Debate) which knowledge you think is most important. Create a prioritized list, and work together to find ways to increase the knowledge richness of your curricula.

- When students receive instruction on and experience with the effective knowledge-building practices laid out in this chapter, all across their school day, they more reliably master them and leave behind ineffective (yet common and time-consuming) practices like mere highlighting and rereading. If an entire school were to focus on teaching, modeling, and requiring just the work in this chapter, students would quickly internalize how the mind builds knowledge in ways that an isolated "study skills" course or infrequent advisory lesson could not accomplish.

CHAPTER FOUR

Argue Purposefully and Often

I tell my students on the first day of school that this year we'll do a lot of arguing. Because I teach ninth graders, this is their first day of high school and most of them are already nervous; when I tell them we'll be arguing a lot, I can sense some of them nearing the verge of fainting because, unfortunately, argument is something that many students conceive of as negative and threatening. And for every child who sees argument as a threat, there are others who, indeed, see argument as a chance to dominate other people, to have their voice be the only one heard and their view the only one accepted. In short, the word *argument* brings fight-or-flight instincts to the fore.

You might be wondering, *Why does this man insist on stoking the primal instincts of his students on their first day of school? What is wrong with you, Dave?*

The reasons are simple: on that very first day, I want to begin challenging the faulty perceptions of argument that my students bring with them to the classroom. For both my shy, often nervous introverts and my outgoing, sometimes dominating extroverts, the redemption of argument is too precious a goal to wait until some designated unit. Furthermore, it's not the year-end tests that

We've come to believe that it would be advantageous to students if we found opportunities throughout the day to immerse them in a culture of debate, or argumentation (in the best sense of the word). And we believe that it would invigorate the school day to find many opportunities, often, for students to take and defend positions, to learn from argument and counterargument. The research is clear that if students have opportunities to do the work orally that we hope they will learn to do as writers, this is advantageous to them.

—CALKINS, EHRENWORTH, AND TARANTO (2013, P. 147)

And that's all an argument is—not wrangling, but a serious and focused conversation among people who are intensely interested in getting to the bottom of things cooperatively.

—WILLIAMS AND MCENERNEY (N.D.)

primarily drive me to push argument all year long—it's the tests of lifelong decision making, including decision making upon which democracies rise or fall. And finally, throughout the year arguments will provide my students with opportunities to exert their intellects in public (and therefore, for many students, pressured) situations—I call these Pop-Up Debates, and we'll go into further detail on those later in this chapter. For these reasons and more, regular and purposeful arguing forms one of the six components of the *These 6 Things* bull's-eye.

The Argument for Argument

When I call argument precious, I don't mean it sarcastically. Something that is precious (from the Latin *pretium*, or price) is highly valuable; it is to be treated with the greatest of care. Like an irreplaceable family heirloom passed down through the generations, argument comes to us not at the behest of some list of standards but rather at the behest of democratic civilizations. The ability to argue makes one able to read critically, to write logically and compellingly, to listen at a level beyond compliance, and to carry on complex conversations aimed at solving problems or settling disputes. Perhaps counterintuitively in a time when argument means citizens yelling at one another on social media, *thoughtful, proper, listening* argumentation is the bedrock not just of the best kinds of schools (as Graff and Birkenstein, 2017, say, "argument is the *lingua franca* of academic discourse") but also the best kinds of families, communities, and organizations. You see—argument *is* precious!

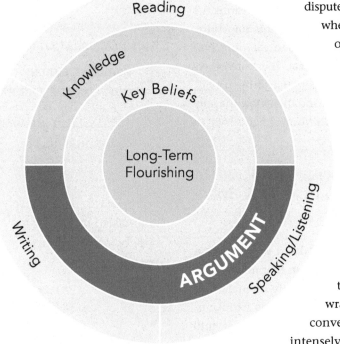

The only way this can make sense is if we conceive of argument as something broader and deeper than a zero-sum showdown. It's "not wrangling, but a serious and focused conversation among people who are intensely interested in getting to the bottom of things cooperatively" (Williams & McEnerney, n.d.). Like Richard Fulkerson (1996), I "want students to see argument in a larger, less militant, and more comprehensive context—one in which the goal is not victory but a good decision, one in which all arguers are at risk of needing to alter their views, one in which a participant takes seriously and fairly the views different from his or her own" (p. 17). Lindsay Ellis (2015) calls for teaching the goal of argument as "com[ing] to the best possible solution to a problem through discussion" (p. 204) and helping our students see that argumentative practices teach us to "develop nuanced positions through a process of critical deliberation" (p. 209).

I've called this "type" of argument all kinds of things over the years: "Fulkersonian," after Richard Fulkerson; "collegial," in the sense of the kind of arguments that great colleagues have together; and "collaborative." The term I finally landed on, however, is "earnest and amicable argument." (I know, I know, it's not going to win me any "naming" awards, but naming has never really been my thing.) Earnest is important in its "sincere and intense conviction" ("Earnest," 2018). It's the opposite of flippant, apathetic, and halfhearted. And amicable is the other side of things, lest we become dreadfully serious. At its Latin heart (*amicus*), this word means "friend." In Late Middle English, amicable started to mean "pleasant or benign" ("Amicable," 2018). Earnest and amicable arguments are both serious and joyful, good for the mind and good for the soul. That's what I'm after in my classroom. Figure 4.1 shows a chart we created in my classroom to remind us of these points.

Conceiving argumentative work like this is so critical to me that it's on my wall, and I harp on its themes with my students every chance that I get (see Figure 4.1). This is the argumentative culture—or maybe it's counterculture—that I'm trying to create in my classroom. So before I regale you with the evidence for the centrality of argument from a college and career readiness bent, allow me to entreat you from the angle of long-term flourishing.

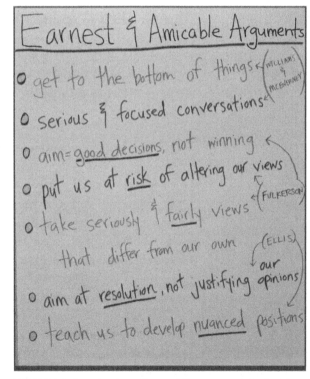

Earnest & Amicable Arguments
- get to the bottom of things (WILLIAMS & MCENERNEY)
- serious & focused conversations
- aim = good decisions, not winning
- put us at risk of altering our views
- take seriously & fairly views that differ from our own (FULKERSON) (ELLIS)
- aim at resolution, not justifying opinions (our)
- teach us to develop nuanced positions

FIGURE 4.1 • Anchor Chart of Earnest and Amicable Argument Attributes

What would the conversations around family dinner tables—or during long car rides, or in those hard moments with a close friend or sibling or spouse—look like if, when disagreement arose, all participants were fluent in this collaborative, resolution-oriented argumentation? How different would televised presidential debates be if getting to the bottom of things cooperatively was the norm? Or the social media chatter around those debates? Would the oft-cited "echo chambers" of 2016's post-election analyses have existed in a world where we were all comfortable with being ever at risk of needing to alter our views?

I concede that not all of our students may need to develop the sharp, technical skills of the competitive debater, but I cannot conceive of a single child whom I don't want to be excellent at having evidence-based conversations in which "the goal is not victory but a good decision, one in which all arguers are at risk of needing to alter their views, one in which a participant takes seriously and fairly the views different from his or her own" (Fulkerson, 1996, p. 17). I can be content if my children don't grow up to be politicians or lawyers; I will feel that I've failed, however, if they lack lots of practice and competence with collaborative, cordial argument by the time they leave my house.

So there's the long-term flourishing argument for argument. Now let's look at how argument relates to schooling. If you're not yet convinced, here's even more evidence for making argument a central part of your classroom and school year:

It's central to the democratization of academia. In his seminal *Clueless in Academe* (2003), Gerald Graff explains that the reason most college students view their post-secondary studies as nothing more than a grueling marathon of producing work that matches the various idiosyncrasies of each of their professors is because academia does a good job of "obscuring the life of the mind." This "cluelessness" is lamentable not just for its contribution to low college completion rates but also because it's avoidable. Students, Graff (2001) contends, are intellectual about the things in their lives—they can debate sports teams or fashion labels or musical artists or video game systems—but when they go into their college classes, there seems to be no place for the "hidden" argumentative intellectualism. This is unfortunate because all of academia *is* a connected web of argumentative cultures—just as much as all of sports or all of music or all of pop culture. Argument literacy, then, is a nonnegotiable part of what it means to be educated.

It's the most substantial intellectual thread across all the core subjects. In their *Framework for K–12 Science Education* (2012), the National Academy of Sciences explains that "engaging in argument from evidence" is a core practice across the science disciplines. In the authors' words: "Science is replete with arguments that take place both informally, in lab meetings and symposia, and formally, in peer review." In the most widely used set of math standards in the United States at the time of this writing, Mathematical Practice 3 calls for "construct[ing] viable arguments and critiqu[ing] the reasoning of others" (National Governors Association Center for Best Practices & Council of Chief State School Officers [NGA & CCSSO], 2010a). In the most widely used standards for English language arts and literacy in history/social studies, science, and technical subjects, only one topic gets referred to as having a "special place" (p. 24 of Appendix A). The topic? Yup, argument.

It's the core of "critical thinking." Critical thinking is a classic example of an important concept killed through buzzwordification. If we seek a definition for critical thinking on Google, we're bound to find a different definition for each of the first ten listings pulled up by the algorithms. I think cognitive scientists probably have the most right to define this, so I like Daniel Willingham's (2007) clarification: "From the cognitive scientist's point of view, the mental activities that are typically called critical thinking are actually a subset of three types of thinking: reasoning, making judgments and decisions, and problem solving" (p. 11). Argument helps us to do all three of these things, but it's a much clearer concept than the overextended term *critical thinking*.

It fits throughout the school day. Argument is one of the few pieces of common ground that the different departments share; there are various disciplinary dialects (hypotheses versus claims versus theses), but "arguespeak" (Graff, 2003) is the common language. How much more coherence would our secondary students experience throughout the school day if we made a concerted effort to make argument's centrality more apparent in every course? How much would our school cultures improve if, in music class, we sometimes asked our students to argue about topics relevant to the mastery of physical education and music and science and mathematics?

In short, I submit that we can help make our students sharper thinkers, readier college-goers, more competent career-pursuers, wiser citizens, and more capable parents and spouses if we immerse them in the work of argumentation.

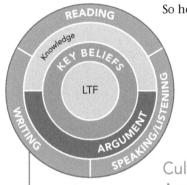

So how do we do this? I have three recommendations:

- Cultivate an earnest and amicable argument culture in your classroom.
- Increase the *quantity* of argumentation in your classroom.
- Improve the *quality* of argumentative thought in your classroom.

Cultivate an Earnest and Amicable Argument Culture

If our students are to produce a good deal of high-quality argumentative thinking and to feel that they all belong to the argumentative, academic communities that we create in our rooms (refer to the Belonging mindset, Chapter 2), then we first need to attend to creating earnest and amicable cultures of argument. Here are some of the ways that I've been able to cultivate a collegial argument culture—much of it learned through trial and error.

CREATE AN ANCHOR CHART WITH DESCRIPTIONS OF THE RIGHT KIND OF ARGUMENT

Remember that chart I mentioned earlier in the chapter, shown in Figure 4.1? As a warm-up early in the school year, I have my students find the chart on the wall, read it, and then summarize its points in their own words. When the warm-up is over, I'll begin the lesson by asking students to share their summaries with a partner, and then I'll call on a few students to share their summaries with the whole class. (This is simply Think–Pair–Share, which I'll discuss in Chapter 7.) I close the warm-up mini-lesson by asking students to consider whether they find that politicians or parents or peers tend to argue in this way. The poster becomes an anchor chart to refer to whenever we are reinforcing the type of argument we'll be doing.

USE ARGUMENTATIVE ICEBREAKERS

On the first day of school, I guide students in getting to know one another by having them write down five facts about themselves. Then I ask them to turn those facts into claims. I model this with a few examples of my own, as demonstrated in Figure 4.2.

TRY THIS

Introduce key ideas about argumentative culture through reading, writing, and discussion.

A FACT ABOUT ME . . .	. . . TURNED INTO A *CLAIM* THAT TELLS YOU SOMETHING ABOUT ME.
I like tacos.	Tacos are the greatest food on Earth.
I like watching University of Michigan football games.	U of M is going to beat OSU this year.
I am a Christian.	Jesus of Nazareth is the most significant figure in world history.

FIGURE 4.2 • I use a fact/claim chart like this to model for students this argumentative ice breaker.

In this way, I begin to reveal to students the argumentative nature of much of our lives. To build community with this activity and reinforce the safe nature of earnest and amicable argument, I ask students to share their claims with their partners. During this time, I walk around, listening to and laughing with students as they share claims and begin enjoying some friendly clashes. After the partner-share time ends, I ask for volunteers to stand up and explain their arguments. As this is happening, I can point out to students the other basic elements of argument that I want them to learn early on. (We'll look at those in a minute.)

This ice breaker exercise can be used at other points in the year, such as after a seating chart change. I can also make it specific to my discipline, asking students to create five debatable claims based on what we've learned during the past unit.

TEACH THE BASIC PARTS OF ARGUMENT

There are plenty of schools of thought on what language we should use for teaching argument and how it should be taught. In my classroom, I teach four basic components of argument, a simplified version of the Toulmin (1958) model of argumentation:

- Claim: A debatable statement.

- Evidence: Data used to corroborate one's claim. In science, this is often experimental data. In history, it's primary source information. In English language arts, it's evidence from a given text.

- Reasoning: Logic used either to connect one's evidence to one's claim or to support one's claim independently.

- Counterclaim: An awareness of what other claims might exist and proactively dealing with such "naysayers" (Graff & Birkenstein, 2014).

These initial components can be introduced as early as the first day of school in the icebreaker assignment described earlier. When volunteer students stand up to share and explain their claims, I may point out how Cade backed up his claim with evidence (e.g., Ohio State University [OSU] will defeat Michigan this year because they have a better quarterback) and then used reasoning to connect his evidence to his claim (. . . and quarterbacks win difficult football games, so the Michigan–OSU contest will come down to who has the best quarterback).

Importantly, when I introduce these terms, I have students start a fresh page in their notebooks for argumentative vocabulary, writing down the terms and their definitions. As we read or speak or listen to arguments in the weeks to come, I ask my students to both identify and create examples of these four argumentative components in action. If we're to become the sort of people who can argue dispassionately and open-mindedly, we need to have a language for analyzing arguments. Using the head, we seek to temper the heart's penchant for single-sidedness.

USE "CHOOSE YOUR OWN ADVENTURE" DECISION-MAKING GROUPS

To force collaborative decision making, I like to present my students with scenarios from time to time, tasking them with deciding between a number of options (sometimes, I leave things open-ended by not providing options, or I challenge their brainstorming abilities by having them come up with as many options as possible).

Afterward, in true Choose-Your-Own-Adventure style, I tell students what would have happened had they taken their decided route. Following are some examples from my class and those of my colleagues in other departments:

- Had you approached the Pharaoh on your own, he would have had you killed for your disrespect of his divinity. And no pyramid for you!
- Had you placed your plant specimens in three pots of soil without controlling for soil moisture, confounding variables would have made your results unreliable.

- Had you simply reread your list of French vocabulary words, you would not have remembered them as well as those who quizzed themselves using flashcards.

Such exercises force small groups to engage in collaborative argument, and they allow teachers to have fun adding gruesome details to the end results of student decisions.

ASSIGN SIDES IN POP-UP DEBATES

For the sake of building an earnest and amicable argumentative culture in my classes, I periodically ask my students to put themselves on a side that they wouldn't naturally choose, thus forcing them to "take seriously and fairly views different from [their] own" (Fulkerson, 1996, p. 17).

There are several ways to assign sides:

Eeny meeny miney mo, "everyone on this side of the room is arguing the affirmative," or some other equally sophisticated random selection method. The benefit is that it's quick; the drawback is that it doesn't ensure that all students are arguing for a side they would not have chosen on their own.

Raise your hand if you agree with the debatable statement today. Thank you. Everyone who just raised your hand, you'll be arguing against the statement today. Those who didn't raise their hands, you'll be arguing for it. This approach tends to get more students arguing opposite the side that they would have chosen, but it can engender distrust if you don't communicate frequently to students about how the best debaters can debate all sides, how sometimes we'll only grow if we argue on sides we wouldn't naturally choose, and how honesty is a critical part of the flourishing life. (After all, when they suspect that I'm about to place them on the side opposite the one they'd like to be on, they will be tempted to lie.)

For your warm-up, you're going to write a response to this debatable prompt. Please use evidence and reasoning to support your argument. One hundred words minimum, please. (I use word counts when I want to spur on my students who are quick to say, "I'm done," when they've written five words with a tangible target.) These warm-ups are collected after five minutes, and then I can quickly sort them into piles based on what side the students took, and I can create groups opposite to those sides chosen in the warm-up.

As is so often the case, the classroom culture makes or breaks teaching efforts like those described earlier. In a classroom where students don't feel like they belong to the academic community or where they don't feel that they can succeed or that the work has value, students will likely be too threatened by such efforts to benefit from them. Once again, there is no escaping the fundamental, oft-ignored nature of the Key Beliefs we discussed in Chapter 2.

COMMON TEACHER HANG-UP

What Do I Do When Debates Get Heated?

Before I approach this question, let me just admit that I typically *avoid* debate prompts that could lend themselves to emotional arguing. Basically, this is because I want students to push themselves during my debates as thinkers, and I don't want to place undue obstacles in their way to arguing in the collaborative, resolution-oriented spirit that I want them arguing. If you watch one of our Pop-Up Debates, don't expect a showdown about whether abortion should be legalized or creationism should be taught in public schools. I've just not found debates on hot-button issues to be super productive learning experiences.

With that said, I do occasionally provide students with a chance to practice the restraint that hot button issues require. For example, in the month leading up to the 2016 U.S. presidential election, my students were given the chance to argue about which of the handful of candidates we had read about in a series of articles was the best candidate for president. Prior to this debate, I was careful to model the measured tones I expected them to use, and I firmly and clearly set the ground rule that we would be discussing and engaging with the candidates' ideas and behaviors, not with blatant attacks on their persons or name calling. My students did a great job. This is largely due, I think, to the preceding weeks in which I sought to build an earnest and amicable argumentative culture in our classroom.

Still, even the blandest debates can get emotionally charged at times. When I begin to sense this, I immediately break into the debate, reminding students of how we engage with ideas, not with people, and that great debates consist of contributions from community members, not attacks on individuals.

Increase the *Quantity* of Argumentation in Your Classroom

To improve the quality of argumentation, there is perhaps no lower hanging fruit than increasing the number of arguments our students are expected to read, write, understand, analyze, summarize, and produce. Quantity is a prerequisite to quality. I have seen this in my own classroom, and I have seen this in schools I've visited across the country. Perfectionism must give way for progress.

POSE LEARNING TARGETS OR ESSENTIAL QUESTIONS OR WRITING PROMPTS AS DEBATABLE PROMPTS

Before students even walk into the room, we can shape our lessons to increase the quantity of arguments they are exposed to by framing our learning targets as debatable prompts. Figure 4.3 shows some examples by course.

COURSE/ CONTENT AREAS	DEBATABLE LEARNING TARGET
World History	• Were the Vikings raiders or traders?
World Language	• What is the best method for improving one's retention of Spanish vocabulary?
Mathematics	• What is the best method for solving for x?
English Language Arts	• In the novel *Things Fall Apart*, is Okonkwo a hero?
Music	• What is the key difference between students who do well in music and students who don't?
Physical Education	• What is more important: speed or strength?
Health	• Should the FDA regulate how much sugar companies can put in their food and drink products?
Business	• When considering Business X and Business Y, which is the better business?
Earth Science	• Is the Earth flat?
Biology	• Are vaccines safe for children? • Is artificial selection ethical?
Government	• Are the checks and balances of the U.S. government currently functioning as they're supposed to?
Economics	• Will lowering taxes create more jobs?

FIGURE 4.3 • Table of Argument-Centered Learning Targets

As you can see, different content areas allow for different possibilities here—many of the core subjects, as well as health and business, could use learning targets posed as debatable prompts for nearly every lesson, whereas for the fine arts and physical education this may be less the case.

If I were to be given control of a high school tomorrow and were directed to improve the quality of argumentative work happening across the school, the key message I would want my teachers to understand is that argument must serve the ultimate aims of the courses in which we situate it. It is, after all, about "getting to the bottom of things" (Williams & McEnerney, n.d.), and therefore, as my imaginary faculty went about converting learning targets into debatable prompts, I would ask them to argue for what they believe is a sensible number of debatable learning targets. After all, in band when we are learning a new song, there's nothing to debate—we just need to learn that song. But there are times when argumentative conversation could make us better band students—for example, a brief, Think–Pair–Share-style discussion on improving the performance quality of a piece of music would likely get students approaching their task from a more strategic angle.

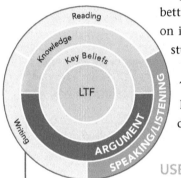

The point? Argument has a place in all of our classes, but it ought not to look identical or to occur with equal frequency all throughout the school day.

USE POP-UP DEBATES TO GET KIDS ARGUING

Years ago, when I was first convinced of the need to increase the volume of arguing my students were doing, I went online searching for how to facilitate classroom debates. The best I could find was a description of something called Lincoln–Douglas Debating, and I won't put you through the confounding exercise of trying to figure out how to make a Lincoln–Douglas debate intelligible to your students because I could never really master what it took to make it intelligible to mine. (Props to those of you who have!) But we did hold several debates in that format, and then we held some more because I was convinced that my students wouldn't become better arguers without actually receiving mandatory opportunities to argue.

As we continued using the Lincoln–Douglas format, I began taking pieces off. No more specific argumentative actions per speech; no more set time limits for a given component of speech; no more hard-and-fast use of binary debate prompts; no more mandatory coming to the front of the class.

TRY THIS

Whole class Pop-Up Debates are student favorites, and they always provide me with teachable moments for instruction, feedback, or modeling on argumentative, speaking, and listening skills.

We ended up with a structure that I called Pop-Up Debate. This is all it is:

1. Every student speaks one time minimum to two times maximum, depending on time constraints as determined by the teacher. (I remove or modify maximums based on the needs of each given debate.)

2. To speak, students simply "pop up" at their desks and talk. The first person to speak has the floor; in other words, the teacher does not serve as the "who spoke first?" judge. When multiple students pop up, students must practice (and initially, they must be taught) politely yielding the floor. Argument is a collaborative endeavor, and collaboration isn't a finger-pointing delivery of "You sit down. I was up first."

Figure 4.4 shows the chart in my classroom.

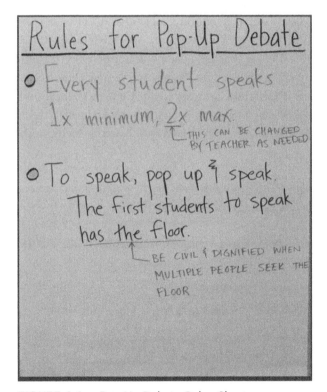

FIGURE 4.4 • Pop-Up Debate Rules Chart

DIG DEEPER

I've found the following resources to be particularly helpful for teaching argument:

- Erik Palmer's *Good Thinking: Teaching Argument, Persuasion, and Reasoning* (2016)

- Gerald Graff and Cathy Birkenstein's *They Say, I Say: The Moves That Matter in Academic Writing* (2014)

- Gerald Graff's *Clueless in Academe: How Schooling Obscures the Life of the Mind* (2003)

- Jennifer Fletcher's *Teaching Arguments: Rhetorical Comprehension, Critique, and Response* (2015) and in a unique style and form

- Joe Miller's *Cross-X: The Amazing True Story of How the Most Unlikely Team from the Most Unlikely of Places Overcame Staggering Obstacles at Home and at School to Challenge the Debate Community on Race, Power, and Education* (2007)

For a full list of the "Dig Deeper" titles mentioned in this book, go to davestuartjr.com/t6t-list.

To make Pop-Up Debates work their best, I try to abide by two foundational guidelines:

- Students use assigned text(s), logic, and/or course content to respond to a debatable prompt and their peers' arguments.

- I precede the Pop-Up Debate by teaching and modeling a target skill, and then, during the debate, I keep track of whether everyone speaks at least once and to what degree they use the target skill (check, check minus, check plus). This is almost always formative data for me to be used in either mid- or post-debate, whole-class feedback.

And that's really all that you need to know to get started with Pop-Up Debates. In the next section, I'll share the things I've learned in conducting over a hundred of these with my various groups of students over the years.

IMPROVE YOUR PROMPTS

Prior to meeting Les Lynn, the founding executive director of the Chicago Debate Commission and the founding executive director of the National Association for Urban Debate Leagues, I had no rhyme or reason for the creation of debatable prompts, but I noticed that some prompts lent themselves to better debates than others. Thankfully, Les's Argument-Centered Education keeps an active blog called *The Debatifier*, and it was here that I discovered Les's five criteria for creating effective prompts: Openness, Balance, Focus, Authenticity, and Interest.

Select a prompt that you might like to have students argue about in a course that you teach. Then, evaluate it for these five criteria

- Openness—There's more than one defensible and credible position.

- Balance—All sides are roughly equal in their defensibility.

- Focus—The prompt centers on a single idea or question.

- Authenticity—It's something that people actually argue about in a discipline, in a culture, in the wider world.

- Intellectual Interest—It's either immediately interesting to students (and you!) or likely to be through study.

davestuartjr.com/les-lynn-blog.

To visit the post in Les Lynn's Debatifier blog where he unpacks five criteria for good prompts, use the link or QR code above.

COMMON STUDENT HANG-UPS

Silo Speaking

One surefire way to make Pop-Up Debates and discussions boring is to allow what I call "silo speaking." Early on in the year, when we're having our first Pop-Up Debates designed to establish universal participation and public speaking comfort, silo speaking is inevitable.

A silo speech happens when students pop up, say what they want to say (or what they have written down), and then sit right back down. They don't respond to what another person has said, they don't paraphrase, and they often overtly repeat other people's arguments. When many silo speeches occur in a given pop-up discussion or debate, there's really not a discussion or debate happening—it's just a string of isolated speakers. This is a far cry from amicable work.

After one of those early-in-the-school-year, silo-filled "debates," I like to ask students to reflect on our class performance, citing things we did well and things we did not. When the kids share these out, I wait for a student to say that we repeated one another an awful lot, and then I give this occurrence a name: "silo speaking." When we all agree that this makes things a bit boring, we can then resolve as a class to not do it anymore.

Before our next pop-up, we're ready to learn about Paraphrase Plus, which you can read about at the end of this chapter. I print the graphic and have them keep it in their binders (see Figure 4.8 later in the chapter on page 126; for a larger graphic, visit davestuartjr.com/paraphrase-plus). If they are to succeed with this lynchpin set of discussion moves, they'll need consistent, live feedback during the next few Pop-Up Debates.

Improve the *Quality* of Argumentation in Your Classroom

As I've sought to expand argument from a mere unit into a part of the fabric of our classroom culture and a regular activity that we engage in through Pop-Up Debates, I have found it much easier to help my students improve the quality of their argumentative thought.

By the end of the first few months of school, Pop-Up Debates begin suffering. Students are used to the format, and some of them really get into it, but others become bored. I can't blame them because student debates start becoming repetitive, and they rarely clash. Perhaps the best way to begin remedying this is to require tracking the argument via note taking (competitive debates call this "flowing").

MAKE POP-UP DEBATES BETTER

It's useful to explain here that Pop-Up Debates in my classroom are not what someone with a competitive debate background would call a debate. In my eyes, they are primarily about increasing the volume of argumentative work that my students will do in a school year, giving us whole-class contexts within which to teach and learn specific argumentative moves, and getting us all comfortable with speaking for a whole room of people to hear (more on that in Chapter 7). I'll describe how to improve the quality of argumentative work that our students do in the next segment, but here, I'd like to share how to make Pop-Up Debates as enjoyable and successful as they can be.

Manage the Room to Minimize Cross Talk

In my experience, it's important to show zero tolerance for cross talk during a Pop-Up Debate. Zero tolerance, mind you, doesn't need to mean draconian death sentences for cross talkers; rather, when a student speaks from her seat or interrupts another student in some other way, I just firmly say, "No cross talk." As discussed in Chapter 2, I want to support all students believing that they belong, that they have a place in the Pop-Up Debates we hold.

You Are the Coach, and Pop-Up Debates Are Scrimmages

I wasn't a huge sporty in high school, but I do remember in my JV soccer days that we would have mock games (scrimmages) in which our coach would let us play a bit, then blow a whistle and interrupt to teach us, give us feedback, model a move for us, point out something that someone did that was excellent, or pinpoint a problem that a few of us were having in our play. That interplay between us playing soccer and our coach using instructive interruptions was important for our skill development. With Pop-Up Debate, I aim to interrupt no more frequently than every three student speeches, and my interruptions can include the following:

- Whole-class specific critique: "All right, has anyone noticed the phrase we keep using to start our speeches? . . . Yes, that's right—we keep saying 'I agree with So-and-so.' Let's try to mix that up."

- Single-student specific critique: "Caleb, I noticed there that you *mentioned* something that Danielle said, but you didn't paraphrase it. I want you to take a look at the sentence starters for paraphrasing (see Paraphrase Plus at the end of this chapter: Figure 4.8 on page 126) so that we know what in Danielle's speech you're referencing."

- Whole-class specific praise: "I'm hearing multiple people clash with opposing views in this debate, but no one is doing it with a snarky or dismissive tone of voice. That's excellent; you all sound like professionals."

- Single-student specific praise: "Tyler, your stance on this issue there was a little provocative, and we all reacted to it, but then you laid out your thinking for us. That helped us see that you're serious, and it helped us take you seriously. Good job."

- Modeling of the pre-debate target skill or a new skill that I'm seeing students struggle with (in these cases, I will often explain the skill and then contribute to the debate in a way that models the skill): "All right, family and team, let me show you something. Prior to the debate, I gave you some sentence templates for *complicating* the issue. We use moves like this to push the discussion into deeper territory, to point out that it's not as simple as we've been letting on. Let me show you how that would look in today's debate. . . ."

- Refocusing the discussion back onto the prompt: "All right, we're getting pretty bogged down on the question of _____, but that's really not our debate prompt. Take a look at that again up here on the board. Who would like to get us back on track?"

Every Kid Needs to Speak

In the first Pop-Up Debate of the school year, it is critical to get every student to stand up and talk. In fact, that is the only instructional goal that I have for the first Pop-Up Debate—every student stands up, says something, and sits down. That first Pop-Up Debate is often very short (students typically stand up and say a sentence or less) and very boring and more than a little awkward. But having every student speak that first time is critical. When they've done it once, they are far more likely to continue doing it. For a discussion of how I work to achieve universal participation (even from shy or anxious students) during that first debate, see Chapter 7.

Great Debaters Can Debate All Sides

As discussed earlier (see p. 111), I often assign sides to promote open-mindedness and argumentative flexibility. This can feel awkward and uncomfortable at first, for both you and your students, but it's worth it. Every year I find it an important learning experience for all my students.

We All Win With a Great Debate

I rarely choose winners in Pop-Up Debates. This isn't because I don't believe in the value of competition; rather, up to this point in my experience with Pop-Up Debate, I have found that selecting a winner results in fewer students continuing the argument after the class period. In other words, when I don't select a winner, it is not uncommon for me to be walking down the hallway later that day and to hear a group of students continuing our argument from class earlier. Score one for increasing argumentative volume!

Teach and Assess One or Two Skills at a Time

Because Pop-Up Debates aren't only exercises in argumentation, the mini-lessons I teach prior to Pop-Up Debates don't always pertain to argumentation. When I do target argumentation, I'm typically after lynchpin moves like paraphrasing, agreeing with additions, disagreeing with reasons, or complicating with questions (see Paraphrase Plus, Figure 4.8). When I target speaking skills, I might teach an element of Erik Palmer's (2011) PVLEGS, or the importance of organizing one's speech with a clearly stated beginning, middle, and end ("Tell 'em what you're going to say, say it, tell 'em what you said"; Palmer calls this "signposting"). I wish I could say that I have a carefully sequenced list of skills that I teach through Pop-Up Debate mini-lessons, but the reality is that I'm taking notes of student strengths and weaknesses during each debate, and I'm using those notes to develop one or two mini-lessons at the start of the next debate. In this way, teaching with Pop-Up Debates is one of the most responsive areas of my practice.

Teach PVLEGS Early and Use It All Year Long

Again, this will be discussed in Chapter 7, but it merits stating here that PVLEGS makes every speaking assignment better and more engaging for all participants. Figure 4.5 shows a classroom chart for quick reference.

Include a Reflection at the End

I've found it educationally profitable to save five minutes at the end of a Pop-Up Debate for students to quickly write what they feel they did well and what they feel they need to work on individually, and then what we as a class did well and what we need to work on collectively. I then ask students to share these out, making note of them on the board and asking the class to vote on which strengths and weaknesses we

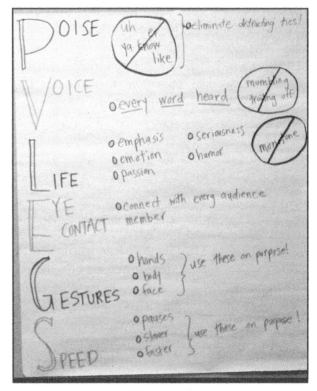

FIGURE 4.5 • Classroom PVLEGS Chart

should work on most with our next Pop-Up Debate. This communicates to students the collaborative nature of our arguments and the degree to which great discussions are always the fruit of great performances by all conversants.

Budget Time Wisely

In an ideal world, I would have students conduct a Pop-Up Debate every two weeks, resulting in twenty or so pop-up experiences over a school year. In doing this, I would be providing them with an unprecedented level of exposure with whole-class, structured, argumentative discussions—not because their previous teachers are inadequate in any way, but because argument is largely undervalued in American education and lost in the noise of the Next Big Thing we all need our kids to be doing. (*Who needs argument when we can put kids on iPads every day!*) In reality, I'm often unable to make pop-ups happen this often because, as it turns out, it takes time to get every kid talking.

In my larger classes of 35+ students, a Pop-Up Debate at the start of the year (when students are shy and lower skill sets yield shorter speeches) can take as little as twenty minutes. As the year matures, the average length of a Pop-Up Debate increases, often up to the thirty-minute mark. Thankfully, there are more efficient means for getting every student to argue among peers (see Conversation Challenge, Chapter 7), but when I do facilitate a Pop-Up Debate, I try to have thirty-five minutes of class time available so as to ensure that we complete it in a single period. This doesn't always work out, but it's always the goal.

Call on Students When the Discussion Stalls

Some students will hesitate to stand up unless called upon; when pop-ups begin to slow, I do call on reluctant students. To ensure that they have something to say, I precede Pop-Up Debate lessons with warm-up quickwrites on the topic of the day's Pop-Up Debate. I ask students to share these quickwrites with their partners (thus giving them a chance to rehearse) and to keep the quickwrites out during the Pop-Up Debate. That way, if they are called upon, they can always read from their quickwrite. As the year progresses, I begin pulling aside the kids I consistently have to call upon, telling them that I want them to work on contributing early on in the conversation, before I can call on them. The fact that this group of students often takes me up on this challenge is likely due to the noncognitive factors I seek to cultivate all year long—the Key Beliefs discussed in Chapter 2.

The point of all this is that we want to shift from simply conducting Pop-Up Debates every so often to becoming students of the craft of getting our kids arguing well.

MANDATORY ARGUMENT TRACKING

To teach tracking, I always begin with a binary debate—one with two sides. Debates with more than two sides can also be tracked, but it's more complicated than I want for my students' initial attempts with the art of tracking an argument. While eventually tracking can be done using a simple chart, I like to begin with a rule-based, more visually oriented flowchart method gleaned from Les Lynn (2017b). Figure 4.6 shows what it looks like.

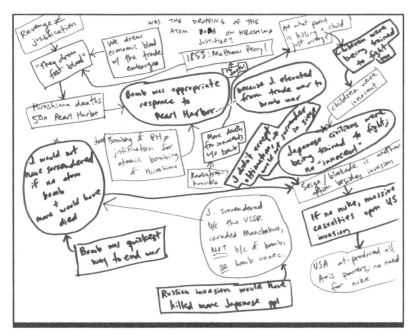

FIGURE 4.6 • Argument Tracking Flowchart

Here is what's going on in Figure 4.6:

- Our debate question is at the top of the page: "Was the USA justified to use atomic force on Hiroshima?"

- This was our second time debating the question; the first time produced enough poor fruit to make me want to revisit the question and add the tracking requirement.

- Each side was assigned a color.

- Each *claim* was circled.

- Each *counterclaim* was boxed and linked to the argument it responds to with an arrow.

- Each refutation (an attempt at defeating a counterargument) is also boxed and linked with an arrow to the counterargument it responds to.

Only new, "additive" argumentation is tracked (Lynn, 2017b). If a student pops up and contributes something that repeats a prior argument or goes on an unproductive tangent, his or her arguments are not recorded.

As I'm doing this on the document camera during the debate, I'm frequently asking arguers to restate or clarify. This signals to them that they have a responsibility to be clear, and this tends to perk the ears of the listeners who are tracking the argument. They shift from passive recipients of Pop-Up Debate speeches into active evaluators.

At times I "call" an argument—for example, I say that the blue team has effectively defended their counterargument against the red team's "Japan received an ultimatum and did not respond, and, therefore, the Hiroshima bombing was justified," and, therefore, the red team loses their argument. Or, if I'm not sure who has won an argument (after all, I typically don't adjudicate Pop-Up Debates, so I don't have a ton of practice), I'll say something like, "Okay, let's call that line of argument a draw—who has a new argument?"

Tracking, in other words, pushes us to improve the quality of our spoken arguments because we've got to be clear and we've got to respond to the arguments and counterarguments that have been put forth by our peers.

PRACTICE "THEY SAY, I SAY," USING CATHY BIRKENSTEIN'S TWO-PARAGRAPH TEMPLATE

While I obviously love the energy and opportunities created through whole-class Pop-Up Debates, these are not the only means by which we can increase the quantity of arguments our students experience. Before I discuss how I guide students in encountering arguments outside of Pop-Up Debates, let me just press home one strong point: when students produce and engage with one another's arguments through speech, argument is as practical, concrete, and "real" to their minds as I've seen it get. Spoken arguments such as those engendered by frequent Pop-Up Debates are the door through which students can more capably enter reading, writing, and listening to arguments.

Whenever I have students read or listen to arguments, I want them to focus on three things:

- First, what is the arguer's argument? This is where all productive arguments begin: with an understanding of what is already being said.

- Second, what are the strengths of the arguer's argument? How about the weaknesses?

- And finally, what do I think, based on what I know right now?

When we respond to arguments, I want my students to begin with what "they say"—what the authors or speakers have already said. Only after accurately summarizing the views they've heard or read should my students launch into whether they agree or disagree. Cathy Birkenstein's (in Graff, 2003, pp. 169–170) generative, two-paragraph set of templates offers the scaffolding my students need. This blank template is seen in Figure 4.7.

> The general argument made by author X in her/his work, _____, is that _____. More specifically, X argues that _____. She/he writes, "_____." In this passage, X is suggesting that _____. In conclusion, X's belief is that _____.
>
> In my view, X is wrong/right because _____. More specifically, I believe that _____. For example, _____. Although X might object that _____, I maintain that _____. Therefore, I conclude that _____.

FIGURE 4.7 • Blank They Say, I Say Two-Paragraph Template

Source: Cathy Birkenstein, from Graff (2003). Used with permission.

Some have criticized Graff and Birkenstein, arguing that such templates, "by teaching students to reduce every argument down to a single-issue conflict . . . inherently limit the possible insights that a writer can draw from normally multi-valent academic debates" (Arthur & Case-Halferty, 2008). While I do agree that no issue my students or I discuss is as simple as our arguments about it generally make it out to be, my students need scaffolding, and this is a good place to start. I want my students to engage with as many of the arguments in my curriculum, my discipline, and our world as possible during their year with me, so I need to give them scaffolding like these templates to help them "get in" at the ground floor. I agree with Graff and Birkenstein (2017); templates like this are, indeed, "generative."

USE THE PARAPHRASE PLUS SET OF TEMPLATES

One way of organizing argumentative templates like those suggested by Graff and Birkenstein is to chunk them into a simple set of moves. I have a set like this that I call "Paraphrase Plus" (see Figure 4.8). This is the central set of "moves" used in good, engaging Pop-Up Debates (and marital conversations, and political arguments with relatives, and rigorous department meetings, and so on).

When my students are ready to learn this baseline set of moves (typically around the third Pop-Up Debate of the year or so, once the nervousness of Pop-Up

PARAPHRASE
_____, you're basically saying _____.
_____, I hear you saying _____.
_____'s key point is _____.

AGREE & ADD-ON
I agree with what you're saying and would even add _____.
You're dead-on, and here's another reason why: _____.
You nailed it. After all, there's the additional point that _____.

DISAGREE WITH REASONS
The primary problem with that is _____.
The reason that your statement can't stand is _____.
I don't agree because _____.

COMPLICATE
I can see why you'd say that—after all, _____.
But I can also see _____ being true.
Isn't it more complicated than that, though? I mean, what about _____?
Do you think you might be missing _____?

FIGURE 4.8 • Paraphrase Plus: A Central Move of Great Discussions

Source: Concept derived from Graff and Birkenstein (2014). Special thanks to Erica Beaton for design inspiration. Image created by Dave Stuart Jr.

Debate has worn off and we're ready to start getting better), I actually re-create Figure 4.8 by hand in front of students, having them do likewise in their notes. I find that this is a more effective way of getting them to think through the templates and how they work than if I were to just hand it out to them, and I also appreciate the chances it gives me to argue for the *value* of using patterns of speech like this, not just in my class but in life as well. It's a pretty noncreative writing moment in the class when we handwrite the Paraphrase Plus tool but an important one nonetheless.

To get them acquainted with Paraphrase Plus, I'll have them discuss several accessible questions with their table partner, such as "What is the most important of the four 'core' subjects: math, science, social studies, or English? What is the least important?" and as they are doing this I will direct them to paraphrase their partner's statements and then use one of the three post-paraphrasing "moves" on the diagram: disagreeing with reasons, agreeing and adding on, or complicating.

Once we've done this, I'll have a few volunteers demonstrate the moves for the class, and then we will launch into that day's Pop-Up Debate, mindful of the fact that Paraphrase Plus is expected of all participants henceforth unless otherwise noted.

PUSH REFUTATION WITH REFUTATION TWO-CHANCE

I often tell teachers that Pop-Up Debate is simple to a fault. One of the faults is that it does not require refutation—which, as I said earlier, occurs when an argument or counterargument is answered by an arguer. "Refutation," Lynn (2017a) says, "is probably the most under-appreciated, under-taught, and the most essential and irreducible of all of the components of academic argument." Language like that from someone as experienced as Les Lynn gets my attention.

To begin doing this, I've used Lynn's Refutation Two-Chance. Here's how it works:

- Students are given a two-sided (binary) debatable prompt and divided into two teams. Students should also be given a balanced evidence set in advance.

- Team 1 has someone stand up to deliver an argument in support of their side. This argument is tracked (written down) by the teacher and the class. If there is any lack of clarity in the argument, the teacher asks for it so that the argument can be accurately written down. Team 1's arguer remains standing (or "popped up").

- Team 2 has someone stand up to deliver a counterargument against the argument that Team 1 just put forward. Again, this counterargument is tracked, and again, the counter-arguer remains standing.

- Team 1 now has two chances to refute Team 2's counterargument. If the first refutation attempt is successful (as judged by the teacher), Team 1 earns two points. If the second refutation attempt is successful, Team 1 earns one point. If neither of the refutations are successful, Team 2 earns two points for successfully counterarguing Team 1's argument.

- Now the roles reverse as Team 2 produces and defends an argument against a Team 1 counterargument.

COMMON TEACHER HANG-UP

What Debate Skills Should I Teach, and When?

My students' previous Pop-Up Debate performances are my primary guide in deciding what skills to target before a given Pop-Up Debate. If you watch me teach over the course of the year, you will not see a terribly systematic or scientific approach to moving students from mediocre to really good. Rather, I watch them, I take notes on how they could improve, I ask them to reflect after each debate on what we can improve, and prior to the next Pop-Up Debate I teach toward one of the areas we need to improve in. With that said, here is the general progression of skills that I teach in a given school year, in chronological order:

1. **Everyone participates.** For a detailed treatment of how I use the first Pop-Up Debate to teach students to overcome their inhibitions with public speaking, see Chapter 7.

2. **Paraphrase Plus.** Students quickly notice that early Pop-Up Debates are bogged down by repetitive or disconnected speeches. Person A stands up and says what he wants to say, and then Person B stands up and says what she wants to say, and so on, and no one is really responding anyone else. Paraphrase Plus (Figure 4.8) helps with that.

3. **PVLEGS.** This acronym from Erik Palmer (2011) for speech delivery is central to the speaking work I ask students to do.

4. **Argue for any side.** I require students to argue for a side they don't agree with.

5. **Mandatory tracking.** I expect all students to take notes on each speech in a debate, and I show them how to do that.

The difficulty with Refutation Two-Chance is that it puts me on the spot to think and communicate clearly about whether a given refutation successfully addresses a given counterargument. As such, this activity improves not just my students' argumentative creation and evaluation skills but also my own!

EXPLORE RHETORIC

In her excellent book *Teaching Arguments*, teacher and professor Jennifer Fletcher (2015) contends that many of our students argue in the same way that a novice photographer uses a brand-new DSLR camera—they point and shoot. Fletcher goes on:

> If we want our students to do more than just point and shoot when it comes to argumentation, we need to teach them what rhetoric is and does. Rhetorical reading and writing are the gateway practices behind effective argumentation. Within rhetoric itself, we find several threshold concepts that change how students approach texts: occasion, audience, purpose, ethos, pathos, and logos. All are integrative and transformation. (p. xiv)

My own teaching practice is barely scratching on the door of a rhetorical approach to argumentation like Fletcher lays out in her book. I mention it here as an example of how argument is a deep pool for our professional exploration and the promotion of our students' long-term flourishing. Exploring rhetoric in detail is beyond the scope of this chapter, but I encourage you to find ways to incorporate rhetoric into your instruction—and Fletcher's book is *the* place to start. I don't foresee getting bored with the many ways in which I can push my practice forward in this area—that is as it should be.

EXPLORE PRAGMA-DIALECTICS

The trouble with teaching students that arguments consist of claims, evidence, reasoning, and counterclaims is that it can communicate to students that the important job is justifying your positions and protecting them from other positions. This difficulty is treated beautifully by Professor Lindsay Ellis (2015), who offers up an alternative model of argumentation that she studied on a research sabbatical at the University of Amsterdam. This "pragma-dialectical" model encourages writers "to move through four phases, not necessarily linearly:

- *the confrontation stage*: identifying a difference of opinion
- *the opening stage*: establishing the terms and common starting points, i.e., the common ground between those who have the difference of opinion, perhaps the writer [or speaker] and the reader [or listener]

- *the argumentation stage*: developing evidence and reasons to support standpoints and respond to critical questions

- and *the concluding stage*: evaluating the results of this argumentation on the merits, sometimes moving into a new confrontation stage when a new difference of opinion within the issue is identified. (p. 204, emphasis added)

Ellis opens up wide and promising territory for Pop-Up Debate teachers who want to take their students deeper into the beautiful, special territory of argument done right.

COMMON TEACHER HANG-UP

I'm Not Ready to Have Kids Debate!
I Don't Know Where to Start!

At this point, I can see how I'd be feeling if I were reading this five years ago. "Ahhh! Argument is way too complicated!" I often meet teachers who feel overwhelmed by how much goes into building a course punctuated with earnest and amicable debates. If that's you right now, let me encourage you to just return to the basic ground rules:

1. Everyone speaks: minimum once, maximum twice

2. To speak, stand up and talk. The teacher isn't the referee. You need to be polite.

While the kids are debating, you the teacher are doing a few basic things with a simple list of student names and a clipboard:

- Keeping track of who has spoken

- Keeping students from cross talking ("Oops, no cross talking Braxton.")

- Taking note of areas for future improvement

- Calling on students who have not spoken yet when there is a lull— don't make space for long awkward gaps in speaking.

That's all. You tell students that you're trying to push the group into new territory, that you believe in arguing well for all the reasons laid out at the start of this chapter, and that you believe in their ability to argue with one another like the best classrooms in the country do. And you get better each time you hold a Pop-Up Debate because each time you learn something new.

The key isn't being perfectly prepared. It's starting.

The Gist

Argument is central to not just a life of the mind, but a life of constructive conversations and good decisions. To create classrooms in which the study and practice of argument is not confined to a unit, we need to cultivate what I call earnest and amicable cultures of argument, we need to give our students a large number of opportunities to study and practice argument, and we need to try our hand at improving the quality of student argumentative thought over time. We are so quick to push for quality in our secondary classrooms, but I've found I can only address quality once my students and I have been immersed in the work we've discussed so far. If argument isn't situated in the context of a life-giving classroom *culture*, it's not going to promote the Key Beliefs we're after. And if argument isn't a normal part of our classroom life—if we don't provide kids with a certain *quantity* of argument—then it will always seem like a detached, one-off kind of exercise. As we increase the quantity of arguing our students are doing throughout the school day, we begin to create opportunities for improving the *quality* of those arguments.

We can work at all three of these areas simultaneously or focus on one at a time. How we approach these three recommendations depends on the time we have, the current state of our curricula, and the number of other things on our plates.

Better Together

Argumentative work, when done frequently and in earnest, yields great fruit at the classroom level. However, it is only when teams, departments, PLCs, and schools work in concert on argumentation, teaching students what argument looks like in each discipline and throughout the school day, that our kids begin to see that argument, indeed, is "the name of the game" in academia (Graff, 2003, p. 3). Here's how we can do better together.

- At your next faculty meeting, hold an impromptu Pop-Up Debate on which course or subject is the most important one taught in your school. Typically, we teachers have readymade and knowledge-rich answers to this question. Afterward, have teachers reflect on the degree to which they could see this Pop-Up Debate format working in their own setting. Brainstorm: What could kids debate about? What problems might arise, and how might we head them off?

- Ask each of your colleagues to bring an argumentative article that they appreciate to your next meeting. Request that this article be relevant to their discipline. At the meeting, swap articles. Afterward, discuss what similarities and differences you noticed in the ways that article authors argued. How might this affect the way that we deliver argument-based instruction in our classrooms?

- If argument is commonplace in your school and you want to take it to the next level, play "Refutation Two-Chance" (see the earlier discussion) at your next staff meeting with a question that is relevant to what your team is currently working on. (See p. 100 for how Wisconsin educator Patty Sankey did something like this.) You will need at least one person to judge whether refutations succeed, so if you have a debate coach in the room, use him or her!

Argument (and school) makes most sense for kids when argument is common throughout the school day. The more we can make this central thread of academia explicit to our kids, the more likely they are to build identities that include academic interests.

Notes

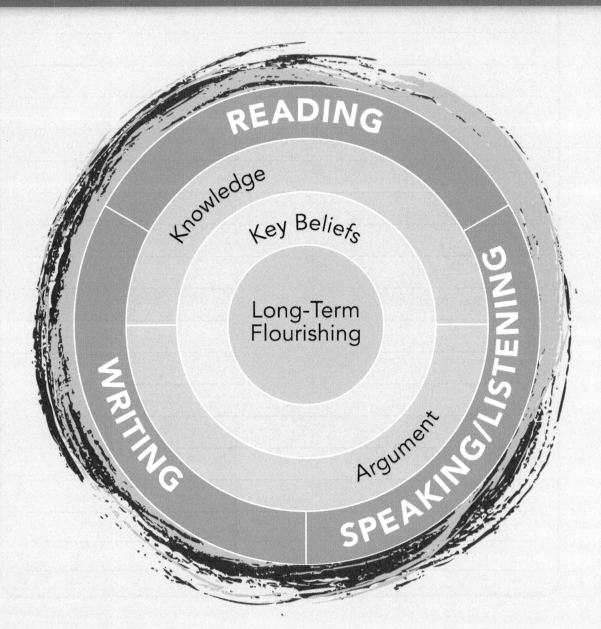

PART III
Literacy-Rich Learning Experiences

READING

Knowledge

Key Beliefs

Long-Term Flourishing

SPEAKING/LISTENING

Argument

WRITING

So far, we've said that any efforts to improve how much and how well we cultivate the key beliefs isn't wasted but is wise; any time that we teach our students more things about the world, we're doing good work; and whenever we get our kids arguing or find ways to make plain to them the links between the argumentative cultures they live in and those that inhabit academic and public life, we're on point. None of this is special or groundbreaking, and that's the point—we're ignoring the distractions of what's new, rooting ourselves instead in three time-tested, evidence-based areas of work. All along the way, we're seeking the mastery of our material—we want our students to become the best world language or health or chemistry or civics or English students they can be.

Now, we move on with our intentionally time-tested work. We examine how these foundational pieces inform the purposeful and frequent reading, writing, speaking, and listening that we ask our students to do.

As we read, the first three components of the *These 6 Things* bull's-eye might urge us to consider the following:

- What knowledge do I want my students to gain from this text? What new vocabulary?
- What arguments might this text bring? What arguments might it support?
- How will I bring to bear the beliefs I've taken such care to cultivate on the challenges this text may confront us with?

As we write, we consider the following:

- What knowledge will students process in this writing exercise? What do they need to know to do this writing well?
- How might this piece of writing make them more capable users of evidence, of reasoning, of claims, of refutation?
- How will I communicate to students the value of this writing assignment? How might I support them in owning the pieces of writing they create and the effort required to make these things exemplary?

And as we speak and listen, we consider the following:

- What knowledge are my students building or rehearsing in today's exercises?
- What critical skills will they bring to the task of listening or speaking today?
- How will what we believe about speaking affect the degree to which my students fully engage in today's speaking and listening work?

These inexhaustive lists serve, I hope, to illustrate how the bull's-eye's components work together and how the ordering of this book represents the order in which they build upon each other.

CHAPTER FIVE

Read Purposefully and Often

Much of a good education consists, as it always has, of a simple combination of one or more good texts matched with an interesting question.

—MIKE SCHMOKER (2011, P. 36)

Teenagers want to read—if we let them.

—PENNY KITTLE (2013, P. 1)

One joy of being a father is having the chance to watch my children transform into readers. To me, this is something that still borders on the magical, even now that I've been able to observe how Haddie's and Laura's teachers have made the magic happen. What amazes me about reading is that it gives my children access to nearly all the world's information. If they someday want to become fitness fanatics or amateur physicists or experts on the writings of C. S. Lewis, they are now gaining what they need, in their earliest years, to do all of those things. Reading, I hope, will be a key way that my children, and my students, engage with the world, learn about it, and understand the intricate conversations taking place all around it.

Before we move on, let's once again situate ourselves in the bull's-eye. We've examined the Key Beliefs that underpin every single act of reading we'll ever ask kids to do, and we've looked at how reading is given its purpose partially from the critical knowledge we hope it helps our students learn or the argumentative skill we seek to strengthen through that particular reading. It is only when we see reading as situated on top of noncognitive factors and between our knowledge and skill objectives that we can maximize a given text's utility in promoting the long-term flourishing of a child.

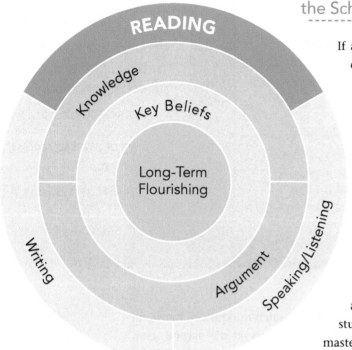

If all reading throughout the school day did was help my English language arts colleagues and me, then I wouldn't advocate for it. Every discipline has enough challenges. However, reading widely is not an ELA issue—it's a long-term flourishing one. In other words, students who read widely in all content area classes reap benefits far beyond the school day.

If you need to be convinced, here are key reasons we ought to have our students reading more on their way to mastery of our course material.

Reading is uniquely tied to college completion.

While I don't believe that college completion should be the sole goal we communicate to our students, I find that my students and their parents generally expect that when students graduate from high school they will be ready for college if they choose to go. This assumption, unfortunately, is often too generous, at least in the United States. According to the National Center for Education Statistics (2008), college completion rates nationwide are at 60 percent, and they are only *36 percent* at institutions with open admissions policies.

Reading, it turns out, is a big part of that story. When students enter college requiring a remedial reading course, they have half the chance of graduating as those who do not, which is why one study on the topic concludes that "the need for remedial reading appears to be the most serious barrier to degree completion" (Wirt et al., 2004).

Professors expect students to be able to learn through reading.

For my own part, I'm almost more convinced of the importance of reading by an anecdote than I am by that data. Some years ago, I was part of a panel at a local, open-enrollment community college. The panel was given to an audience of the college's instructors, and I was the lone representative of K–12 education (a scary thought, I know). During the question-and-answer time, a professor of nursing stood up, looked right at me, and described how her nursing students were incapable of reading an assigned text and preparing to be quizzed on that text's most important ideas. "The greatest weakness I see in my nursing students," she said, "is that they don't know how to learn through reading. They expect me to tell them everything." This was not a professor of literature or someone working with high-level graduate students; rather, she was an instructor at an open-enrollment college that helps fill the growing need for qualified nurses in the United States. And her students, she decried, seemed unable to learn from reading.

Reading equips us for the worlds of work and adult life. Of course, not all of my students will (or need to) attend college, with plenty from our town choosing paths in the military, the trades, or elsewhere. Yet all of them will have situations in which they'll need to read things closely, and, as my colleague Erica Beaton (2016) warns, "an inability to read means a readiness to be taken advantage of." That paper you need to sign? The loan you're considering taking out? These things often need to be read, with the help of additional texts. In general, being informed and well read is *always* an asset, whether working as a lobsterman or a lunar spacecraft engineer.

Reading can increase empathy and social skills. The reading of literary fiction—which this chapter will not limit itself to—has particularly interesting benefits, according to some research. Keith Oatley (2011), a cognitive psychology professor emeritus at the University of Toronto, says that reading literature can provide students with a boost in social skills. Furthermore, in experiments published in *Science*, researchers David Comer Kidd and Emanuele Castano (2013) found that reading literary fiction (versus nonfiction, popular fiction, or nothing at all) temporarily enhances one's ability to understand the mental states of others. (Perhaps of special note to teachers in the fine arts is Kidd and Castano's suggestion that such empathic enhancement may come from engaging with works of art in general.)

Reading builds vocabulary and general knowledge. In Chapter 3, we examined the critical role that knowledge plays in a variety of areas, including wide reading comprehension. As it turns out, the opposite is true, too: reading voluminously helps build knowledge and vocabulary, which in turn makes more reading and knowledge-building possible (Cunningham & Stanovich, 1998). Warren Buffett, in his typical folksy-wisdom style, is said to have summarized this as follows: If you want to be successful, "read 500 pages . . . every day. That's how knowledge works. It builds up, like compound interest. All of you can do it, but I guarantee not many of you will do it" (Housel, 2014). Let's make sure our students read.

A Focused, Sensible Approach to Reading Throughout the School Day for the Long-Term Flourishing of Our Students

In addition to the pro-reading reasons listed earlier, there's one fundamental thing that holds true: Providing widespread opportunities for students to read increases the odds that they'll discover that reading isn't something to have an opinion or feeling about—"Reading is boring" or "I love reading." And it's not just something we do in school. Rather, we want our students to know—to internalize—that reading is something that knowledge builders and informed, engaged arguers *do*; even if they don't all love doing it, reading ought to be something that they competently, consistently do in their pursuit of the flourishing life.

So how do we do it? We need to get practical; there's only so much time in a school day, after all. The remainder of this chapter focuses on my recommendations for drastically increasing the quantity and quality of reading our students do throughout the school day, in a few manageable steps:

- Quantity step 1: Situate reading in the context of content mastery
- Quantity step 2: Give me a number
- Quantity step 3: Strategically increase that number
- Quality step 1: Master the nine simple moves that support readers
- Quality step 2: Increase the complexity of the reading we expect our students to accomplish

Let's work through each of these in turn.

QUANTITY STEP 1: SITUATE READING IN THE CONTEXT OF CONTENT MASTERY

"We're all reading teachers now."

This is probably *not* how we should sell reading-throughout-the-school-day efforts.

Plenty of educators outside the English Language Arts department have heard this line, and I'll bashfully admit that I've been guilty of saying it, too. Virtually always, the line is delivered with great intentions. And virtually always, the line causes dissension rather than unity.

I can still remember a colleague responding to my own early attempt at "we're all reading teachers now" types of arguments. He said, "I became a social studies teacher because I like social studies, not because I wanted to teach reading." I wish I could say that I responded to him with empathy and respect, but the truth is that I judged him. "This guy is burnt out and selfish," I thought. This was not a helpful internal position from which to find common ground with my colleague!

In reality, my colleague and other people who voice similar concerns aren't being selfish—they are being honest. We should honor the fact that people come to teaching because of a love for their content area. This doesn't negate the fact, however, that students could and should be doing far more reading during the school day.

Reading throughout the school day, rightly conceived, aims at the long-term flourishing of kids, specifically by giving them more and better chances to master course material. So my question is this: Is there any way in which reading could enhance mastery of your course material?

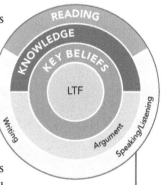

Consider, for example, a Spanish course in which, once per month, students were given an article written by a polyglot (someone who speaks several languages). One month, it's the article "Spanish Numbers: How to Count from 1–1,000+ in Spanish" from Benny the Irish Polyglot's blog *Fluent in 3 Months*. In this rather extensive piece, Lewis unpacks practical tips for learning to count in Spanish, and along the way he gives a glimpse into the methods he's used to learn seven languages. In turn, students might become curious about Benny, and the way that he's used language to unlock world travel could serve as a prop to students' value beliefs. Providing students with the occasional article written by someone who's not us but who is still engaging not only helps our students build knowledge, it increases the degree to which they find our courses valuable.

TRY THIS

Use articles written by people of interest in your discipline or content area.

Within any discipline we can debate matters of curriculum and pedagogy—like which math skills should be mandated by state curricula, or how many labs students should conduct in a chemistry class, or whether project-based approaches are the best means by which to teach a government class. What we can't debate, however, is the value of the knowledge gained in each of these subject areas. This needs to be affirmed not just with lip service but also in how building budgets and professional development sessions are apportioned and in how we approach the challenge of getting more kids reading during the school day.

QUANTITY STEP 2: GIVE ME A NUMBER

With reading properly framed, we come to a simple question: How many texts are your students currently expected to read in the course(s) you teach? Before we can explore whether they could be reading more, we simply need to arrive at a number. This quantification work is essential because it drags us away from the arguments for or against reading across the content areas and plants us firmly in simple, useful data. In each course under your purview, how many texts are students expected to read? Before we get lost in the quality of those texts or the scaffolding around them, we need a number where we can start.

Categorization is helpful here. English teachers, count up novels and poems and articles and short stories. Social studies teachers, add together the textbook excerpts, other secondary sources, primary documents, and articles you ask your students to read. Science teachers, how many journal articles, "science in the news" articles, textbook pages, and reports are your students reading? Do your best to come up with numbers for any course that you teach. Figure 5.1 shows a simple chart I started with my ELA colleagues.

TEXT	TYPE
Things Fall Apart, by Chinua Achebe	novel
"White Man's Burden," by Rudyard Kipling	poem
"Colonialism's Effect on the Kuba Kingdom of the Congo," by William Henry Sheppard	primary source
"An Investigation into Congo Colonialism," by George Washington Williams	primary source
"Colonialism in Africa," excerpted from *Africa: An Encyclopedia for Students* (2002)	secondary source, excerpts

FIGURE 5.1 • Sample Quantification of Texts Read in One of My English 9 Units

Note: It can also be useful to quantify the number of pages read.

Tallying the number of texts that all students are expected to read is not a small task, and it shouldn't be done flippantly. When we undertake this exercise, we want it to end with a picture of present *realities*, not present intentions.

Numbers in hand, we come to our next question: Could we possibly increase that number in a way that enhances, rather than detracts from, deep student engagement with knowledge building in our content area?

If every department in the country quantified the amount of reading students were guaranteed to be expected to read in their courses, then sought to incrementally increase that number over time, the results would be dumbfounding. Right now, I encounter nearly no one who *knows* how much kids are expected to read in their courses. Instead, we have departments around the nation feeding complex (and time-consuming) data collection systems, or comparing summative assessment scores, or chasing after the latest fad. Alternatively, we could spend time seriously grappling with this: How many texts do kids read now, and how might we increase that number this year?

QUANTITY STEP 3: STRATEGICALLY INCREASE THAT NUMBER

When I ask teacher groups around the country whether they could possibly increase the number of texts students are expected to read without abandoning the souls of their disciplines or crushing their students beneath undue amounts of work, they routinely answer with "yes!" Here is what seems to be the quickest approach to "winning" at the quantity problem: incorporating shorter, regularly assigned texts.

In Chapter 3, we examined Kelly Gallagher's popular article of the week assignment as well as the way I've shifted that assignment into the Burning Questions of the Year series, and math teacher Kelly Turner gives a similar assignment called Graph of the Week. I consistently find teachers intrigued by these examples of consistent, low-cost (in terms of in-class and planning time) routines for drastically increasing reading opportunities. Turner also recently introduced a "Great Engineering or Nah" set of prompts, which seem ideal for STEM settings.

http://www
.turnersgraphoftheweek
.com/

Kelly Turner's website can
be found using the QR code
or the URL above.

In many of the content area departments in secondary schools around the world, a regularly assigned (weekly, biweekly, monthly) short text (article or graph, primary source document or mini-biography of a famous musician) is easily the lowest-hanging fruit for increasing the quantity of reading and the incidental knowledge-building opportunities that our students experience. In science and health and career tech classes, there are Lexile-adjustable articles at *Newsela.com,* freely available and conveniently categorized. For math or science teachers, there is Turner's graph of the week. For schools with greater resources (or DonorsChoose funding), there are monthly magazines from Scholastic that cover all manner of subjects. Assigned monthly, such reading increases the number of texts read in a given course by nine or so per year; assigned weekly, the increase moves to four or more texts per month. Each incremental improvement in quantity is potentially life-changing for students, especially when multiplied across the school years. We never know when a text might spark a student's curiosity or capture a child's imagination.

Won't it get old? Of course it will. But a teacher who attempts to explain the value of the assignment is bound to help students to value it themselves. And once in a while, it's worth having students complete a Hulleman-style "Build Connections" warm-up (see Chapter 2) in which they reflect on connections between the regular article or graph-reading assignment and their personal lives.

COMMON TEACHER HANG-UPS

Where Am I Going to Find Time to Grade Written Responses to Weekly or Monthly Texts?

We'll dive into this more in Chapter 6 on writing, but I know that some readers will be itching right now: *I have more than one hundred students, and now this guy wants me to grade a written response to an article or a graph or a mathematician biography every week or month? You've got to be kidding me.*

Nope, I'm not kidding you, but I am also *not* saying you should be grading these closely. Please keep what we're trying to do in view: We're trying to increase the opportunities our students have to read a broad array of texts. Because of that, any writing our students do in response to these texts *need not be micro-graded.* While my students do write plenty of pieces each year that I give careful feedback on (again, we'll discuss this more next chapter, but note that *careful* doesn't mean *lengthy*), their responses to articles of the week are not one of those pieces. I once interviewed Kelly Gallagher, who spoke to a similar approach when I asked him about grading articles of the week:

This may come as a surprise or a shock or a disappointment, but I spend very little time assessing those AoWs. Whether I put an A or a B or 20 points or 16 points for me is really, really not the impetus behind giving that assignment. What's important to me is that the kids are doing the reading and the kids are doing the reflecting. . . . I may look at each paper for a grand total of four seconds. It's really not a grading issue for me. *I think teachers get way, way too hung up on grading.* For me, I just want the kids to be doing the work. I give them enough points to keep them going, and occasionally when they start to slide, I'll pick two or three that are really good ones, and then bring them out and ask the kids, "Why is this a 20? Why is this a 20?" But I actually don't score them in front of the kids because I do them at a hundred miles an hour. (Gallagher, as quoted in Stuart Jr., 2016, emphasis added)

If we're micro-grading everything that our students write in response to readings, then our students will never have the chance to read and respond to as many things as they ought to.

QUALITY STEP 1: MASTER THE NINE SIMPLE MOVES THAT SUPPORT READERS

So now we come to an interesting question: What if we provide all these opportunities to read articles and excerpts and poems and mini-biographies, only to have our students not actually read them? Here we come to the post-quantity problem: quality. How do we encourage and equip all students to get as much as possible from each reading opportunity?

First of all, let's not forget the Key Beliefs that underlie student effort and behaviors. In everything we do in our classrooms, we must bend our minds to cultivating these Key Beliefs. When students believe that they can succeed at reading the texts we give them (efficacy), that they are the kinds of people who read stuff like we ask them to read (belonging), that through effort they can increase their comprehension of any given text (effort), and that the reading they do in our class matters to their actual lives (value), then guess what? They're going to take an earnest swing at doing the reading we ask them to do.

So while I'm sad to inform you that we probably won't get away with simply chucking a bunch of documents at our students and telling them to go to work,

I'm happy to say that we've already covered a key component of the problem with fake reading: student beliefs. I once told a group of great Wisconsin educators that we teachers are in the business of providing opportunities to kids; master teacher Chris Vander Ark responded, "Yes, and the business of selling those opportunities, too." Chris gets at the important role that motivation plays in whether or not students will read and succeed with a given text. See Chapter 2 for in-depth treatment of the beliefs underlying student motivation.

Now, second, let's boil down our objectives with a given text:

- First, we want students to understand what they read
- Second, we want them to do something with that understanding

Before we assign a reading, then, we're wise to ask ourselves Kelly Gallagher's "Four Questions to Ask While Planning" (2004, pp. 198–199; in blue below):

1. Without my assistance, what will my students take from this reading? In other words, what will they understand or be able to do without any help from me?

2. With my assistance, what do I want my students to take from this reading? Now we get to my hopes: what do I want students to understand by reading this? What do I want them to be able to do?

3. What can I do to bridge the gap between what my students would learn on their own and what I want them to learn? Here, our goal is Goldilocks teaching: I want to give my students just enough support—not too much, not too little—to get them where I hope they'll be by the end of this text-based lesson.

4. How will I know if my students "got it"? In other words, what will I be looking for while they're reading and after they're done, and how can I use the information to tell me whether or not we succeeded?

The first question helps us decide how much support our students need, and the rest of the questions unpack how I'm going to provide that support. For all text-based lessons, I pull from nine simple, fairly old-fashioned teacher moves: three before reading, three during reading, and three after reading (see Figure 5.2). What I'd like to suggest in this section of the book is that we're wise to experiment at using just enough of these to give kids a real opportunity to read the texts we assign.

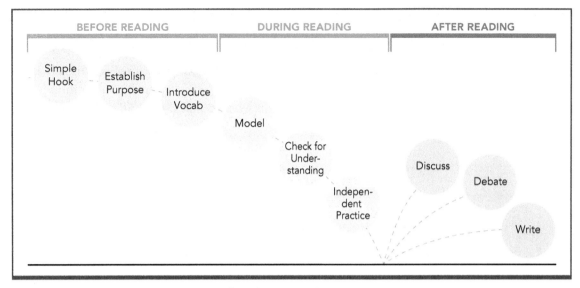

FIGURE 5.2 • Nine Instructional Moves for Teaching With Texts

Source: Concept inspired by Mike Schmoker's "authentic, redundant literacy" template from *Focus* (2011); image concept created with Erica Beaton (ericaleebeaton.com).

The essence of the nine moves comes from Mike Schmoker's (2011, p. 74) "authentic literacy template," with modifications made over the years as a result of conversations between my colleague Erica Beaton and me. As you can see in the graphic, we think of text-based lessons as a bounce pass because in the initial stages of a text-based learning experience, the teacher initiates. Typically, we literally pass a text out to our students. Then, we may

- Attempt to hook students into the text, which can help activate schema or enhance the value belief

- Establish a purpose for reading the text, which makes clear for students what they're to do with the reading and why they're being asked to do it

- Introduce complex vocabulary that we suspect could get in the way of our students' understanding

In all these three moves, our goal is efficiency. We don't want to spend a single second longer in pre-reading work than we think is necessary. After all, our goal is to increase the amount and quality of *reading* that our kids do, not the amount and quality of prereading.

Words Matter

Mike Schmoker's "Authentic Literacy Template"

Schmoker (2011) describes his "template for authentic literacy" as "utterly unoriginal" (p. 76). He summarizes it as follows:

- Close reading/underlining and annotation of a text

- Discussion of the text

- Writing about the text informed by close reading, discussion, or annotation

As the bounce pass approaches the ground, the actual reading takes place. During a reading, we may do the following:

- Model "higher-order reading" for students (Schmoker, 2011, p. 79), which can include note taking, *purposeful* annotating, or think-alouds to show students what's happening in our minds as we read a portion of the text

- Check for understanding, where we walk around the room to look over students' shoulders, confer one-on-one, and support students as needed

- Give kids time for independent practice: actual time in class to silently read some or all of the assigned text

Again, we're after efficiency in these things.

Finally, after our students read, the ball bounces beyond the reading task into authentic, text-based work. Typically, we draw from one or more of the following:

- Discussion, which can be small group or whole class

- Debate, which can be small group or whole class

- Writing, which can take a variety of forms (e.g., summary, response, essay)

Nothing crazy, right? Yet in the beliefs-rich classroom, these are the only moves I find myself needing to pull from to create text-based lessons that my students enjoy.

Let's examine each of these moves in greater detail. For each, I'll use three scenarios.

- An integrated science class during a unit on the solar system. I'll be using an excerpt from Bill Bryson's (2003) nonfiction book *A Short History of Nearly Everything* (specifically, his exploration of how big the solar system is, found on pp. 23–26).

- A health class in which I've incorporated the Burning Questions of the Year model (see Chapter 3). Our Burning Question is, "What does it take to live to one hundred?" and we're going to be reading an article titled "Yes, Sitting Too Long Can Kill You, Even if You Exercise," by Susan Scutti (2017) for *CNN.com*.

- An English 9 class in which we're reading Chinua Achebe's (1958) novel *Things Fall Apart*.

Provide a Simple Hook

There are two situations in which it's a good idea to hook:

- I suspect that my students won't be motivated to read the text, or

- I want them to activate schema so that they'll be ready to understand the text.

There was a time in my career when I would use huge amounts of time to plan and deliver hookish activities. I now aim for the shortest possible path. Here are some useful hook techniques.

Ask a provocative question. For the Bryson excerpt, my goal is for kids to gain a better understanding of the scope of the solar system and the immensity of the space within it, so I'm just going to start the class with a simple, provocative question: *If the Earth were reduced to the size of a tennis ball, how far away would it be from the sun?* Bonus question: *How big would the sun be?*

Play a brief, related video. In the Health class, I've got this article topic that's already pretty provocative; I think the title alone is going to draw kids in, as is the Burning Question in which I've situated this article. I'm not worried about motivation, then.

I am, however, worried that this idea of sitting down as a deadly thing is going to be easy for my students to dismiss, so I want to take a couple of minutes to settle them into the issue. To help with this, I'm going to play a brief video that CNN included with the article. The video is titled *Is Sitting the New Smoking?*

"Take a stand." For novels, I draw from the nine moves at the whole-novel level and at the individual reading assignment level. Before we begin reading Achebe's novel, then, I know my students will need some hooking because their lives are pretty far removed from Okonkwo's and his Ibo neighbors'. One good method for hooking kids into a novel like this is asking them whether they agree or disagree with a few questions that are germane to the book.

So, for example, consider these questions for Achebe's book:

- Are all religions equally valid?

- Do men have the right to be the leaders of the household?

- If people want to have multiple spouses, should they be allowed to?

These questions are meant to get kids thinking about issues that will be brought up in the novel. If I have time, I'll have students respond to these during a warm-up at the start of class, stating their stance and their reasons for it.

Then, I have them show their take physically: if you answer with a strong affirmative, stand up on your chair; if you answer with an affirmative, stand up; if you answer with a negative, stay seated; if you answer with a strong negative, kneel or crouch on the floor. (Prior to doing this, I make the requisite remarks about not breaking things or people during this activity.)

This can take as little as five minutes, but if I want to extend the exercise a bit I'll ask for volunteers (or call on students randomly) to explain their positions.

As an alternative to the physical movements of this activity, students can process the questions via Think–Pair–Share or Conversation Challenge, which we'll explore more in Chapter 7.

It can be tempting to get carried away with creating hooks for texts—be wary of this. Not all texts require a hook—an article on cell phones in school, for example, will get my kids' attention just fine on its own, and they don't need much schema activation—and hooks need never be elaborate. In my experience, the beliefs-rich classroom is inherently a place of joy; elaborate hooks aren't needed, but a simple hook can come in handy from time to time.

BEFORE READING

Simple Hook

ESTABLISH PURPOSE

Introduce Vocab

Establish Purpose

This is where we explain—again, in as simple and quick a fashion as possible—*why* we're reading this text today and *what* we're going to do with it once we've read it. The *what*, my students know, is almost always going to consist of one or more of the following: writing, discussing, or debating. I want to be sure to share with them any pertinent information about those after-reading tasks (e.g., whether there is a specific writing prompt).

Emphasize understanding. The first purpose of reading any text is to understand it. In fact, I try to get my students to view reading *as* understanding. As Daniel Willingham (2006b) puts it, understanding that a non-understood text is a non-read text "confers a significant advantage to comprehension" (p. 45).

Early in the year, then, I create a simple anchor chart for my students, like the one shown in Figure 5.3.

As the year progresses, I'll start adding things that are specific to my discipline. For example, "Use graphic organizers for comparison, causation, continuity/change, and periodization," or "Locate unfamiliar geographical references." I also use Thomas Frank's "Crash Course" Reading Assignments video on YouTube to introduce my students to SQ3R, a strategy that is well-documented on the web.

I also like using Kelly Gallagher's (2004, pp. 86–91) "Three Key Questions" for texts, found in his book *Deeper Reading*:

- What does it say? This is literal comprehension.

- What does it mean? Here we attend to argumentation, synthesis, analysis, or opinion.

- What does it matter? Here we examine significance. So what? Why is this relevant? This targets the value belief, as well.

Provide response options. For the Bill Bryson text, I might tell students that, after reading the excerpt, they are going to write a 200-word response to some or all of the following questions:

> **Reading = Understanding**
> That's why we...
> o Re-read confusing or difficult passages
> o Look up unfamiliar words
> o Locate unfamiliar place names
> o Take notes that summarize main ideas & illustrate with details
> o Identify our unsolvable question marks & take them to peers or Mr. Stuart
> o Survey Question 3 Read Recite Review

FIGURE 5.3 • Classroom "Reading = Understanding" Chart

https://youtu.be/ WAlUkjsZ5xQ

To access Thomas Frank's "Reading Assignments" video, use the QR code or the URL above.

- What in this text surprise you? Why? Be specific!

- Okay, so the solar system is big. Who cares? Why does that matter to your actual life?

- How does Bryson help us to "get" the immensity of space? What techniques does he use to make the facts easier to grasp?

Set Knowledge and Argument objectives. We can also set objectives for a reading based on our preceding two chapters, Knowledge and Argument. For example, in the Health class article on sitting, I can set both a Knowledge objective—I want my students to learn about the surprising health risks of sitting too much—and an Argument objective—I want my students to continue considering our Burning Question. How seriously should "sitting" be taken in a conversation about the keys to living to one hundred years old?

Discuss "unkillable" questions. For *Things Fall Apart*, I may tell students that their job in the first chapter is to record as many questions as possible about the reading. I'll say, "Listen, Okonkwo's world is pretty different from our own, so you'll know that you're understanding this first chapter if questions start rattling around in your mind and you begin feeling confused. All that I want you to do as you read this first chapter is to write those questions down—let's say at least five. And then tomorrow, we'll discuss them."

The next day, I'll have students go through their questions with a partner (via Think–Pair–Share; see Chapter 7) or in a small group (via Conversation Challenge; see Chapter 7), and I'll instruct them to move on from questions that they are unable to answer so that they can get through as many as possible before time expires for the discussion. Then, I'll have students share out questions that their partner or group couldn't answer. I'll show students how to answer the questions that can be answered using outside resources (e.g., "Is Amalinze the Cat actually a cat?" can be answered with context clues; "What does the word *fare* mean?" can be answered with a Google search). Questions that can't be answered without reading further into the novel (e.g., "Why is Ikemefuna referred to as an 'ill-fated lad'?") are posted on the wall so we can keep track of them as the novel progresses. I find that this "Unkillable Questions" exercise teaches students to ask more questions, answer more questions, and ask better questions, all at the same time. It also helps my students to value the class, and for my kids who lack reading confidence, the assignment provides a feeling of success.

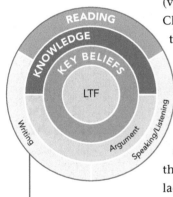

TRY THIS

Assign "unkillable questions."

Introduce Complex Vocabulary

If there are any words in the text likely to impede students' understanding, I want to introduce those efficiently before they dive into the task. My goal isn't to introduce every possible unknown word, of course—that gets really boring. We want to be picky, and here are some ideas.

For shorter texts, lead students in annotating quick, functional definitions. In most cases, I briefly preview complex vocabulary by pointing them out to students on the document camera and leading students in annotating brief, functional definitions in the margins. (If it's a text we can't write on, I'll have them do this on a spare sheet of notebook paper.) I'm not after vocabulary memorization here; I just want to optimize access to the text.

For the Bryson passage, here are some terms I would ask students to locate in their photocopies, circle, and annotate:

- Speed of light: 7.5× around Earth in 1 second (!)
- Lumbering: slow
- Prospect: chance, way

For the Scutti article on sitting, I might preview the following:

- Mortality: death
- Verify: confirm that they are correct
- Sedentary: sitting still, not moving
- Duration: how long something lasts

For novels, use a glossary. In the English 9 scenario, I want to show my readers how to manage vocabulary needs themselves. To help with this, I find a glossary to the novel online, and I copy and paste this into a Google Doc and shrink the text size to about 10 pt. This makes it possible to give kids a fairly comprehensive glossary of the book using only a couple of sheets of paper. During our initial readings of the book, I'll preview words that come up in a reading assignment by having kids highlight them in the glossary we've printed out. As the unit progresses, I'll be less directive here, releasing students to take responsibility for consulting the glossary as needed.

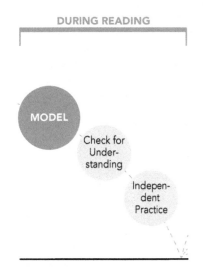

DURING READING

MODEL

Check for Under-standing

Indepen-dent Practice

http://www.davestuartjr.com/purposeful-annotation-close-reading/

For an in-depth look at purposeful annotation, including several video explanations, use the QR code or the URL above.

During Reading: Model Higher-Order Reading

By reading aloud a paragraph or so and thinking aloud for my students, I can show them how I approach the various subtasks that come with this particular text-based lesson. For example, if I've asked them to focus on learning the material by taking notes on a given textbook section, I read a paragraph and model how I would go about deciding what to write in my notes and what to leave out. If, instead, students are reading a primary source document, I would show them how I read the sourcing material and begin to make predictions about what stance the document's author will take on the question or issue we are exploring.

Let's take a look at a couple of key approaches for modeling.

Purposeful Annotation

Annotation got caught up in the buzzwordification of close reading after the widespread adoption of the Common Core State Standards. Through informally polling teachers over the years, I've found that most people come to annotation in a manner similar to my own story. I arrived at college, I was told to buy all these books, and then I was given these incredible reading assignments; I had to read and comprehend and do something with really complex texts. And so, because the books were mine, I started annotating as a survival instinct. In the margins, I would summarize dense passages, paraphrase difficult sentences, and make note of any bits of interest that might come in handy when I was sitting down to write an essay or participate in discussion later on.

In short, annotation was never a task assigned to me; it was a technique that I used to succeed at my assigned task. This, then, is what I want my students to do with annotation: I want them to *purposefully* annotate as a means to help themselves during and after a reading.

Here's how I would model this with the Bill Bryson passage:

All right, class, someone remind me what we're going to be doing after we read this excerpt. . . . Yes, that's right. We're going to write in response to one or more of the response options I introduced you to a moment ago. So two of these response options are things that we can annotate for while we're reading:

- *What in this text surprised you? Why? Be specific!*
- *How does Bryson help us to "get" the immensity of space? What techniques does he use to make the facts easier to grasp?*

If you think about it, there's no reason we should get to the end of reading and have nothing to say here. For that first prompt, when Bryson writes something that surprises us, we can mark it—let's say, with an exclamation mark. Now we'll have specific things we can come back to for reference if we choose to go with that prompt.

For the second prompt, we'll have to think a little harder. Let me demonstrate what this might look like.

At this point, I would read aloud the first two paragraphs of the Bryson excerpt on the document camera as students follow along on their own copies. When I arrive at a bit where Bryson tells us it will take us seven hours to get to Pluto if we hop aboard a rocket ship that travels at the speed of light, I'll annotate, "He turns the distance into a travel time, helps us imagine traveling it."

Point out a pattern. In my health class, I've asked students to consider how serious this whole sitting problem is. Where does it rank in our consideration of the Burning Question of how we're all going to live to one hundred? So I'm going to model for students how we can figure out whether to trust Susan Scutti by pointing out how she gives a brief background on each of her sources. For example, she doesn't just cite a study; she cites a study "published Monday in *Annals of Internal Medicine*." In other words, the research is recent, and it's appeared in a formal journal.

After pointing out another example or two of this technique, I'm done. It's time for students to get reading on their own.

Questioning. For *Things Fall Apart,* I might read aloud several paragraphs to model for students what it looks like to ask productive questions during a reading. I find that my students struggle with struggle; they can be quick to shut down when things get confusing. Kelly Gallagher (2004, p. viii) has a good mantra for this that he uses in his classroom: "embrace confusion."

Words Matter

Purposeful Annotation

When we show students how to annotate on purpose–to help themselves understand a text or to prepare themselves for a post-reading discussion, debate, or writing assignment– then we're giving them practice with an authentic skill. Teach purposeful annotation. For help, visit http://www.davestuartjr.com/purposeful-annotation or use the QR code below, where I've explored the concept in depth using videos and classroom examples.

Words Matter

Productive Curiosity

Being curious isn't automatically helpful. It's possible to be curious and not learn much at all. I want my students to be productively curious, to cultivate the habit of not just wondering about random stuff but of asking good questions, making predictions, analyzing, learning, and growing. Read a fuller treatment using the QR code or URL on page 156.

www.davestuartjr.com/
productive-curiosity-billion-
dollar-character-strength/

Read more about productive
curiosity using the QR code
or the URL above.

In my own class, I like to speak to my students about "productive curiosity": don't just wonder something; do something about that wondering! This is part of the reason I assign Unkillable Questions when we're beginning *Things Fall Apart*. I want students to see how we'll track these questions, working to eliminate plot questions as the story progresses and fact, word, or concept questions by using resources like the glossary I've provided or the internet.

Check for Understanding + Independent Practice

Although I'd love it if I could reasonably expect all of my students to do the reading outside of class, I know that's not possible. For this reason, I work hard to make my text-based instructional routines efficient; I need time in class for kids to read if all of my kids are going to do it.

DURING READING

As I release students to do the reading in class, I walk around, checking for understanding. This is when note taking or annotating is helpful as formative data: I can see whether students are doing too much (e.g., writing down a sentence in their notes for every sentence in the text, or underlining every paragraph in the name of annotation) or too little, and I can also see whether or not they understand the task (i.e., are they annotating in a manner that will help them respond to the post-reading writing prompt?). As I walk around, I provide support as needed.

In the Integrated Science scenario, I'm looking over students' shoulders to see their annotations. If I find a kid annotating in every square millimeter of the margin, I'll check in to see what's going on. Is this purposeful? Why so much? Typically, I find that students do this kind of "over-annotating" when they think it's what I want.

In the Health class, I might try to engage a couple of my more reluctant readers in a brief, quiet conversation at their desk about the Burning Question and how it relates to their life and what they're reading: *So we're looking at this BQ of how to live to one hundred. What do you think about that? Do you think it's even a good question? What are you taking from this sitting thing? Is it really "the new smoking"?* My goal here is to engage kids in the reading, specifically by targeting their belief in my credibility (I'm showing I care about them and what they think), the value of the task (I'm prompting them to search for value in the BQ I've situated this text within), and their feeling of belonging (I'm trying to guide them toward seeing themselves as the type of person who reads this kind of article).

And in the English 9 class, perhaps I'll try to pull students in the hallway for quick, two-minute conferences on the book, targeting kids who I think might have a lot to say about the book but haven't had a chance yet today to really talk about it.

Discuss, Debate, or Write About the Text

After we read something, I want us go a step further and either discuss, debate, or write about what they've just written. Each of these three things has an entire chapter dedicated to it in this book, so I'll be brief in my remarks here to demonstrate how post-reading exercises need not always be lengthy. Let's imagine that each of our sample classes had only ten minutes at the end of a class period in which to "do something" with their reading.

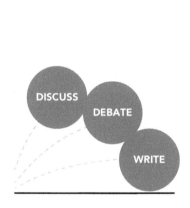

In the Integrated Science classroom, I've always showed students their options for responding to Bryson's excerpt on the size of the solar system, so I can spend our final ten minutes having them write toward their 200-word target. If time permits, I would love to have them share one line from their written response with a partner.

In the Health classroom, I might make way for an impromptu Conversation Challenge (see Chapter 7), which is just a small-group discussion that fits easily within ten minutes. To spark conversation, I might write the following questions on the board:

- Is sitting the new smoking, or is that an overstatement? Explain.
- What in this article surprised you?

As students conversed in their small groups, I would be walking around listening.

In the English 9 classroom, I might use my final ten minutes to hold an impromptu Pop-Up Debate on a recurring question in our class: Is Okonkwo a hero? With so little time, it wouldn't be possible for everyone in the class to participate in the Pop-Up Debate, so to ensure that everyone said at least something in response to the prompt, I might precede the Pop-Up Debate with a brief Think–Pair–Share (see Chapter 7).

If teachers across the content areas were allowed to become experts at using just these nine moves with any given text, we'd see a lot more quality reading instruction happening throughout the school day. Remember: the goal is always to use as few of these as possible so as to increase the efficiency with which we can work through texts in the classroom. Less time per text leads to more time available leads to more texts that we have time to read and learn from.

COMMON TEACHER HANG-UP

But Kids Won't Read Teacher-Selected Texts!

Saying that all kids don't read is like saying that all white people can't dance. It's condescending. I am in the business of providing an elite, equitable education to my students. This means I want them having the same opportunities as the schools down the road with lower free/reduced-price lunch populations and more BMWs in the student parking lot. So frankly, this means I give my students lots of chances to read and to learn through reading.

What I can't do, however, is assume that just because I assign something, kids will read it. I need to become a master at the nine moves—particularly those that target Key Beliefs, like hooking and purpose setting—and I must become efficient in my overall instruction so that more time is provided for reading in class.

QUALITY STEP 2: INCREASE THE COMPLEXITY OF THE READING WE EXPECT OUR STUDENTS TO ACCOMPLISH

Finally, equipped with a quantity to build upon and a set of basic moves to improve the degree to which all of our students benefit from those quantities, the final frontier is increasing the challenge. Opponents of teacher-assigned reading cite widespread, student-reported "fake reading" as an argument against having much teacher-assigned reading at all, but if we use our knowledge of the lever-like Key Beliefs from Chapter 2, we can begin to draw different conclusions from the "fake reading" phenomenon.

Namely, reading is something we'd like our students to carefully do, and what our students believe about a given reading assignment has a largely predictive effect on whether or not they'll give a reading an effortful attempt. The solution to non-existent academic behaviors and poor effort isn't abandoning the expectation that students engage in academic behaviors. In my classroom, it's approaching the problem from the angle of academic beliefs.

First, we must take care to build classroom communities in which reading is something we do—not because it's assigned but because it's beneficial, because if we're going to be in school we might as well make the most of our time, because we aren't going to waste these years of our lives disengaged and running from challenge. As we assign more texts, we should also aim to test just how challenging we can make the reading we assign—and how we can build classroom cultures in which doing challenging reading is the norm and is a part of our identity as learners. Those who abandon assigned reading because "students don't read" are taking too lightly the degree to which a teacher can build an environment in which hard reading (and good, quality discussion, debate, and writing afterward) is the norm.

Second, we need to attend to how we scale up the reading we expect our kids to do if we want them to believe that their skill can improve with effort. At the start of the year, I slow down when using the nine moves so that my students experience success. As the year progresses, I assign increasingly challenging readings so students can get a sense of how their hard work is paying off.

Third, we define success with a given text clearly for our kids so that they can build the mindset that they can succeed in the reading tasks we assign. At the start of the year, my criteria with textbook reading is to take a page of notes. Then, it is to succeed on a quiz focused on vocabulary from the reading. Next, it is to answer higher-level questions using the material from the reading. And so on. As they succeed, I raise the bar.

Finally, we leverage what we can to make the work valuable to students. We give them occasional opportunities to reflect on why

DIG DEEPER

For deeper, more focused treatments of helping students to read more and better, I recommend these resources:

- Douglas Fisher and Nancy Frey's *Text-Dependent Questions: Pathways to Close and Critical Reading, Grades 6–12* (2015) and *Rigorous Reading: Five Access Points for Comprehending Complex Texts* (2013)

- Kylene Beers and Robert Probst's *Notice and Note: Strategies for Close Reading* (2013)

- Laura Robb's *Vocabulary Is Comprehension: Getting to the Root of Text Complexity* (2014)

For English teachers in particular, I recommend these:

- Ariel Sacks's *Whole Novels for the Whole Class: A Student-Centered Approach* (2014)

- Berit Gordon's *No More Fake Reading: Merging the Classics With Independent Reading to Create Joyful, Lifelong Readers* (2017)

- Penny Kittle's *Book Love: Developing Depth, Stamina, and Passion in Adolescent Readers* (2013)

Also, it's worth noting that my favorite book on reading is Mortimer J. Adler and Charles Van Doren's classic *How to Read a Book: The Classic Guide to Intelligent Reading* (1940). That book has made me the professional reader that I am today.

For a full list of the "Dig Deeper" titles mentioned in this book, go to davestuartjr.com/t6t-list.

reading matters to them—Teri Lesesne's (2010) reading ladders are an excellent example of this, and Chris Hulleman's Making Connections exercise (see Chapter 2) is a simpler form. Value can also be created by stories shared with our students of how reading has improved our own lives and how successful people have used reading to advance themselves. Ultimately, we make reading more relevant when we give kids a chance to discuss, debate, or write about what they've read and when we frame that work as intentionally challenging.

The Gist

One needless cause of the literacy decline is a lack of reading volume in secondary schools. Each one of us can combat this without sacrificing content knowledge. We start by quantifying the reading we assign in each course and brainstorming "low-hanging fruit" methods for increasing that quantity. As we increase the quantity of texts read, we also need to increase the simplicity and effectiveness with which we support students and their reading—the nine moves in this chapter can suffice. And finally, when kids don't do the reading, we must do more than throw in the towel; we can use the Key Beliefs to identify means by which to increase the likelihood that our kids do the reading and do it with care.

Better Together

Like all the others, the action steps laid out in this chapter can be completed by individual teachers to good effect. For great results, however, we're better off doing this work together. Here are some examples of how the work laid out in this chapter gets both easier and more effective when done in teams, PLCs, or as a whole school:

- Calculate the number of texts students are given the chance to read per course. I would categorize these as laid out in this chapter, keeping in mind that there is no sense in "fudging" this work. The goal of the exercise is to get a real picture of what kids are expected to read. During the exercise, don't get bogged down in whether or not kids are actually *doing* the reading—that comes next and is a separate issue.

- From there, discuss with colleagues what impressions you all have about the degree to which students read and engage with the texts they're assigned. What beliefs from Chapter 2 could you work to target in relation to your reading expectations?

- Alternatively, once you have documented how many texts you expect of students, discuss this question as a group: Is that the best we can do? I always ask myself, "How much reading are the kids at the elite schools of my county expecting students to do? How does that compare to the reading expectations at my school?"

- Pick one of the nine moves from this chapter and compile a list of best practices. For example, what "simple hook" techniques have your colleagues found that work well?

- Reap the benefits of regular reading experiences throughout the school day. Once kids begin to view reading as a key act in the learning process, the "why do we have to do this?" questions diminish, and student beliefs about value and efficacy around reading increase.

CHAPTER SIX

Write Purposefully and Often

> *Writing is not something students use in the English class alone; all scientists and historians write constantly, using the same mental habits and organizational and rhetorical devices that writers in all disciplines use.*
>
> **—JIM BURKE (2003, P. 21)**

> *Writing well is not just an option for young people— it is a necessity.*
>
> **—GRAHAM AND PERIN (2007, P. 3)**

If we were presented with a magical button that turned all of our students into proficient writers, we'd push it. None of us would *not* push it. But in a way that none of the other components quite replicates, our biggest obstacle when seeking the actual writing proficiency of our students is *time*. In this chapter, I'll argue that we do not understand how little time it could take to drastically improve the writing proficiency of the average American diploma holder by writing throughout the school day. This is good news. We can cast off the cart of baggage—the worries about stress, complexity, papers, grading, and time— that comes with improving writing volume across the school day.

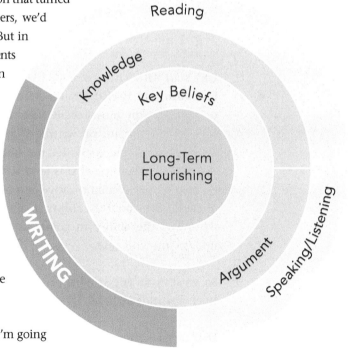

So let me not be cute—in this chapter, I'm going to attempt to argue four things:

- Writing is critical to both mastery now and long-term flourishing in the future. It's not an English thing—it's a life in a literate society thing.

Words Matter

Satisfice

Satisfice is a verb created by Nobel laureate Herbert Simon in the 1950s as the combination of the words *satisfy* and *suffice*. I tend to describe it to people as *satisfying* the requirements of a task while *sacrificing* the optimal level of completing that task. Due to the inordinate number of expectations that we face as educators, knowing when and how to satisfice is a critical skill for flourishing as a teacher.

- **Quantity comes first.** Increasing the quantity of writing that our students do during the school day is job number one. When we approach this strategically, huge gains are possible with next to no added time grading.

- **After quantity, we need to increase quality,** and all quality-improvement efforts should start with zero-grading approaches that are time-tested and straightforward.

- **Grades don't make writers better, but feedback does.** With the preceding pieces in place, we need to address the confusion around grading and feedback. Too many of us conflate the two, and this conflation costs our students. Timely feedback is what counts, and there's no room for unrealistic idealism if we're going to get better here. Feedback must be satisficed. (See sidebar.)

The Case for Writing Throughout the School Day

Let's start with a fun game: I'd like you to guess what percentage of students in eighth and twelfth grades were found to be able to write proficiently or better on the most recent National Assessment of Educational Progress (NAEP) Report Card on writing (National Center for Education Statistics, 2012). Before you guess, let me note how the NAEP defines proficient: "Students performing at this level have clearly demonstrated the ability to accomplish the communicative purpose of their writing." In other words, no one is talking about the ability to mimic Shakespeare here; rather, proficient writing is the ability to compose an email that someone can read and understand with ease.

So, what's your guess? What percentage of students were capable of at least this level of writing ability in 2011?

Did you guess around one quarter? Did you feel dirty guessing that, like you are harshly judging the youth of America?

Well, don't feel dirty—feel despair because you're right. *It's 27 percent.*

I'm joking about the despair thing; despair is not the right emotion here. But sobriety, urgency, determination, fire . . . those are called for. Consider the many benefits of being able to write proficiently.

Words Matter

National Assessment of Educational Progress

NAEP reports are frequently referred to as "the Nation's Report Card." NAEP is mandated by congress, and it was established in 1969 to measure national student achievement. It is meant to be a nationally representative assessment, and it is administered by the National Center for Education Statistics. NAEP is not administered every year; at the time of this writing, results are forthcoming for the NAEP in Writing that was administered in early 2017.

Writing uncovers poor understanding. When a science teacher asks his students if they understand photosynthesis, his students may nod their heads even though they do not understand it. This isn't because they're lying; it's because they are *familiar,* and that familiarity is making them suffer an illusion of competence (see Chapter 3). This tragic state need not be terminal, however, as the illusion quickly vaporizes when we ask students to write a paragraph explaining photosynthesis using the terms *autotroph, chlorophyll, chloroplast, pigment,* and *reactants.*

Writing clarifies thinking. I like how two-time Pulitzer Prize winner David McCullough puts it: "Writing is thinking. To write well is to think clearly. That's why it's so hard" (Cole, 2003). When we write, unlike when we speak, the words we produce stare back at us rather than vanishing into the air. In a time when our civic life is under duress and our decisions yoke us with astronomic levels of debt per capita, clear thinking isn't something I want a mere 27 percent of my students to have access to.

Writing provides access to work. From an economic perspective, writing is important, too. An increasing number of jobs require writing, and writing doesn't seem to be on the short list of "Next Things for Technology to Make Obsolete." Actually, it seems to be the opposite. More jobs today require writing than was the case ten years ago, and ten years ago that same statistic held true for jobs ten years prior to that. A 2004 report from the National Commission on Writing for America's Families, Schools, and Colleges illustrates writing's role as a "ticket to work," specifically how it provides access to jobs, promotion opportunities, and salaried positions in a variety of industries (p. 7; see Figure 6.1). I want all of my students to have access to these things so that they're as likely to flourish as possible. The report also estimates that companies spend $3.1 billion annually to remedy writing deficiencies in employees (p. 29) to help employees produce clearer emails, presentations, memos, and reports. In short, employers are eager to hire competent workers who can also competently write.

Writing aids reading achievement. According to a Carnegie Corporation of New York report, when students engage in simple kinds of writing (e.g., summaries,

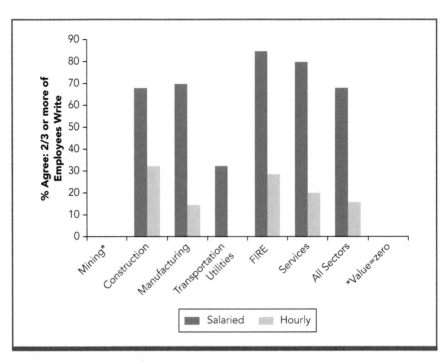

FIGURE 6.1 • Most Professional Employees Are Expected to Write

Source: Writing: A Ticket to Work . . . Or a Ticket Out © 2004. The College Board. Reproduced with permission.

Note: FIRE stands for Finance, Insurance, and Real Estate.

note taking, answering questions in response to reading) and when they write more, their reading achievement scores go up (Graham & Hebert, 2010). By having our kids practice one key life skill—writing—we help them do better in another—reading. I like it.

Writing well will be an enormous advantage for future workers. Journalist Esther Cepeda (2012) has memorably quipped that those students fortunate enough to be part of the 27 percent will be "the rock stars of their generation." What she means is that this minority of proficient writers is going to have first dibs on the many opportunities that call for proficient writing. Whether they want to forge their own path building an online business, work their way up the ranks of a manufacturing company like General Motors, or advocate for policy changes on Capitol Hill, those who possess writing ability will have an all-too-rare superpower.

Writing supports a life of the mind and a readiness for life's challenges and responsibilities. Mike Schmoker (n.d.) puts this powerfully in his timeless essay, "Write More, Grade Less": "Make no mistake: When students write—especially about what they have carefully and closely read—they enlarge their intellects and prepare themselves for college, careers, and civic participation in a way that can't be surpassed." I want every one of my students, whether they plan to pursue diesel mechanics, pediatric brain surgery, or professional writing, to regularly engage in the expansion of their intellects.

Writing reduces worry by externalizing the brain. As neuroscientist Daniel Levitin (2015) explains in *The Organized Mind*,

> When we have something on our minds that is important—especially a To Do item—we're afraid we'll forget it, so our brain rehearses it, tossing it around and around in circles in something that cognitive psychologists actually refer to as the rehearsal loop, a network of brain regions that ties together the frontal cortex just behind your eyeballs and the hippocampus in the center of your brain. The rehearsal loop evolved in a world that had no pens and paper, no smartphones or other physical extension of the human brain; it was all we had for tens of thousands of years and during that time, it became quite effective at remembering things. The problem is that it works too well, keeping items in rehearsal until we attend to them. Writing them down gives both implicit and explicit permission to the rehearsal loop to let them go, to relax its neural circuits so that we can focus on something else. Writing things down conserves the mental energy expended in worrying that you might forget something and in trying not to forget it. (p. 68)

It seems that more and more of my ninth-grade students are burdened with debilitating levels of anxiety, depression, and other mental health struggles. If writing things down can help with that while simultaneously making my students smarter and more knowledgeable, sign me up.

In short, writing proficiency lines up with our shared top-level objective: the long-term flourishing of kids. It makes them smarter, more capable people with access to greater choice throughout their lives. I struggle to imagine putting together a solid argument for why we wouldn't want all of our students to be capable writers when they graduate. This problem is relevant outside the English classroom. Writing well is an obvious good, for all the reasons mentioned earlier, and it can support the content mastery we're after. While much fuss was made about newfangled twenty-first-century skills, one very old skill

Words Matter

Life of the Mind

Though the phrase "life of the mind" is typically used in reference to a life spent in academics, I envision the life of the mind more broadly as the thoughtful, richly intellectual conversations that permeate both popular culture and the academic disciplines. In this way, my views have been largely shaped by Jerry Graff's *Clueless in Academe: How Schooling Obscures the Life of the Mind* (2003).

To further explore the rich worlds that writing opens for our students and how we might best help our students enter them, consider the following texts:

- Jim Burke's *The 6 Academic Writing Assignments: Designing the User's Journey* (2018)

- Kelly Gallagher's *Write Like This: Teaching Real-World Writing Through Modeling and Mentor Texts* (2011)

- ReLeah Cossett Lent's *This Is Disciplinary Literacy: Reading, Writing, Thinking, and Doing, Content Area by Content Area* (2015)

- Penny Kittle's *Write Beside Them: Risk, Voice, and Clarity in High School Writing* (2008)

For a full list of the "Dig Deeper" titles mentioned in this book, go to davestuartjr.com/t6t-list.

that seems to be only increasing in importance is writing. A proficient writer is able to journal through mental health struggles, articulate complex thoughts, and communicate in a measured manner. Writing makes us better readers, better thinkers, better speakers, and better listeners. Through writing, we can inform, explain, argue, entertain, and inspire. This isn't just for teacher/blogger/nerdy types (I don't know any of those, of course); it's for mothers, employees, citizens, dreamers, and spouses.

So where do we go, in light of all these things? I think career- and college-readiness expert David Conley (2007) points the best way: "If we could institute only one change to make students more college ready, it should be to increase the amount and quality of writing students are expected to produce" (p. 26). To paraphrase Dr. Conley (who, for what it's worth, was researching college and career readiness years and years prior to the Common Core popularizing the term), this is what it takes to make the next NAEP report card a better one. I call this the Conley Challenge:

1. Increase the quantity of writing students are expected to produce.

2. Increase the quality of writing students are expected to produce.

That's what we'll tackle for the rest of this chapter: how to increase quantity and how to improve quality, all while doing fewer things so as to do them better.

A Focused, Sensible Approach to Writing Throughout the School Day for the Long-Term Flourishing of Our Students

If these four steps were followed in all content areas, we'd move the ball forward and have better NAEP scores next time around:

- Quantity step 1: Validate content mastery

- Quantity step 2: Strategically increase volume in ways that honor and support content mastery

- Quality step 1: Improve quality of student writing without increasing our paper load
- Quality step 2: Improve quality of student writing with simple, robust feedback

Let's work through each of these in turn.

QUANTITY STEP 1: VALIDATE CONTENT MASTERY

There's no sure path to flourishing that doesn't include the manifold benefits possessed by those who write proficiently. The first step to improving the percentage of our kids who are capable writers is to increase how much writing they do. Typically, the classes with the greatest opportunities to do this are the non-ELA ones.

Now, I imagine everything I've written so far has the English teachers nodding vigorously, thinking of all the other people in their lives who need to read and take to heart these words. Meanwhile, the content area teachers are saying, "Okay, I get it—writing is important for long-term flourishing. But so is my class, and my standards, and my time! While I could certainly eat up more of my time teaching writing, that sacrifice wouldn't be balanced out by my English colleagues spending more of their time teaching mathematics or science or health or history. When are we ever going to have an initiative that supports the work in my discipline?"

These are valid concerns. So here is the only way, in my opinion, that writing in all the disciplines makes sense—and this is still assuming that I'm going to help you get past common grading and writing assignment roadblocks. Writing in the disciplines *must* support content mastery. In my opinion, that's the only kind of writing that makes sense in non-ELA classes. Here are a couple examples:

- If kids are going to write anything in a math class, it ought to be writing that helps them unpack their problem-solving thought processes, or argue for the merits and demerits of certain approaches, or review what they've learned today. Representing their mathematical thinking in writing helps them achieve greater clarity of thought and gives them a type of retrieval practice (see Chapter 3) that can be valuable. I'm not recommending your students start writing poems about differential equations.

- If kids are going to write a single word in a physical education class, then it had better be solely the kind of writing that makes them smarter about their bodies and their physical fitness. Exercise journaling? Check. Tracking personal fitness statistics? Check. Writing a one-page free response to a quarterly one- or two-page article on physical fitness? You're overachieving here, and I like it. But there's no reason to ask a physical education or music or drama teacher to do as much writing as the social studies or English teachers.

You get the idea—writing in non-ELA courses must be 100 percent focused on mastery of content area material, concepts, and skills. Otherwise, it just doesn't make sense and neither teachers nor students will buy in.

So, for example, if we want to help our science colleagues to have students writing more, the place to start is by saying, explicitly,

- In this school, we want to graduate the strongest science students possible.
- Writing is a means by which our students can strengthen both their scientific thinking and their scientific content knowledge, so we want our science teachers to explore what writing currently happens in their classes and experiment with how we can increase that using the Pyramid of Writing Priorities (coming in a few pages).

In words and in truth, writing in science needs to aim at increasing mastery of science, and writing anywhere else outside of the ELA classroom needs that same kind of mastery-oriented bent. If writing is done just for writing's sake, a lot of the potential gains of the initiative are left on the table because it seems so disconnected to both the teacher and the students. That discredits our teachers and devalues our students.

In short, if we want more writing in science (or social studies, or health, or business, or band), we need to ask, "How can writing strengthen student performance in _____ course?" instead of "How can you non-ELA teachers get your kids doing more writing?" Again and again, the emphasis of secondary school leaders must be aimed at long-term flourishing. Writing proficiency is a part of that picture. But writing in the content areas—math, science, social studies, business, health, and so on—only makes sense when it reinforces discipline-appropriate knowledge or skills. If we don't approach the task of increasing the quantity of writing our kids do from this angle—the angle of improving mastery in the content areas—then things get confusing for both us and our kids.

COMMON TEACHER HANG-UP

Do I Need Hip, Catchy Writing Prompts?

I don't get too hung up on what percentage of the writing my students do is explanatory versus argumentative versus creative versus narrative and so on. My questions are simpler: "What do I want students to learn, and how can I help them strengthen and demonstrate that learning through writing?" So in terms of genre, I always pick that which makes the most sense—and over the past few years, I've found that rarely involves something like "Write a tweet by Hong Xiquan during the Taiping Rebellion" or "Pretend you're an Austrian peasant—create a Facebook profile that you'd be comfortable sharing with the local priest." I'm not trying to cast aspersion onto these kinds of assignments, but I am trying to say that we don't need to feel like hip or catchy assignments like this are the way to get kids engaged in the work. Beliefs—not hip, catchy assignments—are what drive engagement. A well-crafted assignment can certainly cultivate the Key Beliefs we explored in Chapter 2, but it's not the only inroad to belief cultivation. In a great school with lots of student engagement, I wouldn't be surprised to find that most writing prompts started with mundane-sounding stems like those found in Burke and Gilmore's *Academic Moves for College and Career Readiness* (2015):

- Identify and explain _____
- Summarize _____
- Compare/contrast _____
- Analyze _____

And so on. Such prompts need not drain the life out of a classroom—we have to get away from this idea that "fun" assignments are the key to invigorating a classroom. The keys to invigorating a classroom are the Key Beliefs (see Chapter 2).

I know of no better or saner way to take up the Conley Challenge than through the three kinds of writing laid out in the "Writing to Learn" chapter of *The Core Six* by Perini, Dewing, and Silver (2012). Here the authors introduce a way of thinking about writing that has greatly clarified for me how to approach the Conley Challenge. Over the past several years of speaking to fellow teachers about Perini et al.'s ideas, I've come to conceive of them as a pyramid of writing priorities (see Figure 6.2).

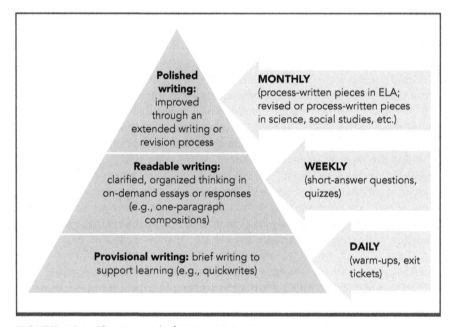

FIGURE 6.2 • The Pyramid of Writing Priorities

Source: Three kinds of writing from Perini et al. (2012). Implementation recommendations and image by the author (DaveStuartJr.com).

If we want to drastically improve writing volume, we should start at the bottom with daily provisional writing and work up—and we ought only to work up to polished writing in appropriate subject areas. When students walk in the door each day, have a prompt or two for them written on the board—something that will get them thinking about the material of today's lesson or get them reviewing material from yesterday or last week—and give them a specific word count minimum. For my ninth graders, I set this at one hundred words in five minutes. Early on in the school year, I demonstrate for them that they are capable of producing well over one hundred words in a minute, and I tell them that the challenge of our warm-ups will be quickly transitioning from hallway craziness to on-topic writing. I earnestly frame our warm-ups as a challenge, as something uncommon for ninth graders. I frame them this way to help students value the warm-up writing, and over time this daily production of one hundred words helps my students develop a sense of efficacy—fewer and fewer of them say things like "I can't write that much" or "I don't have anything to write about."

Let's imagine a social studies department at No Writing High School that is doing no writing at all—zero words written per semester. (My hunch is that there's no social studies department in the world like this, but since I'm a social studies teacher at the time of this writing, I'll pick on my own disciplinary team.)

The NWHS social studies department's first objective should be to incorporate daily provisional writing. Provisional writing is only for the purpose of learning. It does not need to communicate to anyone except oneself. This would include written warm-ups, written exit tickets, even notes based on reading or listening activities. In adding this, the department goes from zero words written per semester to tens of thousands (assuming an average of one hundred words written during each lesson). But even if we move from zero words to one hundred words, we've achieved infinite percentage growth—not bad.

Next, the department builds on this foundation with readable writing tasks. In this case, student writers are writing for an audience, but that audience is likely limited to peers or the teacher. The prime example of readable writing would be single-paragraph responses to questions about key content knowledge in every course. At this level, readability is important, so skills like crafting clear topic sentences, capitalizing proper nouns, using evidence to support arguments, and so on are important. For a list of writing skills valued by the respondents to the survey in *Writing: A Ticket to Work . . . or a Ticket Out* (National Commission on Writing for America's Families, Schools, and Colleges, 2004, p. 28), see Figure 6.3.

TRY THIS

Daily provisional writing.

To help teach these skills, we would want to (a) model with exemplars and (b) provide periodic, focused feedback. Because the teaching and grading/feedback demands are higher for readable writing, the objective at the end of the project would be to master the art and science of students completing one readable writing assignment per week, on average. Compared to the incorporation of provisional writing, this is an in-depth project. It is my estimation that few schools have successfully built this into their social studies classes, so upon

HOW IMPORTANT IS	EXTREMELY IMPORTANT (%)	IMPORTANT (%)	TOTAL (%)
Accuracy?	95.2	1.6	96.8
Clarity?	74.6	22.2	96.8
Spelling, punctuation, and grammar?	58.7	36.5	95.2
Conciseness?	41.3	50.8	92.1
Scientific precision?	36.5	33.3	69.8
Visual appeal?	11.1	68.3	79.4

FIGURE 6.3 • Percentage of Responding Employers Who Valued Key Writing Skills

Source: *Writing: A Ticket to Work . . . Or a Ticket Out* © 2004. The College Board. Reproduced with permission.

completion of this task, the social studies department would really be doing standard-setting work.

Finally, the department will enter world-class status when, on top of the work above, it begins teaching and expecting students to produce one polished piece of writing per month. This was not uncommon in my college history courses, but it's exceedingly uncommon in high school social studies classes.

If you want to know how monthly polished writing can be done in high school social studies courses, you'll need to find a more advanced book because I'm not the guy to tell you how to do it—I am still working at the readable writing goal. However, despite not having reached the top of the pyramid yet, my ninth-grade AP World History students have routinely exceeded the percentage of students who write in the top quartile on the free-response section of the national exam. How did they do it? Not through outrageous innovation, and not through a teacher willing to sacrifice his family life on the altar of student success. No—they leveraged noncognitive factors (e.g., they worked hard, had great attitudes, and monitored their beliefs) to make much of my plodding attempts to work my curriculum up the Pyramid of Writing Priorities, one assignment at a time.

To close out this section, I invite you or your team to consider a few prompts for reflection.

- What level of the Pyramid of Writing Priorities do you need to start at for your course(s) as they currently are: provisional, readable, or polished writing? (It helps to quantify the current writing expectations of your courses, organizing them by the three types of writing laid out in this section.)

- Being as practical as possible, how could you increase quantity in that area?

- If you do have a writing-rich curriculum already in place, what tweaks are you contemplating? (For example, many ELA classrooms have lots of writing already happening, but in my experience we can be prone to missing those daily provisional and weekly readable opportunities).

COMMON TEACHER HANG-UP

If We Don't Grade Provisional Writing, Is It Really Going to Help Kids Get Better at Writing?

Provisional writing is powerful, despite its gradelessness, for the following reasons:

- It requires so little extra time for teachers.

- It significantly increases the volume of writing that students do. Volume, by itself, doesn't make our students far better writers, but it does provide a "base" of writing experience. It helps build writing stamina, much like my students on our school's cross-country team are told to run a certain number of miles over their summers to develop a base. This summer work for the runners doesn't involve intensive coaching; its goal is for students to develop basic endurance and familiarity with running and to not hurt themselves in the process. Those are some pretty good goals for our provisional writing, too.

- It clarifies for students what they do and don't know to a far greater degree than a multiple-choice test item can (see Common Student Hang-Up: "But I Studied!" in Chapter 3).

QUALITY STEP 1: IMPROVE QUALITY OF STUDENT WRITING WITHOUT INCREASING OUR PAPER LOAD

We've already covered ground that helps us overcome some of the most common writing hang-ups, but so far we've only addressed the *quantity* of writing our

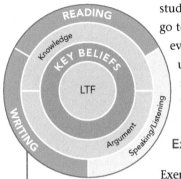

students do, not the quality of that work. The first thing that teachers tend to go to when we get into this conversation is the paper load issue. Yet before we even pick up a stack of papers, there are simple, powerful techniques we can use to improve the quality of writing our students produce: scaffolding with sentence templates, modeling with exemplars, vetting work in progress, and using a skull and crossbones list.

Exemplars

TRY THIS

Show students exemplar pieces of the work you're asking them to produce.

Exemplars show our kids what we mean by a clear topic sentence, a defensible thesis, a blended quote, a non-fluffy lab report introduction, and the like. It is one thing to teach these skills in isolation; it is another to read through an exemplar paragraph as a class while pointing these things out, having students take notes or annotate as appropriate. In an exemplar, our students experience a real piece of writing that does the things we want all of our students to do. When using exemplars, I select one to three specific skills I want my students to pay attention to, and I have students annotate the exemplar pieces along with me so that I can be sure they see what the target work looks like. This makes abstract writing concepts clear to students, which increases their confidence in being able to do it—reinforcing the efficacy belief.

Producing exemplars takes some planning time—we have to either write them ourselves, or find good examples in our students' work, or find professional texts—but the time is short compared to how long it takes to give feedback on a set of student pieces of work. So using exemplars in writing instruction is the epitome of working smarter over the long term. When we make good writing explicit for our kids through the use of exemplars, we increase the odds that they'll become exemplar-producing writers themselves.

Sentence Templates

Sentence templates serve a similar function as exemplar pieces, but they provide even more scaffolding and work at the sentence level. Typically, I use sentence templates more in the beginning of the year and then as needed with kids who struggle as the year progresses. While there are a slew of sentence templates in Graff and Birkenstein's *They Say, I Say* (2014), they can also be created on the fly. For example, I asked my students to respond to the following prompt, and I provided them with a template to help.

Prompt: Analyze similarities and differences between two ancient civilizations from the list we've studied this past week. Use the sentence template below to help.

Sentence Template: While the _____ and _____ civilizations were similar in how they _____, they differed in how they _____.

With templates, we certainly scaffold for our weaker writers, but we do much more than that, too. We show *all* of our students the moves that proficient writers use to communicate their ideas. Importantly, these templates are generative in nature—they don't give students ideas, but they do help get students started with the kinds of "moves" (as Graff and Birkenstein call them) that writers make. In my own classroom, I'm continually amazed at how a simple sentence template can help a student feel confident in his ability to complete a given writing task—again, that reinforces the efficacy belief.

Vetting Work in Progress

One challenge that comes of over-planning lessons is the loss of responsive teaching time. With complex lesson plans, a single unplanned event can send an entire lesson careening off track, but isn't that when true learning might occur?

One clear example of the need for responsive teaching comes with regularly vetting student writing as it's in progress instead after it's completed (Schmoker, n.d.). While our students are writing—be it readable or polished work—we can walk around and check for understanding. The insights we gain from looking over the shoulder of five random students per class will inform our instructive efforts, and these, in turn, give our students a chance to improve before we ever get out the feedback pen. If we find that four out of the five kids we've sampled aren't doing something well—say, they're mishandling evidence in their development of arguments—then we can pause the whole class, construct an exemplar on the board (or show a student exemplar from within the room), and have them all revise for that particular problem. Such responsive instruction is critical in our efforts to spend less time sitting with a stack of papers or a set of complex rubrics.

Skull and Crossbones List

In my interactions with teachers around the country these past few years, I've come to find that I'm not alone in being frustrated by the silly mistakes students include in their submitted work. A part of this, I know, is simply human error—this is why I still hire a proofreader to comb through my blog because I know there will be instances of *your/you're* or *it's/its* or whatever other annoying error I produce. But too frequently, my students submit errors again and again and again that they are simply not trying to eradicate. This is how the skull and crossbones list was born (see Figure 6.4). This is essentially a list of writing sins that are unacceptable at the secondary level, such as the following:

- Lack of capitalization (first-person pronoun *I*, first letter of a sentence, proper nouns)
- Omitting end-of-sentence punctuation
- Failing to indent new paragraphs
- Misspelling words that are readily available (e.g., Stuart, an author's name, America)
- Using emojis or text-message abbreviations

Here's an example from a science department that I once worked with at Powers Catholic High School in Flint, Michigan:

- No "I think . . .," "I believe . . . ," or feelings. Not your opinion!
- Straight to the point! (No fluff!)
- All claims need evidence!

In this case, the entire science department has developed a skull and crossbones list—that's working smarter and better together.

As the year's first pieces of writing come across my desk, I identify five or fewer basic problems like those above. I'm thinking about things that ninth graders have most certainly been taught and things that aren't recursive. (For example, placing commas correctly is recursive because it is something that gets harder over time as the kinds of sentences students are trying to create get more complex. But capitalizing things doesn't really do that. It's not recursive.)

As I'm identifying these things, I don't mark a single thing on the student papers—I'm just populating the skull and crossbones list. If I have to input a grade, it's credit/no credit.

The next day, I give the pieces back, and I tell students to create a page in their notebooks with a skull and crossbones drawn at the top. I then create this on one of those big poster-sized sticky note things or a sheet of white butcher paper. This will hang up in the classroom all year, always available as a reference.

I introduce each one of the items to students, being sure to give an example of the problem. We record the item. I ask students to demonstrate for me on a scratch sheet of paper what the problem looks like and what the solution looks like. For example,

- Problem: i strive for excellence.
- Solution: I strive for excellence.

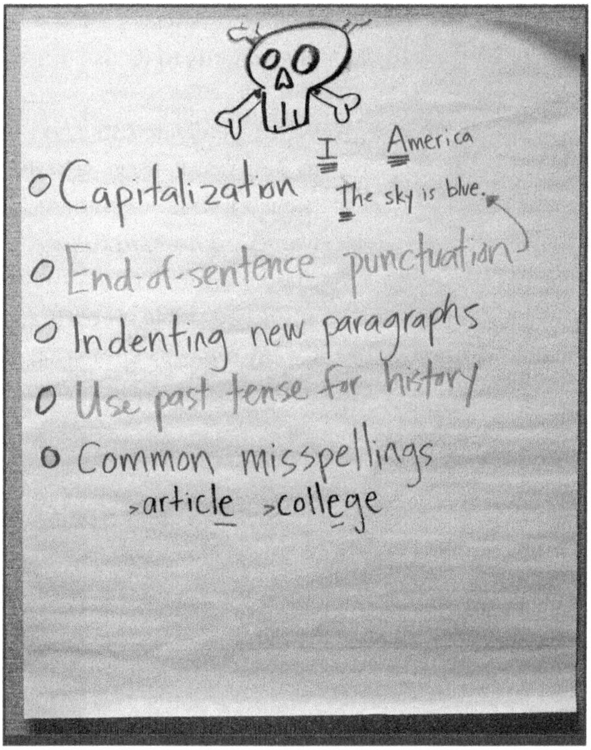

FIGURE 6.4 • Skull and Crossbones List of Unacceptable Writing Errors in My World History Class

I tell the students that, henceforth, any time that I see a skull and crossbones error in a piece of readable or polished writing, I'm just going to draw a little, simple skull and crossbones symbol at the top and return that work to the student. It won't go into the gradebook as anything but a zero until the student fixes whatever's wrong. (That part is important from a parent/guardian standpoint. I think one reason that parents don't tend to complain about this is because the student is free to fix his or her problems and resubmit.) I don't identify on the paper what's wrong with it because, after all, the skull and crossbones list isn't terribly long, and it's always hanging up in the classroom as a reference, and we had that whole mini-lesson thing where we wrote this in our notebooks and students demonstrated understanding, and this is really just a list of early elementary standards . . . You get the idea. I'm working smarter, and my students are working harder on something that matters. Because details do matter!

As time progresses, I add to the skull and crossbones list only as needed. I want my students to focus on their most common unforced errors.

When we create lists and policies like this in our classrooms, we're not trying to be jerks. Rather, we're just expecting that a basic level of care be put into the work that our students do. If a team of athletes wanted to be elite—if they wanted to do hard things—they'd be silly to expect sloppy habits to get them there. I want all of my students to have the chance *now* to be held unemotionally accountable for basic attention to detail by someone who loves them (me). I want them to know that, in truth, details do matter—that it pays to attend to them.

COMMON STUDENT HANG-UP

Quote Bombing

When a student is writing an argument and then suddenly drops a quote into the paper with no introduction or explanation, that's a quote bomb. While I "invented" this phrase in my own practice, a simple Google search demonstrates that it's not all that original.

My colleague Erica Beaton explains it to students like this: Quote bombing is akin to a courtroom scene where the prosecuting attorney stands up with a glove while stating, "The defendant is guilty. This is a bloody glove. The defendant is guilty." It would be a laughable scene in a film; it's a painful scene for someone who's trying to take an arguer seriously. Without the reasoning that links the evidence to the claim, there isn't an argument.

Importantly, no student ever learns to quote bomb by himself or herself. They've learned that their essays need evidence, but they've not really learned how to use quotations as evidence or maybe even how evidence works. To help with this, we can give our students more opportunities to argue with evidence in class. I introduce the use of evidence through modeling at the start of a Pop-Up Debate, and then, when a student uses evidence effectively during the discussion, I interrupt to explain why what they did worked.

After a Pop-Up Debate like this, students are ready to learn from an exemplar before writing one-paragraph arguments of their own that use textual evidence to support their topic sentence claims.

QUALITY STEP 2: IMPROVE QUALITY OF STUDENT WRITING WITH SIMPLE, ROBUST FEEDBACK

To help my students improve their writing as much as they can, I need a simple, robust set of feedback moves to pull from. Feedback is key, but it's not possible if I'm not very strategic and realistic. Toward creating that, I only choose from Five Kinds of Feedback. I'll explain each one, going from the least individualized and quickest to the most individualized and slowest:

1. Roots and shoots list

2. Coding

3. Simple rubric

4. Conferring (in-person or digital)

5. Extensive notes on each student's paper

Roots and Shoots List

All right, so let's say I have a stack of readable student writing in front of me, and I want to give my students some feedback. Prior to receiving this stack, I've used some or all of the feedback-free methods mentioned earlier: I read through an exemplar with students, pointing out areas where I wanted them to improve; I walked around the room checking for understanding while they were writing the piece; I referred them to sentence templates to help them use the academic moves appropriate for this piece; and I reminded them of the skull-and-crossbones errors that will result in me not even reading their piece. In other words, this stack in front of me is much better than it would have been had I just given an assignment and waited to see what came up.

I've got a notepad next to me, and it's the only thing I'm going to write on. I read through a handful of the student pieces, making mental note of any weaknesses. As I get to the fifth piece or so, I start writing patterns of weakness on my notepad: for example, "vague claims," "no evidence," "lack of topic sentences that directly address the prompt." I read through five or so more pieces, and then I look at my list.

I'm trying to collect one to three specific things that my students can work on. If I've noticed one to three things so far in my reading that multiple papers have as weaknesses, then I'm done with the stack. I'm going to limit myself to three skills maximum because anything more than that is going to be overwhelming for students. If I need to put a grade in the gradebook, then I'll simply give a credit/no credit grade—say, five points if you turned in the piece, zero points if you didn't.

(It's worth noting here that the long-term flourishing of kids is important to me, and the nitty gritty of grading is not. Grades don't make my students better writers. I grade because it's something I need to do in order to be a teacher in my school. My target in grading is to make my practices sensible and fair to all stakeholders: students, parents/guardians, administrators, and myself.)

Before I finish my time with the student papers—and notice, I haven't read even close to all of them—I select a couple of pieces that I'd like to photocopy as exemplars. Specifically, I'm looking for pieces that demonstrate the skill(s) I've selected from my notepad. If there aren't any exemplar pieces or I'm concerned about sharing anonymized student work, I type up an exemplar of my own.

The next day in class, I hand back the student work, and my students say, "Hey, there's nothing on these papers." And I say, *"Yes, I know. Open up to a fresh page in your spiral notebooks, and title the page, 'Roots and Shoots.' I'm going to teach you the three things that these papers showed me that we need to work on as a class."* I call it Roots and Shoots because these are skills we're trying to grow this year . . . get it?

I then spend no more than five minutes per skill, and typically I go through this process:

> *One skill I noticed that we need to work on is using a clear topic sentence that directly answers or links back to the prompt. On your page of notes, write what I'm writing on our anchor chart: "Clear, responsive topic sentence."*

I show the exemplar on the document camera, or I pass out photocopies. "This is what a clear, responsive topic sentence looked like on the piece of writing you just turned in." I read the exemplar topic sentence aloud. "Do you see how this links back to our prompt?"

> *Now, look at the piece of writing you turned in yesterday. Is your topic sentence clear and responsive like the exemplar? I'd like you to underline your topic sentence right now if it is responsive, and I'd like you to fix it if it's not. It's possible that you don't have a topic sentence at all; in that case, I'd like you to create one at the top of that piece of writing you turned in, drawing an*

arrow to where it should have gone. I'll walk around and check to see that you understand this while you work.

I walk around, quickly scanning to make sure students are demonstrating that they understand what a clear, responsive topic sentence is.

Okay, it looks like we understand this skill. There's one more thing I'd like you to do before we move to the next skill I noticed. I want you to write "(TS)" next to "Clear, responsive topic sentence." In the future, if you see TS+ on your writing, it means that I see that you've written an effective topic sentence. If you see TS–, it means that you're either missing a topic sentence or that yours is ineffective.

Over several months, this class creates a working roots and shoots list of skills that students have learned through modeling, exemplars, and quick revision exercises like the one modeled earlier. This type of feedback is certainly not individualized, but I can prep it in about fifteen to twenty minutes, and that means I can reliably give this type of feedback the next day. Timeliness, in my experience, is the most critical ingredient in feedback. It's also the thing I struggle with most when I'm not using stripped down feedback methods like the roots and shoots list.

www.davestuartjr.com/five-key-beliefs-writing/

For help motivating students to take full advantage of opportunities like learning from exemplars and roots and shoots lists, see my blog article "The Five Key Beliefs that Motivate Student Writers" by using the QR code or the URL above.

Coding

Once the roots and shoots list has several items on it, each with a corresponding code (e.g., "TS" as described earlier), I can start giving quick, individualized feedback using the codes that we've developed. So if I have that stack of papers in front of me again, I'm now going to read every one of them, but only as far as it takes to place a maximum of three codes, at least two of which should be areas for students to improve. For some papers, this means I'll read the entire piece of writing, and I may not get to three. That's fine. For others, I might read the first three sentences, already have three codes to write, and then I set the paper aside and move on.

Although this way of limiting my feedback on each paper certainly saves me time (and thus improves my ability to get these coded papers back the next day), it's also pragmatic in the sense that I've not found people (myself included) to be terribly receptive to five, ten, or fifteen pieces of feedback at a time. Three is a good number—I find that most of my students can deal productively with three pieces of feedback.

On the following day when I return the papers, I point students to the codes on our anchor chart and hand their work back. Once they've had a minute to look things over, I ask them to complete a provisional piece of writing for me in which they respond to the following prompt:

- In what specific ways can you improve as a writer based on the feedback you've received on yesterday's piece of writing?

It's also possible during this time to add something to our roots and shoots list if I noticed a trend in the papers that we've not yet addressed.

Using a Simple Rubric

Rubrics are only feedback in as much as writers understand the rubric. Whenever I'm given a complex, overwrought rubric to use with my students, I simply give a grade as quickly as I can, err on the side of a too-generous grade, and move on. If the rubric makes no sense, then there's no sense in spending any more time on it than is necessary.

In my role as an AP World History teacher for ninth graders, I've been given (1) a point/no-point–style rubric, which has been very clarifying, and this rubric (2) aims at high-level, complex skills, and I'm tasked with (3) making this rubric sensible to my ninth-grade students. Let me break each one of these down in turn, but please keep in mind that I'm not a rubric expert. What I am an expert in is seeing that simple is best, and I see a lot of wise simplicity in these three elements:

1. A point/no-point-style rubric. The College Board's rubrics for the AP history classes follows an asset model, meaning that graders are to look for the items on the rubric and award points when they see them. If they don't see these items, then the point is not awarded. This asset-based approach to grading means that graders are ignoring erroneous or unnecessary material. While such an approach might not be appropriate for an English class where matters of style and mechanics are taught and assessed, it makes great sense for the rest of the classes where discipline-appropriate content, thinking skills, and argumentation are prized.

So, for example, on the Long Essay Question rubric, the College Board (2017b) awards one point for a thesis that "responds to the prompt with a historically defensible thesis/claim that establishes a line of reasoning" and then goes on to explain that this point is earned when writers "make a claim that responds to the prompt, rather than merely restating or rephrasing the prompt. The thesis must consist of one or more sentences located in one place, either in the introduction or the conclusion."

And the rubric goes on to describe five additional points. Just six things for a college-level essay, and for each of these points there's not a scale—the teacher simply decides, "Yes, this meets the criteria," or "No, this doesn't."

2. High-level, externally vetted, complex skills. I find it valuable to use a list of skills that an entity outside of me has created, especially one like College Board that has such a history of working with colleges to identify what matters most for each Advanced Placement course. At the start of this book, I warned against what we could call the Everest Island approach where we define Everest for ourselves and shut our doors and work toward it. The trouble with Everest Island approaches is that we're guaranteed to reinvent the wheel, and we're bound to do it more poorly than someone else has done.

When we begin to realize that long-term flourishing is what every authentic stakeholder in education is after, we can start to look outside ourselves for the things we need to do our work as best as possible, and I think a place where we certainly need this kind of help is in identifying what writing skills matter most for our particular disciplines. In the years to come, I hope to take the College Board's AP histories rubrics and scaffold them down into all of the general-level history courses in our school.

3. Making our rubrics sensible to our students. Once we identify a focused set of skills and we define what it looks like to demonstrate those skills, then we move into the challenge of making this targeted list of skills sensible to our students. In the words that have preceded this section, we've already looked at how we can do this. When I approach the College Board's (2017b) treatment of the thesis skill described earlier, I make it clear to my students through exemplars, sentence templates, checks for understanding, the roots and shoots list, and coding. With learning experiences like these behind us, I can be confident that, yes, when my students see a 1 or a 0 on their rubric for the thesis point, they know where to look in their essay to see why they did or did not earn that point, and they know what to do with that information. In other words, the rubric becomes feedback.

In-Person or Digital Conferring

Conferring—sitting down with a student to discuss that student's writing—is the gold standard of feedback. It's individualized and in depth, and its usefulness is reflected in how much better the book you're holding is now than it was before I began talking with readers about its material. With that said, conferring also tends to be quite time-consuming, and just the thought of it makes many non-English Language Arts teachers balk—"You want me to do *what?*"

Before I briefly explain some efficient means for conferring with students on their writing, let me emphatically state that we could see dramatic writing improvement in our students just through the use of the feedback-free methods we've discussed in this chapter—using exemplars, sentence templates, vetting early work, and skull and crossbones lists—and we'd see even more by using the very efficient means laid out so far in this section—roots and shoots list, coding, and simple rubrics. Frankly, until a teacher has *mastered* all the things I've shared up until this point, I can't imagine recommending that teachers use conferring.

With that said, here are the simple means by which I sometimes confer with my own writers.

In-person conferring. **Conferring with students in person is challenging to pull off, given the constraints that many secondary teachers face. In my own setting, I have classes of thirty to thirty-five students, and my class periods are sixty minutes long. This means that, even when I get close to limiting myself to two minutes per student, I still need more than one full class period to get this done. That's difficult to afford very frequently, *especially* outside of an English course.**

Here's what it looks like.

1. I get the class working on a substantial piece of independent work, something that could take at least two class periods. Obviously, I need to be mindful about what my students believe about this work; otherwise, they are going to become disengaged.

2. I tell them that during their independent work, I'll be calling them to an open desk in the back of the room, and I'd like them to bring their spiral notebooks with them with a fresh page labeled, "Notes on Conferring about [Assignment Name]."

3. When I call them back, I read through a couple target paragraphs of their essay with them, commenting on what I see that they can work on and giving specific compliments as I see them. In particular, I want to emphasize how they've grown so far this year, so I look for compliments along those lines.

4. As I talk, students take notes in their spiral notebooks, and they ask any questions they might have.

5. I thank the students for their time, tell them I'm proud of them, and call on the next student.

Because this method of feedback costs so much class time, I typically only do it once or twice each semester (or, for my AP students, prior to their AP test). I try to time teacher-student writing conferences for when there is an upcoming writing assignment that my students especially care about doing well on, and I want them to take the feedback I give them in these mini-conferences into account when preparing for this upcoming summative assignment.

The digital approach. Although I'm something of a Luddite when it comes to the use of in-class technology, I was once giving a workshop in Lebanon, Ohio, and when we discussed conferring, a colleague raised her hand and told me about an app called Vocaroo that allows a teacher to record oral feedback for students. This teacher describes how she sets her timer for three minutes per paper, and as she's recording she reads a student's paper aloud and provides feedback similar to what I've described for conferences. She then asks students to access the link to their individual Vocaroo recordings during the next day's class period, and in this way each of her students receives verbal feedback on a paper in perhaps ten total minutes of class time—a drastic improvement.

In my own setting, I've experimented with using the Talk and Comment Google Chrome extension to leave comments on students' Google Docs. I had to do some deep breathing exercises when I did this because, you know, technology can be challenging to us Luddites, but overall students seemed to appreciate this. There are plenty of apps that allow voice recording, so play around to find what works for you and your students. (Maybe even ask them to help find the best one.)

Conferring, like all other forms of feedback, is most effective when it's timely. If you don't have time to quickly do conferences for a given piece of writing, I would recommend using the roots and shoots list, coding, or simple rubric methods we've already explored.

Extensive Notes on Each Student's Paper

I don't have much to say here except this: I never do this. I used to, and I used to feel guilty when I didn't, but as my career progressed I realized a couple of things:

- The reason I'm prone to over-commenting on papers is because I loved lots of comments on my papers. It was the closest thing to a payday that I experienced in school. I ate them up. So imagine my surprise when, as an early career teacher, I discovered that not every teenager is a super nerd. There's nothing more heartbreaking that seeing a waste bin full of returned essays covered in my handwritten marginalia.

- Even more problematic, when I insist on extensively commenting on each student paper, there's no way I'll give the feedback in a timely fashion—we're talking at least one week, and probably longer. Once feedback is more than a week old, it becomes next to useless for 99% of our student writers.

So if you've got students that are far different from mine in that they *all* crave and benefit from extensive commenting, *and* you've figured out how to provide this level of detailed feedback on the next day of instruction, then by all means keep doing what you're doing.

But if you're like me, just stop doing the extensive notes thing—even if you teach honors classes, even if your students' parents insist on it. Timely, intelligible feedback is much more effective than tardy, extensive feedback. In my experience, students all across the spectrum are more appreciative of next-day, focused feedback than they are of the late, extensive kind.

Sanity Check: Mentally Disentangling Grading From Feedback and Better, Saner Tips for Tackling Both

Back in Chapter 2, I mentioned how I equate college and career readiness to becoming a Navy SEAL of life. Here's another good line from the world of SEALs, as cited by Eric Barker (2015) on his blog:

> One of the key strengths of the SEAL Teams is the culture of constant self-improvement. No one ever says "That's good enough." On almost

every real world mission I was on—even the most successful ones—we spent 90% of our post-mission debrief focusing on what we did wrong or could have done better.

For feedback to work in my classroom, I aim at three components that Barker points me toward. Good feedback needs to be

1. quick

2. critical

3. focused on improvement

That's simple, substantial guidance. I like it.

But before we get there, we need to cover some critical ground so that we think clearly about feedback, grading, and what makes writers better.

So far in this chapter, we've examined how we might increase the amount of writing students do throughout the school day without us spending much time or energy reading, responding to, or grading student work. This will take our writers further, but it won't maximize their performance.

Words Matter

Feedback versus Grading

Feedback: providing useful, critical, improvement-oriented information on a person's performance so that person may improve.

Grading: assessing a performance to give it a score, a letter, or the degree to which it has met a standard.

Let's clarify a few points, then. First, it's feedback, not grading, that makes writers better. Think about a tennis player. He doesn't improve because of the score of his last match—his grade, if you will. Rather, he improves because of the feedback he gets from his coaches or teammates during and after his last match. The only exception to this would be if the factors behind a given game's score are clear to the tennis player. When the score is intelligible and actionable to the player, then the score can be feedback.

If we hop back into the classroom, we see the same dynamic at play. The feedback we give student writers can make them better, but an unintelligibly sourced score or grade won't. If we take pains to use scoring tools (e.g., simple rubrics, discussed later in this chapter) that make sense to our students, then grades can act as feedback. But even in these cases, it's the feedback that empowers our students to improve, not the grade.

A few principles arise from this line of thinking; we'll unpack these directly:

- Because I do teach in a system in which grades are expected, yet I know that grades aren't particularly transformative for my students all by themselves, I need to satisfice my grading efforts.

- The purpose of a given writing assignment ought to dictate why and how I grade it or give it feedback. If the purpose is increasing the amount of writing my students do, such as provisional writing, then I won't grade it; if the purpose is improving student writing quality, then I'll give efficient, manageable feedback.

- Because I don't want to be a husband and father who is always carrying around a stack of papers to respond to—and because I want the feedback I give students to be timely—I need to work at reading, grading, and giving feedback faster.

- And because I don't adore the process of reading, grading, or preparing feedback on student writing, I need to keep the task confined to focused grading or feedback sessions rather than the classic "grading a stack of papers at night with a glass of wine."

Now let's look at these principles in more detail—and I'll show you how I've learned to manage grading and feedback.

BETTER AND SANER GRADING/FEEDBACK TIP: SATISFICE ANY GRADING THAT'S NOT FEEDBACK

Before we get to feedback, I want to introduce a term that should probably be emblazoned in every teacher preparation program and professional development session: *satisfice*. I first came across this wonderful move in Daniel Levitin's *The Organized Mind: Thinking Straight in the Age of Information Overload* (2015):

> Satisficing [is] a term coined by the Nobel Prize winner Herbert Simon, one of the founders of the fields of organization theory and information processing. Simon wanted a word to describe not getting the very best option but one that was good enough. For things that don't matter critically, we make a choice that satisfies us and is deemed sufficient. You don't really know if your dry cleaner is the best—you only know that they're good enough. And that's what

helps you get by. You don't have time to sample all the dry cleaners within a twenty-four-block radius of your home . . . Satisficing is one of the foundations of productive human behavior; it prevails when we don't waste time on decisions that don't matter, or more accurately, when we don't waste time trying to find improvements that are not going to make a significant difference in our happiness or satisfaction. (p. 4)

The tricky thing about teaching is that of the thousands of decisions we make every day, some may literally be matters of life and death, quite a few are matters of long-term flourishing, but an incredible number are not mind-shatteringly important. Satisficing is a nonnegotiable competency that all long-term teachers must possess.

Here's how to do it:

Step 1. Make sure you're clear on your top-level goals, which should be nestled right beneath long-term flourishing.

Step 2. Run tasks through the filter of your top-level goals. How close is that task to the top-level goal? The stuff that's closest to the top-level goal gets your best effort and your first chunks of noninstructional time.

Step 3. The stuff that's furthest away from the top-level goal gets either satisficed or ignored. Because we probably can't get away with totally ignoring emails or grades or keeping our classrooms looking nice, the next best thing is to satisfice that work.

Now, let's apply this to the matter at hand: helping our student writers improve through the use of feedback.

BETTER AND SANER GRADING/FEEDBACK TIP: ONLY GIVE FEEDBACK ON ASSIGNMENTS WHOSE PURPOSE IS TO IMPROVE WRITING QUALITY

Providing feedback on student writing is hard, mental work, and non-satisficed grading is, too. Therefore, when I have to do these things, this is what I'm after: *efficiency*. For the sake of really zeroing in here, let's be clear on the meaning of efficient—it comes from the Latin *efficere*, which means "accomplish." When I say grading must always be efficient, I mean that it must always accomplish what I'm trying to make it accomplish—nothing more, no wasted effort.

In other words, when I grade, I want to

- Achieve maximum productivity with minimum wasted effort or expense

- Prevent the wasting of particular resources (in this case, time)

- And, to go back to that Latin root, I want my grading to "accomplish" something

In order for me to understand whether I'm efficient or not, I have to know what the point of grading this particular assignment is.

Consider two kinds of work I ask my students to do repeatedly in my courses: they write 250-word responses to weekly articles in our Burning Questions of the Year series, and they write on-demand, document-based question (DBQ) essays.

Here's what I'm after in having my students complete BQY assignments, in order of priority. I want them to

- Build knowledge about the world

- Increase the amount of reading and writing that they do for my class

- Practice their amicable argumentation skills through argumentative reading

From these fairly general purposes flows my fairly general (and fast) approach to grading BQY written responses. Essentially, I take five seconds or so to scan student work, I affix a low-stakes grade out of ten to the paper, and I put the number into the gradebook. When I find that quality of student work is slipping, I'll pull an exemplar to share with students next Monday, reviewing with them what we're trying to achieve with a BQY. This is virtually the same approach that Gallagher uses when grading articles of the week, as described in Chapter 4.

So, heresy though it may seem, I'm hardly reading what my students write for their BQY responses, and I can grade a set of one hundred AoWs in about ten minutes. When I give feedback on these assignments, it's at the whole-class or small-group level—hardly ever the individual level—because skill building isn't the top priority. I *satisfice* the task: there's a grade in the gradebook, which my school, students, and students' parents like to see, and I keep my sanity. For the win.

I simply can't afford to hold to the evidence-lite idea that everything I assign must be painstakingly graded. It sounds nice—I can almost see the sparkle of such a majestic mountain of idealism shining from here—but nice ideas won't magically promote the long-term flourishing of my students. I'm a realistic idealist. I must have my students writing more than I can grade, and that works itself out in me satisficing the heck out of grading BQY responses.

On the other hand, here are my objectives with document-based question essays, in order of priority:

Build specific writing skills pertinent to effective, evidence-based, historical arguments. Namely, I'm after the seven specific skills laid out by the College Board's (2017a) AP World History curriculum document:

- Craft a historically defensible, on-topic thesis that establishes a line of reasoning

- Describe a broader historical context relevant to the prompt

- Use evidence from all of the provided documents to support the thesis

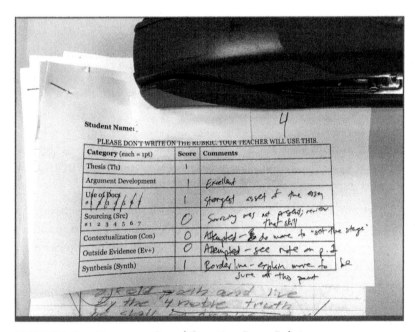

FIGURE 6.5 • Document-Based Question Essay Rubric

Note: Each category receives a 1 if proficiency is shown or a 0 if it's not quite there yet.

- Source documents by analyzing how a document's content is affected by author's point of view, author's purpose, audience, or the historical context

- Develop an argument by showing how documents corroborate, qualify, or contradict one another

- Use outside evidence to support the thesis

- Contextualize the overall argument

- Synthesize the overall argument by extending it into a different time, place, theme, or discipline

From my intense focus here on the development of specific, discrete skills flows my very specific (and more time-intensive) grading of DBQ essays. In general, these each take me four to six minutes to grade, as I'm completing a seven-point rubric (see Figure 6.5) and writing comments as appropriate. (Reading a two- or three-page, on-demand DBQ essay and giving this level of feedback takes me three to five minutes per essay.)

In short, the purpose of an assignment dictates our approach to grading it. This helps us grade more efficiently, which in turn makes us better and saner at our work.

BETTER AND SANER GRADING/FEEDBACK TIP: GET OUT THE STOPWATCH AND MARK LIKE AN ATHLETE

Efficiency depends on speed, too. Have you ever considered using a stopwatch to improve in this area? Here's how it works:

Step 1. Sit down with a stack of papers, a stack of rubrics, and a beverage. (Based on personal experimentation, stimulants tend to work better than sedatives here.) Most important, don't sit down with anything else.

Step 2. Get out a stopwatch. I use the one on my phone, but there are also free ones online. Or, you may even still be able to find a real stopwatch in a sporting goods store, I think. A "Lap" or "Split" feature on the stopwatch or app is strongly recommended.

Step 3. Start the stopwatch and grade an essay. Do whatever it is that you do when you grade this kind of essay. Make comments, mark things, write on the rubric, assign a percentage, and so on.

Step 4. When you are totally finished, set the essay aside and click "Lap" on your stopwatch. This will help you track how long it took you to complete that first "lap" of grading. If your stopwatch doesn't have a "Lap" button, you could simply record how long it took to grade that paper, reset the stopwatch, and then start it again as you move on to grading Paper Two. See Figure 6.6 for a screenshot of my stopwatch.

Step 5. Grade, hit Lap, grade, hit Lap, grade. Grade up to five papers in this fashion, hitting Lap between each one. (Or writing down how long each lap takes if you don't have the Lap thing.) You should probably not check out your Snapchat Story Line during this string of grading. Stay focused. Keep the eagle eye. You've only got to do this for five total papers.

Step 6. After five grading laps, stop. Breathe. Stretch. Stand up. Go get a refill. Taking this mini-break helps the ol' brain stay sharp.

Step 7. Analyze your speed performance. What was your average time per grading lap? How do you explain the laps that went long versus the laps that didn't? Are any of the things you do during a grading lap unlikely to help your students become better writers? Might you experiment with satisficing those things (or skipping them altogether) in the next round of five papers so as to improve your pace?

I've experienced a few benefits when I stopwatch my grading:

FIGURE 6.6 • Smartphone Stopwatch

Note: This is what my stopwatch looks like after grading a few essays. I like that it puts my best "lap" in green and my worst in red. I can take a quick glance over at this every time I hit Lap and see how I'm doing.

- Timing each paper keeps me focused. I'm far less likely to get distracted by the news or Twitter or [insert whatever distractions I use to make grading much more prolonged and much more painful].

- Timing forces quicker decision making. I can't dither about what to write or not write; I just have to move forward with the task of helping this writer and assigning a score. This quick decision making creates a momentum that helps me avoid the existential crises that have so often accompanied my grading sessions in the past.

- Timing prevents the urge to cover a paper with comments and markings. Me acting as a professional copy editor is, at the risk of overgeneralizing, a pointless waste of my time.

- Timing makes it easy to determine how long grading this particular assignment takes, and that allows me to schedule the proper time slots for future assignments, to get them done in a timely fashion. After doing several rounds of five grading laps, I can pretty accurately calculate how much longer I need to grade the whole pile of essays. No more wondering, no more dreading—I just know that this will take three more hours because I have forty-five more papers and each paper takes me an average of four minutes to grade. Then I'm free to schedule those blocks of time into my next working day (I prefer one-hour chunks), and that increases the odds that I'll get these essays back to kids in a timely fashion and not feel The Guilt of the Stack that so often plagues me.

BETTER AND SANER GRADING/FEEDBACK TIP: STOP "RELAXING" WHILE GRADING

It might be painful to survey how many teachers make a habit of "relaxing" at night with a stack of student writing in their laps and a show they've been wanting to watch on Netflix. I've done this plenty of times myself.

But here is the problem: grading or giving feedback on student writing is active, mental work. Trying to grade while watching Netflix is akin to trying to jog while reading a book.

If you're jogging and trying to read, then you're constantly switching between the two activities—you can either really slow down your jog so that you can actually see the page and keep it from bouncing around, or you can really slow down your reading by trying to do it while your jogging is bouncing everything around. There's this constant lack of quality in either the reading or the jogging, the cost of which would be an hour-long jogging/reading session in which you probably did far less reading and jogging than you could have had you just given thirty minutes to exclusively reading and thirty minutes to exclusively jogging.

This is basically what happens in our brains when we do the whole "relaxing while grading" thing. Watching TV is definitely more passive than reading a book, but grading is definitely more mentally active than jogging. So you're sitting here, forcing your brain to try constantly switching between the show or the grading task. After an hour of this, you end up, again, with probably much less enjoyment from the show and much less productivity with the grading than you could have gotten by giving an exclusive thirty minutes to each.

I've used watching a TV show as an example here, but I think the same logic works for other popular recreations like checking one's Facebook timeline or getting on the ol' Twitter. Daniel T. Willingham (2010) sums the message up from a research perspective: "The literature is clear on this point. Engaging in any mentally challenging task should be done on its own—not while also watching television or carrying on a conversation."

It's probably not a stretch to say that our grading-while-"relaxing" habits aren't good for us. At best, they decrease the quality of our evenings and increase the amount of time it takes to complete tasks. At worst, I wouldn't be surprised if we're damaging our brains, decreasing our ability over time to deeply engage with mentally challenging work for periods of, say, sixty minutes at a time.

The morals of the story:

- When it's time to relax, relax.
- When it's time to be done working, be done working.
- Embrace the constraints of single-tasking.

Simple adjustments in our approach to grading can drastically improve both how well we do it and how sane we are when we're through.

The Gist

Whether we want to prepare our students to be "the rock stars of their generation" (Cepeda, 2012) or simply participants in the middle class, proficient writing matters. If our schools did a better job honoring content-appropriate, mastery-supporting writing throughout the school day, we'd be closer to meeting the Conley Challenge and improving our next dose of NAEP writing results. Unless we're pragmatic in how we approach increased writing volume during the school day (the Pyramid of Writing Priorities in Figure 6.2 can help), we're going to create short-lived, unsustainable initiatives around writing every single time. But once we are smart about improved writing quantity, we can begin

COMMON TEACHER HANG-UP

It Takes Me Forever to Return
My Students' Graded Work

I was once on a panel at the National Council of Teachers of English conference, and I asked the audience members to raise their hands if they currently had a stack of student writing that was more than a week old. Nearly every hand in the audience of more than 200 people went up, including mine. "This isn't good!" I said. "We know this isn't good!"

Imagine a coach—say, a basketball coach—who consistently gave her players feedback a week or more after a given athletic performance. "Coach," the players would say, "thanks for putting this time into giving us some pointers and all, but here's the thing: We don't even really remember the game you're talking about anymore. It was too long ago!" Such a coach would be quickly looking for new employment. That's no way to help players improve.

Why do we act as if writing is so different? For every day that a piece of writing sits in our possession awaiting feedback, more and more students move on from the piece, mentally and emotionally. Instead of giving tardy feedback, we're better off giving less but quicker feedback. The better, saner tips we just explored can help with that.

systematically advancing writing quality: first, with grading-free approaches to making good writing sensible and concrete to our students, and second, with a satisficed approach to providing timely, next-day feedback. Finally, we have to examine how we're approaching the dreaded task of grading. The simple, robust approaches we adopt need to be focused and aimed at speed.

Better Together

Here are some helpful ways to do the work in this chapter with your team, department, or school:

- In Wisconsin, literacy coach Norah Olig once asked her teachers to quantify the amount of writing students did in their courses. The exercise was all the group needed to start noticing that they weren't expecting much writing. From this place of mutual understanding, the group began exploring how they might increase quantity and quality in their courses without forsaking content mastery or teacher sanity.

- Compile a list of writing prompts that work well by unit or course concept. As a bonus, categorize these in ways that make sense. For example, you might make a list of warm-up prompts, short-answer question prompts, and so on. When you meet as a team, share prompts that worked well, prompts that didn't, and explore what makes the difference.

- At Cedar Springs High School in Michigan, the English department is given two working days per school year to come together to grade shared, SAT-styled writing assessments. During the first few hours of the workday, the group sits in a room, exchanges stacks of papers, and then goes through a norming exercise led by the department chair. Then, teachers grade work from other teachers' classrooms, making note of any essays in which the grade variance passes a certain threshold (papers with variance are graded by a third reader). These workdays serve to keep the department consistent in its grading practices, and they also give teachers a chance to get quicker at accurately scoring papers.

- At Powers Catholic High School in Flint, Michigan, the science department decided to spend a day categorizing and clarifying expectations for writing throughout the department. They identified four types of writing that they expect students to do in a given course: lab reports, writing in response to reading, research papers, and conflicting viewpoints. They then identified what is essentially a skull and crossbones list for all writing in science—a list of no-no's for scientific writing. These included refraining from phrases like "I think" or "I believe," getting straight to the point ("no fluff"), and supporting all claims with evidence. Finally, the team agreed upon language to use when teaching students to do each of the four kinds of writing.

Notes

CHAPTER SEVEN

Speak and Listen Purposefully and Often

> *Reading and writing float on a sea of talk.*
>
> —JAMES BRITTON (1983, P. 11)

> *It can be easier to build an app than to have a conversation.*
>
> —SHERRY TURKLE (2015, P. 361)

Rebekah felt like she was going to throw up. Her nausea was all she could think about, and her mind raced with how she was going to escape the classroom immediately and not return for a number of days. Up front, her teacher was explaining the rules for something he called "Pop-Up Debate," which he was describing as stupidly simple. But nothing about this unexpected challenge seemed simple to Rebekah's racing mind and upset stomach.

I teach students like Rebekah every single school year, and early in my career I would not have dreamed of *requiring* them to speak in front of their peers. Inviting them, sure. Coaching them toward it, yes. But requiring them to stand up and speak? I would not have dared because it was something I always hated in school; I was an anxious introvert myself.

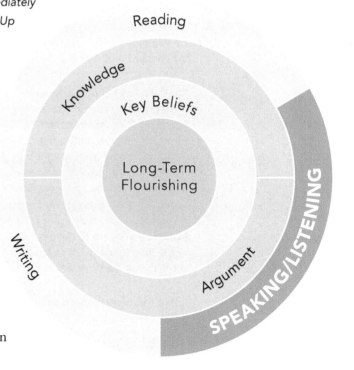

The trouble with not pushing our anxious or introverted kids to grapple with the many challenges of public speaking is that we create classes in which debilitating anxiety can take firmer root in the hearts and minds of students. As I mentioned toward the end of Chapter 2, my classroom is a place where extroverts are challenged by the amount of independent reading and writing we do, yet before I became convinced of the need to give all students access to ample, mandatory opportunities to speak publicly before their peers, my shy or introverted students had no like experience.

Rebekah did end up standing and speaking that day, and I can still remember how her lip quivered, her eyes shining as she was near tears. I do not take

COMMON TEACHER HANG-UP

But There's Official Documentation Saying This Student Can't Speak to Groups!

I sometimes receive documentation—a 504 plan, an IEP, or a note from a doctor or counselor—that excuses a student from public speaking situations in the classroom. At the workshops I lead for teachers, they'll sometimes ask, do you require those students to speak, too? And the answer is that I don't. Whenever there's official documentation, I always follow it.

On the other hand, if a student comes up to me and says, "I have severe anxiety and get panic attacks when I'm asked to speak," then I respond to the student that I appreciate them telling me this and that I will take it into consideration in the things I ask them to do throughout the year. And I do—I ask myself how I might best promote this child's long-term flourishing in the area of speaking and listening, given his acute difficulty. How would I want to be treated if I were him? And so I seek to communicate care and appreciation to him all year long, while at the same time communicating that he needs to take a swing at our whole-class speaking opportunities. "Hey, today we're going to have a Pop-Up Debate, and what I want you to do is to speak first. You'll get it over with, and you'll feel *so much better* than sitting there the whole time waiting to be called on like you did last time."

I have found no magical solution to individual situations like these, but later in this chapter I'll share a series of steps that I've found very helpful in reducing student fears of public speaking.

enjoyment in such discomfort, but I find great reward in what can happen for our socially anxious students when we endeavor to "normalize" public speaking (Palmer, n.d.)—to make it something other than The Big Speech in April or Class Discussions I Can Ignore and, instead, a normal part of what we *all* do in this class. By the end of the year, Rebekah had become one of the strongest debaters in the classroom. Her lip had stopped quivering, and her face shone not with terror but with adrenaline; she was like a person who hates heights getting addicted to skydiving. At the time of this writing, Rebekah is pursuing a degree in teaching. I can take little credit for the good things my students end up doing with their lives, but I am fortunate to report that Rebekah cites the regular chances to debate and discuss as critical in her exploration of her life's calling.

The Case for Speaking and Listening Throughout the School Day

The outer ring of the *These 6 Things* bull's-eye contains two components that receive countless hours of attention in professional development and education coursework: reading and writing. Speaking and listening, on the other hand, are too often killed by "assumicide": we assume that because our students can speak, their skills in oral communication and comprehension don't need to be targeted. Aptly, author and consultant Erik Palmer (2014) calls speaking and listening "the forgotten language arts." It is my hope, then, that even though this is the last component of the bull's-eye, you won't relegate it to last place in your classroom. Instead, I encourage you to incorporate speaking and listening throughout the entire school day, in every discipline. Here's why.

When my students speak, I find out what they know and don't know. The provisional types of writing that we explored in Chapter 6 are certainly useful in helping our students discover what they know and don't know. The problem is those kinds of writing don't really tell us teachers the same information. Speaking, on the other hand, quickly shows us where kids need help, especially when we enact simple means to ensure that all students speak on a regular basis.

Speaking builds confidence and normalizes nervousness. In a classroom where speaking is regularly taught and expected of all students, kids are quickly trying to do many things each time they speak. In their heads, they are keeping track of what they want to say, how they want to organize what they want to say, how they are delivering what they're saying, what they're doing with their hands while they're speaking, and so on. That's a large cognitive load they're carrying. This high challenge, in turn, builds student confidence as the year progresses—especially for our nervous or shy kids. As Martín recently shared in a post-speaking reflection, "I've come to see that nervousness actually helps me a little bit because it keeps me really focused on what I'm doing." In a speaking-lite classroom, students like Martín would not come to such realizations.

Speaking is the main way we communicate on a daily basis, even in today's techno-infused world. It drives my wife Crystal crazy how frequently people text. She and I grew up in a time before texting, so I get where she's coming from: the texting thing can get a little crazy, and it often leads us to sloppy, unnecessary, or superficial communication. But even in a world of GIF texts and emoticons, speaking is still the predominant way that most of us communicate. Whether at the dinner table, the water cooler, the cafeteria, or the job interview, talking still matters. Teaching our kids to talk and listen better, then, matters too.

Speaking makes writing more concrete. I used to find it difficult to teach my students to write argumentative essays. Everything seemed so abstract and fuzzy. That all changed when we started having regular, whole-class Pop-Up Debates. Suddenly, argumentative essays became written forms of the best kinds of Pop-Up Debate speeches. In this way, speaking is a much more malleable and concrete mode of communication by which we can teach the skills that will make our students better writers.

Speaking builds class culture. When we regularly create and teach toward whole-class speaking events, we increase the likelihood that our students will develop the identity belief—people like me do work like we do in this class. Classes filled with kids who feel like they belong and are being challenged are always classes that I enjoy teaching and that kids enjoy being a part of.

Good talk "stimulates the intellect and is the enemy of boredom" (Schmoker, 2006, p. 67, paraphrasing Graff, 2003). When we've done the work laid out in this book so far, students tend to enjoy and engage with opportunities to discuss big ideas and complex texts. I've yet to meet a student who doesn't think it's cool when all of a sudden we "sound smart" in a discussion around some issue that, three weeks prior, none of us had ever heard about. When we invest in making classes where great talk happens, our classes become the kinds of places that kids value and are glad to belong to.

Speaking helps our introverts learn how to adapt to a world that cherishes the Extrovert Ideal. In *Quiet*, Susan Cain (2013) argues that in American society there exists "the omnipresent belief that the ideal self is gregarious, alpha, and comfortable in the spotlight." She calls this the "extrovert ideal," providing a sharp and effective critique of its presence in businesses, pop culture, and, importantly, schools. In this chapter, I don't want to give the impression that I support the Extrovert Ideal. That's not it at all. The short of it is that if my classes are going to equip students to flourish long term, then I've got to push both my introverted *and* my extroverted students. If you've been reading straight through this book, then you've seen plenty of activities that challenge my extroverts, such as reading or writing silently or placing a maximum on the number of speeches in Pop-Up Debates. And so it is that in this chapter, we'll be talking about speaking—something that certainly does challenge my introverted students.

A Focused, Sensible Approach to Speaking and Listening Throughout the School Day for the Long-Term Flourishing of Our Students

Now that we know all the ways students (and their teachers) can benefit from more and better opportunities for speaking and listening in all their courses, we've got to face some hard realities. Kids are really different when it comes to speaking. Some groups are easier to manage in speaking situations than others. Some students are painfully shy.

Hold on—let's take this one step at a time. Creating more and better speaking and listening opportunities throughout the school day doesn't have to be difficult. As we've seen in previous chapters, there are practical, doable ways to build speaking and listening into your course content on a regular basis. Start small. Scale up. As with other areas, it's about quantity *and* quality, and it doesn't all have to happen at once. Here's how I recommend we increase the amount and quality of speaking and listening our students do throughout the school day:

- Quantity Step 1: Strategically increase quantity with three structures: Pop-Up Debate, Conversation Challenge, and Think–Pair–Share

- Quantity Step 2: Ensure all students speak—and keep track

- Quality Key 1: Responsive instruction

- Quality Key 2: Frequent reflection

Let's work through each of these in turn.

QUANTITY STEP 1: STRATEGICALLY INCREASE QUANTITY WITH THREE STRUCTURES

I must have used dozens of structures for facilitating in-class speaking early in my career. I thought having a hundred structures at my disposal was the mark of the master teacher. So one week we'd be using A-B-C-Share for speaking, and then the next week we'd try Socratic Seminars, and the next week 1-2-3-Repeato (all right, I made that one up), and so on. But then I started calculating just how much time I was spending each week teaching my students the latest structure. The sum was troubling: dozens of minutes per week, and all of them minutes that couldn't be put toward teaching kids to actually improve as speakers (versus as 1-2-3-Repeato users).

Now, my approach is simple. I use three structures for speaking all year long—Think–Pair–Share, Conversation Challenge, and Pop-Up Debates—and my objective is to help my classes become the best users of these structures in the country. (I frame it that way for my students to build the sense that speaking is a team sport [the belonging belief] and that our aim is high [the value belief].) Figure 7.1 gives an overview, along with how frequently I use them, what I use them for, and what I perceive as their structural strengths and weaknesses.

Within the first month of the school year, I introduce each of these structures, and for the rest of the school year we are using these three structures as contexts within which we can build knowledge, practice arguments, discuss what we've read, or prepare for writing.

The Pair Structure: Think–Pair–Share

Think–Pair–Share (Lyman, 1981) is, like me, a child of the 80s. It's simple enough to introduce in a few minutes:

1. Teacher or student provides a content-related question.
2. Whole class thinks or writes in response to the question (this is Think mode).
3. Students discuss the question in partners (this is Pair mode).

4. Students share out answers as a whole class, both through volunteering and random selection (this is Share mode).

5. (optional) Teacher provides students with speaking skills or social intelligence mini lesson and/or the opportunity for partners to give feedback to one another on their conversation. (This step aims to aid skill acquisition; Steps 1–4 will initially increase student skill, but this skill growth will taper off without further instruction and feedback.)

STRUCTURE + TIME IT TAKES	FREQUENCY	USES	STRENGTHS	WEAKNESSES
Think–Pair–Share Takes 3–6 minutes total: (1–2 for Think, 1–2 for Pair, 1–2 for Share)	Daily	• Processing new information • Reviewing old information • Brainstorming prior to a Conversation Challenge or Pop-Up Debate	• Quick • The "Share" mode allows me to randomly call on several students. • I can walk around and listen in on a sampling of Pair conversations.	I don't have a ton of control; someone in the opposite corner of the room could be off task or reinforcing a misunderstanding, and I may not find out or be able to do anything about it.
Conversation Challenge Takes about 10 minutes total: 2–4 for introduction, 2–4 for Conversation, 2–4 for Reflection	Weekly	• Practicing social intelligence • Cultivating the ability to carry on a conversation with a group of people you didn't choose on a topic you didn't choose	Challenges students to grapple with social dynamics and their public speaking concerns, yet it's still quick	As with Think–Pair–Share, Conversation Challenge doesn't give me total control of what's happening in the room—this is why cultivating the key beliefs in my students is so critical.
Pop-Up Debate For a class of 35 students, takes about 30–45 minutes total: 5 for introductory mini lesson, 30–35 for speaking, 5 for closing reflection	Monthly	• End-of-unit summative discussions • Motivating students • Work on argumentative skills	• Challenges students to learn how to deal with public speaking nerves • Provides numerous "teachable moments" for teacher to provide quick instruction around	• Time-consuming • If prompt is inadequate, the debate can become exhausted before all students have spoken

FIGURE 7.1 • An Overview of the Three Structures for Facilitating In-Class Speaking

Because of its simplicity and its age, I'm almost embarrassed when I discuss Think–Pair–Share (TPS) in my workshops with fellow teachers. My hunch is that the reason many of us have heard about TPS but rarely give it the share of classroom speaking time that it deserves is because it is just not fancy enough. When used well, TPS is a lean, mean machine of the focused classroom, marvelous for its simplicity and efficiency (see Figure 7.2). Smokey Daniels and Nancy Steineke (2014) put it just right: TPS is "the most instantaneously transformational structure we can add to our classrooms. Suddenly, it's not just us doing all the thinking, talking, and working; now the kids are taking responsibility and driving the learning, too" (p. 77).

And remember, efficient doesn't mean "rushed"; it means "gets the job done with as little waste as possible." I am a realist when it comes to classroom instructional time: each of the sixty minutes per day that I have with my students is precious; I cannot squander one minute of class time per day because, by the end of a 180-day school year, that amounts to 180 minutes or three full class periods. That's a justice issue in my book. Too many of my students cannot afford to lose three days of English 9 or World History.

Here are some things I've learned the hard way while using TPS in my classroom over the years.

Use mini lessons to teach students important ideas or skills related to TPS. For example, "How do you ask follow-up questions?" or "What do we do when someone's only giving monosyllabic contributions?" You don't need an answer key for teaching these things—as someone who has graduated from college, you know everything you need to teach kids to do TPS well.

Ensure that every student is talking. When you see pairs in which one student is not talking, observe, inquire, and study that situation. Like an observant scientist, your goal is to determine what is blocking that student from participating in the conversation.

Brainstorm what makes a good partner. Students can come up with great lists of positive partner behaviors. These can serve as an anchor chart throughout the school year.

Build the norm that "everyone works with everyone" (Daniels & Steineke, 2014, p. 40). One way to do this is to ensure that students work with as many different

General Get-to-Know-You	• Find three things that you and your partner have in common, including at least one interest outside of school. • What is the most interesting subject in school? Share with your partner. • If you could travel anywhere in the world, where would you go and why?
ELA	• What was the most important thing you learned about writing personal essays today? • Today we learned about comma usage. So what? Why does understanding comma usage matter? • How does *Romeo and Juliet* connect to life in this high school? Where do you see themes in *R+J* playing out in our halls?
World History	• What if there had never been a Zheng He? How might the world have been different today? • What is the most important event of the 1700s? • What is similar about the Han and Roman empires? Why might these similarities exist? • Given the Tokugawa Shogunate's decision to isolate from much of the world, what do you expect might happen in Japan in our next unit?
Algebra	• What are some types of relationships that can be demonstrated by graphs? • What do rational and irrational numbers have in common? • How are variables useful in understanding other courses or areas of life?
Biology	• With your partner, review the most important thing learned today about cell biology. • Where, specifically, do you see the perpetuation of species playing out in our world today? • We've been learning about microorganisms—so what? What do microorganisms have to do with our actual lives?
Health	• What stress management techniques that we learned about today have you used before or do you plan to use in the future? • Whose responsibility is the health of a teenager? The teen's? The parents'? The school's? Explain. • Which daily health habits are the hardest to keep up, and why?

FIGURE 7.2 • Sample Think–Pair–Share Prompts

partners as possible during the initial weeks. To do this, I change the seating chart every day for the first couple weeks, simply taking the index cards we made on the first day of school and placing them around the room before the students walk in. This sometimes becomes frenetic for me as I race to do it between classes, but the end results are worth it because, at the end of a few weeks,

a. my students are better acquainted with one another,

b. I'm more aware of how my students mix with their peers, and

c. students have internalized the fact that, like my mentor Gerome Dixon in Baltimore used to say, my classroom is "my house," and as such there are some small decisions (e.g., where we will sit) that I'll take care of each day.

Explain why the conversational skills practiced in TPS are far from just school stuff. TPS helps us with important situations like interviewing or dating. These are skills, then, that we all want—and though the work will be hard, it will also be fun as we do it together this year, day in and day out. This targets the value belief.

Establish a "back to order" routine. I used to think the "raising your hand for attention" thing was for elementary teachers until I realized that it's just a sane, peaceful way to bring back attention for any group. Whatever signal it is that you want to use is fine—I've come to making a salute motion, standing like a statue, and creating a weird "Cht!" sound—as long as students understand it and you consistently use it. Think–Pair–Share is so much more enjoyable for everyone when there's a clear signal that Pair time has ended.

The Small-Group Structure: Conversation Challenge

While I appreciate the daily practicality of Think–Pair–Share, I need something that gives my students the chance to practice speaking to more than one person and managing their roles in group conversations. The Conversation Challenge structure requires less classroom time than TPS and helps bridge partner sharing and whole-class pop-ups, providing a structure that I can use in as little as ten minutes of class time.

I introduce the Conversation Challenge structure by telling students that young people often find it difficult to carry on a conversation with people who aren't their family or friends, especially on a topic that they haven't chosen. I tell them that some of this is a skill issue—they lack the tools required for this kind of thing, and they lack the practice—and some of this is a social intelligence issue. I then unpack social intelligence for them like this:

- If you're socially intelligent, you
  - find solutions for conflicts,
  - show that you respect the feelings of others,

COMMON TEACHER HANG-UP

How Am I Supposed to Grade Student Speaking?

Teachers often ask me how I grade things like Pop-Up Debate and Conversation Challenge. My answer is that yes, I do often put a grade in the gradebook for these things—after all, I want to communicate to the parents, administrators and students who view the gradebook that speaking is a valuable part of the work we do in the classroom—but this grade is virtually never the product of intensive thought or an elaborate rubric. My rationale for this is the same as it's been the past few chapters: feedback and practice make people better at things; grading doesn't. If every time I want to hold a Pop-Up Debate or Conversation Challenge in my classroom I know that there's an unwieldy rubric or time-consuming grading process I have to complete, then guess what? I'm going to find reasons to provide fewer of these critical learning opportunities for my students.

Instead of focusing on grades during these speaking situations, I'm focused on two questions:

1. What are we doing well?
2. What can we do better?

My instructional focus, then, is on how I transform items that answer the second question today into items that answer the first question tomorrow. That, and not grading, is how we leverage speaking situations into the long-term flourishing of our kids.

- o adapt well to different social situations, and
- o refrain from behaviors that annoy others (Character Lab, n.d.).

"In light of this," I tell them, "this year I want you to become good at holding conversations with small groups of people in our classroom. We'll start with a short time goal—two minutes—and over the year we'll work up to a longer time goal—four minutes. In each conversation, I'll set a topic that's relevant to something we've been studying or something that's been happening in the world or something that's relevant to your life outside school, and it's going to be your group's job to keep that conversation alive and on topic for the full time limit. Every person needs to speak at least once, and if I find that single people are dominating conversations and carrying the team, I may set a limit on the maximum number of times you can speak, just like we tend to do for Pop-Up Debates."

With these brief instructions in place, I set the topic for the first Conversation Challenge, I get out my watch, and I say go. As students are conversing, I'm walking around listening in on bits and pieces of conversations, trying to find areas of weakness that we can address both after this Conversation Challenge and prior to our next one. The few minutes before and after a speaking exercise are ripe for skill growth; this is why I rarely—no, I never—use rubrics for speaking situations. It's not that I don't believe in grading them—I do tend to put a simple credit/no credit score in the gradebook for parents and students to see because grades are expected by my stakeholders—but rather, it's that I'm going to be most successful moving my student speakers if I'm fully listening in on what they are doing, taking notes on what I'm noticing, and giving whole-class feedback afterward. If I am trying to manage a rubric during a live speaking event and filling that out and getting it back to them the next day, I'll miss things.

To summarize this in steps:

Step 1: Introduce the topic of the Conversation Challenge and the target skill.

Step 2: Remind students that it's the Conversation Challenge for a reason—you're *challenging* them to keep the discussion going for the full time limit. Make sure they know what group they're in; I always just group students with the three to five people nearest them.

Step 3: Get out your timer, say, "Go!" and start keeping time. At regular intervals, call out time updates (e.g., "One minute remaining").

Step 4: Walk around and listen in on a few of their conversations, specifically looking for examples of what students are doing well and what they need to work on. Don't worry about a rubric or grading.

Step 5: When the time's up, have students resituate themselves and answer the following reflection questions, either shared out to the whole class or in writing:

- What did your group do well?
- What can your group do better next time?

Step 6: Discuss as a class what key skills we need to target for next time.

Conversation Challenge is an interesting structure because of various things that can go wrong (and thus, the various teachable moments that it faithfully produces). Here are some tips I've learned along the way.

Ask, "What made that awkward?" After a Conversation Challenge is over, I'll often ask students to write or share any awkward moments that arose. (This is after, of course, I've advised them on not using any information that could make things embarrassing. And it's also worth noting that in my class I naturally provide plenty of opportunities for kids to see that it's okay to be awkward. We look at these moments objectively and talk about how they could have been improved. So what I'm saying is, if you're awkward, that will help you talk about awkwardness in Conversation Challenge with your students.)

Here are some awkward moments students reported in a recent Conversation Challenge in my classroom, along with the questions I asked the class to push their thinking on how to better meet the Conversation Challenge next time around:

- "There was a long pause after everyone had spoken."
  - Did anyone have a moment where this happened and then someone stepped in and fixed it?
  - How could you as a group member fix a situation like this?
- "Some people were speaking really quietly and you couldn't hear them."
  - What kinds of things can you say in a group conversation when you can't hear someone?
  - What is it that makes you not want to ask someone to repeat themselves more loudly?
- "Someone was trying to be funny, but no one laughed or got the joke."
  - Is it possible for a single member of a group to smooth situations like this over?
  - What is the best way to respond in a group conversation like this to humor that you don't understand?

Listen for distracting speaking tics, and then poll the class on them afterward. I like to occasionally ask kids, "How many of you were in a group where at least one person spoke in a way that you found, like, you know, like, um, uh, erhm, kind of, like, distracting?" To help my students deal with their distracting speaking tics, one simple method I use is to keep bringing them up. That's what this prompt does. When the students see hands going up from members of their group, they think, "Hmm . . . was I one of the people my group members are thinking about right now?"

Get right in there. There was a time when I felt like my presence "messed up" a Conversation Challenge, so I didn't want to stand too close to groups while they were talking. I don't think this is necessary. Instead, I tell students prior to the first few Conversation Challenges, "Hey guys, I'll be listening in on your groups so I can help us get better, so it's your job just to ignore me." Then, I just walk around the room with my clipboard, standing right next to groups so that I can listen to what's going on and make note. There's no need to be coy—I'm their coach, and I'm trying to figure out how to help them do better.

Build knowledge first. I once was giving my students a series of articles around the Burning Question, "Who are the presidential primary contenders, and which would be the best president?" and the first article in the series was on Bernie Sanders. I had an extra ten minutes at the end of my lesson that Friday, so I had students engage in an open-ended Conversation Challenge around the article. (There was my first mistake: a vague, essentially nonexistent prompt.) What I found in walking around and listening to my students discuss the article is that their comments were lacking in substance and thought. Upon reflecting on this, I realized that my students just didn't know enough about Bernie Sanders or the Burning Question to have a good conversation here. Weeks later, when I gave them a similarly vague prompt (Discuss Trump, Cruz, Clinton, and Sanders, the four candidates we've read about so far in this BQY), and the greater deal of knowledge that my students brought to their conversations created a much higher quality of discussion.

The Whole-Class Structure: Pop-Up Debate

In Chapter 4, we explored Pop-Up Debates as a means for putting argument on its feet and getting kids immersed in live, whole-class critical thinking. In this chapter, I want to demonstrate how the pop-up structure can be used in nonargumentative situations as well. Any time that I want to create a whole-class speaking situation, I use the pop-up method. The structure can facilitate whole-class communications of any kind, including impromptu discussions or end-of-year toasts.

Let's examine what these creative applications of the pop-up structure can look like.

Impromptu pop-up discussions. Sometimes, our students will pose questions during a lesson that get the rest of the class excited. Suddenly, we've got multiple kids wanting to speak at the same time to answer the student's question or to argue with its premise. In these situations, we can use the pop-up method to either hold a brief, whole-class discussion right then and there, or we can tell students that the final five minutes of class will be used to have a pop-up discussion or debate about the question just posed.

In this kind of circumstance, not all students will speak—after all, five minutes is not enough time to make that happen, especially on a topic that people are eager to speak about. In these cases, then, we're not getting every student to speak like we need to do in a regular Pop-Up Debate, but we are providing an organized outlet to spontaneous, student-driven discussion prompt, thereby creating a speaking opportunity that cultivates key beliefs in our students.

Pop-up toasts. I've used pop-up toasts for the past few years to end the year on a high note. Its name says it all: instead of having kids end the year with me by madly scrawling down the final bits of their exams, I plan to have my students finish their exams with at least 30 minutes to spare so that we can end the year giving toasts to one another. I give them advance warning of this activity in case they'd like to prepare, and I share with them how toast-making can come in handy at special occasions.

Basically, during these final thirty minutes of the school year, my students and I take turns standing up with mini cups of soda or water (I provide these), using sentence starters if needed (e.g., "I'd like to make a toast to _____."), and ending with "Cheers" and the occasional laughter, applause, or tears.

The kind of speech is unique, but the structure is well worn by this point: it's just a pop-up.

Whole-class, mandatory participation speaking events serve some of the same purposes as mandatory, whole-class reading experiences: they help us build a shared language and a catalog of shared experiences. They also allow us to

davestuartjr.com/
last-day-of-school/

Use this link or QR code to
access my full rundown of
Pop-Up Toasts.

actively teach speaking in the context of live, real speaking work. Though I don't
want to be interrupting pop-up events after every single contribution, I do want
to be interrupting every three to five minutes so that I can call out good things,
model things that I want students to work on, or redirect the conversation when
it's veering into the weeds. As I said in Chapter 4, pop-up events are like the
whole-team scrimmages that athletic coaches sometimes use to help players prepare for games. In the scrimmage, we want actual gameplay to happen, but we
also don't want to miss capitalizing on a handful of teachable moments. In this
way, whole class speaking structures like the pop-up format serve as teachable
moment machines, and those teachable moments are available for the whole
class to experience.

COMMON STUDENT HANG-UP

"I'm Terrified of Public Speaking!"

Our students who are anxious about public speaking tend to see themselves
as people who *never* speak in front of the whole class. This belief about their
identity is both debilitating and self-fulfilling. To help our students establish
a different identity—say, as a person who doesn't go out of his or her way to
speak in front of the whole class, but who can and does do it when needed—
we can gradually move from mandatory Think–Pair–Share experiences to
low-stakes, whole-class Pop-Up Debates.

I use the following steps at the start of the year to maximize the
odds that even my most anxious students will participate in pop-ups
each year.

During the first three weeks of school, I create Think–Pair–Share prompts
every day (see sample list of prompts in Figure 7.2). Sometimes these can be
personal, "get-to-know-you" style prompts (e.g., What would your friends
say is your greatest strength?), but more often they are related to what
we're doing in class right now (e.g., "Our BQY articles this month have been
on important life skills. Which life skill do you believe is most important, and
why?"; see Chapter 3). During Think mode, I want students writing—just a
couple of sentences, very quickly. During Pair mode, I want them speaking
to their partner. I walk around to monitor this and help things along where
students are struggling. And then, during Share mode, I call on four or five

students at random, using my deck of index cards for the students in each class. My goal in randomly calling on students like this is to ensure that they all experience, at least once per week during those first three weeks of school, that it's possible to speak to the whole class without perishing. To make sure I don't miss a student, I also keep track of Share participations on my clipboard. It is critical that every student provides an answer during at least one Share time.

During the fourth week of school, students complete a provisional writing warm-up on the prompt they'll be debating that day. They don't know they are about to debate this—they just know that it's another day in Stuart's class, and that means another writing-based warm-up.

After they complete the warm-up, I introduce the day's Pop-Up Debate like this:

> Over the past few weeks of school, we've been reading weekly articles and discussing this idea of critical life skills. What life skills are most important, and how do we develop these in ourselves prior to high school graduation? I've tried to impress upon you the idea that these skills aren't guaranteed—that if we want them, we're going to have to make sure that we work to get them.
>
> Today, I want us to practice one of the life skills that has been hardest for me to develop—the ability to speak in front of a whole group. So what we're going to do is use a structure that I call Pop-Up Debate. It's pretty simple:

(I write the essence of the following two bullet points on the board as I explain them.)

- *Every student needs to speak at least one time, and no one may speak more than once until I say otherwise.*

- *To speak, you'll simply stand up and speak. I'm not the referee, so you'll need to practice social intelligence by being polite and yielding the floor—or giving it up to someone else who wants to speak—as necessary.*

I mentioned a minute ago that public speaking was a skill that I stumbled over for a long time. I was the kid in class who did not want to speak, thank you very much. And for most of my adult life, it's been a real

(Continued)

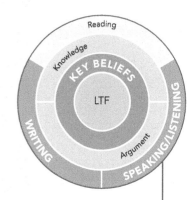

TRY THIS

Gradually work toward whole-class speaking events.

(Continued)

struggle overcoming that. So today, if you're nervous, all you need to do is just stand up and read your one-sentence answer to the first prompt we wrote about today: What life skill do you think is the most important? As you all speak, I'll have a volunteer come up here and keep record of what you're saying.

> *Okay, to recap: everyone speaks, to speak you just stand up where you are and start talking, and if you're nervous all you need to do is read a one-sentence response to the prompt we just wrote about— you can read it straight off your paper.*

While they're speaking, I'm doing three things:

1. I'm **keeping record** on my clipboard of who has spoken, and I'm taking note of my observations on where we can improve. I'll use these observations to help shape our post-debate reflection, and I'll use the record of who has spoken to call on people as needed.

2. As soon as there's a lull in the debate, **I start calling on people who haven't spoken** yet. My voice is unemotional and matter-of-fact. I say the student's name, keeping my eyes on my clipboard. If the student hesitates, I say with a smile, "Go ahead, Bailey—just stand up and speak. Feel free to read from your paper." And then I look back down. I think the point here is to not make this some dramatic event—I don't want to speak down to them, and I don't want to offer empty encouragement. Rather, I just want to matter-of-factly call them to stand and speak.

3. Finally, I'm focused on **shaping the culture** I want for these debates. Any hint of snarkiness, rudeness, or meanness, I handle. If students start doing the whole "Hey this is a fun game, let's all stand up and speak at the same time, and then we can point at each other and yell about who spoke first" thing, then I show them how it should actually look, with almost exaggerated politeness, "Oh, I'm sorry Aiden—you go right ahead."

When everyone has spoken, I bring attention back to me:

> *All right, that was a good start! We're on our way. Now, let me ask you a question. Feel free to be honest. How many of you felt at least 1 percent nervous at some point during that debate?*

This is a key moment because I want the majority of the kids to raise their hands—that's why I phrase it as "at least 1 percent nervous," and that's why I save our first Pop-Up Debate for four weeks into the school year. Students need to be comfortable enough to be a little bit vulnerable. When almost all of the hands in the class shoot up, something important happens and I seek to capitalize on it.

> Wow—look at that. I want my shy and anxious students in the room right now to make note of all those hands because I know that some of you felt sick to your stomach when I started class today by saying everyone was going to have to stand up and speak. Do you see how normal it is to feel nervous prior to public speaking? Do you also see how survivable the nervousness is?
>
> Let's close with this. Get your spiral notebooks back out, start a fresh section, and respond to these two questions. We'll discuss them in just a couple of minutes:
>
> - What did we do well today, as a class, in our Pop-Up Debate? What should we be proud of?
> - What can we do better? Where do we need to improve for the future?

I've seen this simple progression—three weeks of daily Think–Pair–Shares with mandatory Share participation at least once per week, followed by a low-stakes "surprise" Pop-Up Debate in Week Four—nearly eliminate nonparticipation by students. Several years ago, I even measured the effects of this sequence with the help of a Character Lab Teacher Innovator grant and found that it had a significant effect on public speaking comfort.

QUANTITY STEP 2: ENSURE ALL STUDENTS SPEAK—AND KEEP TRACK

If we want all of our students to grow as speakers and listeners during their time with us, then we need to ensure that every one of them speaks, purposefully and professionally, as regularly as possible. I have two questions to help us get started here:

1. What mechanisms or techniques do you use to ensure that *all* students speak?

To become better at teaching, speaking, and listening, we need to become students of these oft-neglected disciplines ourselves. To dig deeper into the instructional aspects of teaching, speaking, and listening, I recommend the following resources:

- Erik Palmer's *Well-Spoken: Teaching Speaking to All Students* (2011)

- the speaking and listening chapter of Kelly Gallagher's *In the Best Interest of Students: Staying True to What Works in the ELA Classroom* (2015)

To dig deeper into speaking and listening in general, consider these texts:

- Sherry Turkle's *Reclaiming Conversation: The Power of Talk in a Digital Age* (2015)

- Erik Palmer's *Own Any Occasion: Mastering the Art of Speaking and Presenting* (2017)

- Carmine Gallo's *Talk Like TED: The 9 Public-Speaking Secrets of the World's Top Minds* (2015)

Perhaps nothing, of course, can make us better at teaching speaking than to go out and speak in a way or for an audience that scares you. You know: that one.

For a full list of the "Dig Deeper" titles mentioned in this book, go to davestuartjr.com/t6t-list.

2. What specific speaking opportunities have your students had to speak and listen at the following levels during your past month of instruction: in pairs, in small groups, and as a whole class?

When teachers reflect on these questions, I often watch them shift uncomfortably at the first question—"Well, uh, I just, I just know, you know?"—or scratch their heads at the second question, surprised to see that they've gone a whole month without one or more of the three levels of speaking I listed.

As we've explored, each of the three speaking structures brings its own opportunities and obstacles. In a class where we neglect any of these three kinds of levels of speaking, we're leaving potential speaking/listening growth untouched. This is where Figure 7.1 can come in handy—it gives us an idea of when and how frequently to aim for each kind of speaking opportunity.

To ensure that all students speak, I use low-tech, simple solutions: a stack of index cards (I told you how I create this stack in Chapter 2) and a clipboard with a list of kids' names on it. (I copy and paste my class lists from our online attendance-taking software into a spreadsheet so that all the students I teach are on a single sheet of paper.)

When I'm randomly calling on students, I use the stack of index cards to ensure that I'm working through the whole class list. When I'm tracking participation in a whole-class Pop-Up Debate, I use the clipboard to mark who has spoken. When there's a lull in the debate, I call on the names that haven't been marked yet.

There are other techniques out there (e.g., Erik Palmer, n.d., suggests giving poker chips to students when they walk into the room and then having students "spend" those chips each time they speak), but the key, to me, is that you have some way of ensuring that all of your students—not just the ones who raise their hands—are speaking for the whole class to hear on a regular basis. The simpler your method for this, the better.

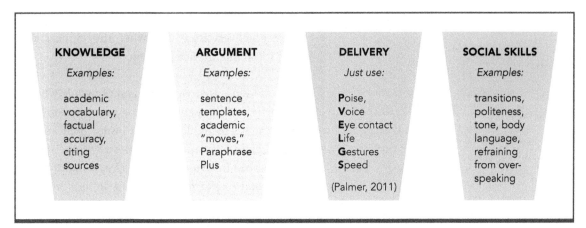

KNOWLEDGE	ARGUMENT	DELIVERY	SOCIAL SKILLS
Examples:	Examples:	Just use:	Examples:
academic vocabulary, factual accuracy, citing sources	sentence templates, academic "moves," Paraphrase Plus	**P**oise, **V**oice **E**ye contact **L**ife **G**estures **S**peed (Palmer, 2011)	transitions, politeness, tone, body language, refraining from over-speaking

FIGURE 7.3 • Buckets of Speaking Instruction

With those three structures in place—Pop-Up Debate, Conversation Challenge, and Think–Pair–Share—and a means for keeping track of when and how frequently each of our students speaks, we can now stop worrying about getting proficient with dozens of strategies, and we can start settling in to becoming experts at three. I find that a relief—to know that I get to just zero in on three simple structures, for years. This is going to free me up to aggressively start targeting the *quality* of speaking my students produce.

QUALITY KEY 1: RESPONSIVE INSTRUCTION

The most critical principle in improving student speaking quality is responsivity. We need to look at and analyze where our students are weak, and we need to offer simple, clear instruction from there. Responsivity requires frequent reflection, as well, which is why these two Quality Keys walk side by side. However, you'll rarely find me hauling around a rubric during a speaking activity. Instead, to be as responsive as possible, I've got my clipboard and I'm listening to the kids, making note of things I'd like to push them to get better at. I want to identify where we need help. There are four "buckets" within which my observations typically fall: knowledge issues, argument issues, delivery issues, or issues with social skills (see Figure 7.3).

When I hear students misusing or misunderstanding a concept or academic vocabulary word, I make note of that as a knowledge issue. When they are difficult to follow or understand, that's often an argument problem—it's a problem with clearly presenting ideas. When their distracting behaviors are, like, um, driving me, like, insane, that's a delivery issue. And when they appear rude, "salty," or disengaged, that's a social intelligence problem.

The best way for me to create the sense that we're a group of people who are pushing ourselves as speakers (the identity belief) *and* the best way for me to show my students how to get better is by modeling what I want them to work on. For example, if I hear them repeatedly misusing the word *suffrage* to mean "suffering"—a knowledge issue—I can interrupt and say, *"Hey class, just a quick note here. I've heard a few of you getting confused about the word suffrage. Suffrage is one of our academic vocab words this unit, but it doesn't mean 'suffering'—it means 'the right to vote.' So if I wanted to use that word, I'd have to link our current conversation back to voting, something like, 'This reminds me of when the women's suffrage movement was happening in New Zealand.'"*

Knowledge or content issues are the easiest and quickest to solve. For the other buckets, I provide modeling and instruction as follows.

When students are struggling with argument, their thinking is often difficult to follow. Sentence templates work best here, and the most frequently used set of templates in my classroom are contained in the Paraphrase Plus set of speaking moves that I introduce early in the school year (see Chapter 4).

www.pvlegs.com

To access Erik Palmer's website, use the QR code or the URL above.

For delivery, I've found nothing better than PVLEGS, teacher and author Erik Palmer's (2011) brainchild. I introduce PVLEGS to my students around the end of the first quarter. By this time, students are well acquainted with the speaking structures I use, they are comfortable with one another, and those who began the year with a debilitating public speaking fear have learned to wrangle it into submission. I ask students to open their spiral notebooks and create a page labeled "Speaking Delivery: PVLEGS." I then ask them to write down the following information as I spend five or ten minutes explaining it. (Refer to Figure 4.5 in Chapter 4 for an anchor chart that summarizes PVLEGS.)

I end this mini lecture by asking students to quickwrite in response to the following prompt: Which element of PVLEGS do you think you struggle with most? Why do you think that is a struggle for you? Finally, I ask students to share their quickwrite with their partners, and then we launch into the day's Pop-Up Debate or Conversation Challenge. (Notice that this Think–Pair–Share activity is a form of reflection—Quality Key 2.)

In future speaking situations, I'll interrupt students to model particular elements of PVLEGS, doing this in front of the whole class and then explaining what I've done.

To help with social skills, as with all the other buckets, I watch for problems and then responsively teach or coach toward solving those. One common problem for students is how to get through situations that they describe as "awkward." There are many ways that so-called awkward moments are created: when a student gets overly heated in a conversation; when someone in the class pops up and says something completely off topic; when a partner in Think–Pair–Share refuses to speak. I often bring these problems to the whole class's consideration by first asking students to share anything they noticed in the preceding speaking activity that was awkward—and it could have been something they saw in their own group or pair or something they saw somewhere else. This generally brings forward some cases for us to problem solve as a class. I'll ask my students, "What can you do in a situation like this?" Often enough, students come up with answers that are just as good as my own, if not better.

My goal in treating social skills situations like this is to normalize situations in which social skills are needed. I want my kids to see that such analysis is a regular part of the constructive, flourishing life.

A Note on Feedback

You will notice that the kind of responsive instruction that I use in speaking situations has feedback woven into it. I believe that students grow as speakers in my class, mostly because I provide ample opportunities to speak, and these opportunities are strengthened through instruction and modeling with feedback embedded.

Sometimes, I will give individualized feedback—almost always, this happens as my students are leaving the room after a lesson. I'll key in on one student I want to speak with, and before he or she walks out the door I'll ask for a quick word. Sometimes, I just offer a specific word of encouragement (e.g., "Mariah, I noticed today that I didn't need to call on you during the Pop-Up Debate. You stood up on your own. Great job."). Other times, I'll give specific, critical attention (e.g., "Caleb, today you were frequently sillier than I thought you needed to be, and from what I could tell it lowered the overall quality of our debate. Is something going on? What can I do to help?").

What I will most frequently do, however, is give my students whole-class feedback, focusing on things that more than a few of us need to work on. To instill a family and team atmosphere, I ask all my students to record this feedback in their spiral notebooks. I want us all to be mindful of the things many of us need to work on and improve. Individualized feedback is certainly ideal, but it is not the only way to move students much further ahead.

QUALITY KEY 2: FREQUENT REFLECTION

If our students don't reflect on what they're learning about themselves as speakers, they're less likely to transfer that learning beyond the walls of our classrooms. To facilitate reflection, I provide frequent, efficient opportunities for my students to reflect on a given speaking event, and I occasionally give my kids a chance to watch their speaking performances via video.

Frequent, Efficient Self-Reflection

Whenever possible, I like to give my students three to five minutes to reflect on what they noticed about their individual speaking performance in a given day's exercise. I commonly will also have them reflect on the group's performance as a whole, too. In this way, I seek to instill in my kids the idea that speaking is both individual and collective. It's the closest thing to a team sport that they'll find in academia. It's not enough for just *me* to be a great speaker; I need to look for ways to help the group out as well.

After a speaking event, we can help kids develop value, efficacy, and identify beliefs by giving them a chance to reflect, first in writing and then as a whole class. I find it best to start such times of reflection with a couple of minutes of reflective writing, and then to follow that with a whole-class debrief. This creates a strong sense among the class that, first, group speaking events are similar to a team sport and, second, we take the craft of speaking seriously in here. I frequently find that the skills I need to teach before our next speaking situation come out of these whole-class debriefs.

TRY THIS

Reflective writing and conversation after a speaking event.

Such reflection doesn't cost me much class time, and it serves as a multiplier to the speaking work I'll have my students do throughout the year. I think this happens because simple opportunities for reflection help my kids cultivate the key beliefs we explored in Chapter 2.

Painful, Gainful Reflection Via Video

Whenever my students see the camera set up prior to a Pop-Up Debate, many of them groan. This isn't an anxiety thing, per se—I never incorporate video recording earlier than late October, and my students know that we're not going to rewatch debates as a whole class or anything potentially embarrassing like that. Rather, my students groan because they know that they are going to have to watch their speech performance during our following lesson, and they know that this is typically a painful process.

There is probably no more powerful a way for me to provide feedback to my students as speakers than to teach them the basics of the four buckets outlined in Figure 7.3—not via lecture, of course, but via frequent speaking opportunities with lots of embedded, responsive instruction—and then to have them reflect on what they notice when they watch a video of themselves during a Pop-Up Debate. There are lots of neat ways to have kids watch themselves on tape, and with our ever-changing technology I don't want to get too nitty gritty here beyond these basic pointers:

- The type of camera you use isn't critical, but getting good audio is. Participants in my workshops for teachers often chuckle when I show them a video of a Pop-Up Debate. When I ask why, it's almost always because there's a kid running around from speaker to speaker holding on to a yardstick with a little wireless microphone attached. I can't tell you the science behind how lavalier mics work, but I can tell you that they're easily attached to a yardstick and they make it beautifully simpler to *hear* what everyone in a crowded room of kids is saying during a pop-up speech.

- I film through the whole pop-up event, and I advise students to mark down when, roughly, they speak during the day's debate or discussion. This way, they'll be able to more quickly find their part in the clip when we access it the next school day.

- To protect my students' privacy, I upload Pop-Up Debate videos to my school-based Google Drive, and then I share that Google Drive file with my students through Google Classroom. That is a lot of Google, I know.

- One-to-one technology setup is critical for this kind of event because when each one of my students has a device through which he or she can access the previous day's debate video, I can set a timer for ten minutes and move on with the lesson after that. This one-to-one limitation is one of many reasons why I don't frequently have my students engage in this kind of video-based reflection.

I'll close this chapter with something a student shared after our most recent video-based reflection. We had finished watching the videos and writing reflectively about what we had seen, and I asked the class if a few people would like to share what was painful about the activity. A young man raised his hand and said, first, that he was surprised at how nervous he felt that he looked in the video. Yet he continued, saying, "Even though it was hard seeing myself look so nervous, I also realized that I said some really strong things in response to Michael's argument, and I came off as pretty respectful while I did it. I think that my nervousness helped me to do that—it actually made me more focused. So nervousness, then, can actually be a strength when it comes to public speaking. I never thought of that before."

I can't even count how many moments of awareness like this that the simple structures and practices in this chapter have produced for my students. It's not because I'm doing anything special as a teacher; rather, I'm allowing my students and I time and space to get good at this.

The Gist

Speaking and listening are often neglected in our literacy teaching. These life-critical skills become the hapless victims of assumicide: because our students, for the most part, enter our classrooms speaking and listening, we assume that we don't need to give them instructions, practice, and feedback in these areas. This costs us more than we're aware of in terms of how well our students engage in and value our classes, and it costs our students more than they're aware of, too. In the class that our shy or anxious students appreciate today because of its lack of public speaking, we find the culprit behind future, high-stakes failures in public speaking, whether on job interviews or first dates.

My solutions to this problem are, I hope, simple, predictable, and unoriginal. We first need to address quantity, and this can be done through the use of three kinds of speaking structures. And then we address quality through the simple no-paper-load means of responsive instruction, modeling, feedback, and reflection. In the speaking-rich classroom, all the other components of the Foundations for Flourishing bull's-eye are easier to work on.

Better Together

When we do the work of this chapter in teams, PLCs, or whole faculties, the benefits begin to multiply:

- It's one thing to normalize public speaking in my classroom; it's another when public speaking becomes a normal, instruction-supported activity throughout the school day. Even the use of shared language like Palmer's PVLEGS helps speaking instruction to stick for students in ways that it can't when teachers work in isolation.

- Some might fear that having an entire team, PLC, or school using only three structures for speaking could get boring for students. To this I would emphatically respond that students are not so simple! There are many ways to target the key beliefs underlying student engagement. In a school where teachers are working together to develop best practices around Conversation Challenges and Pop-Up Debates, there could actually be an increase in student engagement as kids could spend more time engaging with one another and course-relevant ideas rather than learning a bunch of different speaking structures.

- At team, PLC, or faculty meetings, teachers can take turns sharing videos of the speaking work that takes place in their classroom. Such videos serve as invaluable professional development for teachers, as they can observe the nuances that each individual teacher brings to even the same basic structures.

CHAPTER EIGHT

Onward and Upward

> *If priorities aren't incessantly simplified and clarified, they are always at the mercy of the next new thing.*
>
> **—MIKE SCHMOKER (2011, P. 16)**

> *Complexity interferes with turning knowledge into action.*
>
> **—JEFFREY PFEFFER AND ROBERT SUTTON (2000, P. 55)**

> *When I work with teachers, I propose the 5 percent rule—that each year they need to open 5 percent of their practice up to change, keeping the other 95 percent intact.*
>
> **—THOMAS NEWKIRK, IN GLOVER AND KEENE (2015, P. 217)**

We've covered a lot of territory together, and I now want to point you back to the Everest exercise we began with. Remember how I argued that our jobs are a lot harder than a mountain climber's? Well, I left out some really good news.

Even though our jobs this year are harder than Edmund Hillary and Tenzing Norgay's, they are *so much more meaningful*. Why do people climb Everest? Here are some reasons they give:

- "Because it's there," George Mallory once quipped.
- "Because I've climbed the other six continents' tallest peaks, and I need Everest to finish my list."
- "Because when I'm on a mountain, it's like all my problems fade away."

Everest climbers get to boast that they were there, all the rest of their days. Their grandkids get to be proud. They join an elite group. They achieve some level of personal greatness, sure, but ultimately their accomplishment serves little long-term societal good. Climbing Everest, it turns out, doesn't do much good at all.

Teaching, in its purest form, is almost the exact opposite. You achieve no real fame, and from an outsider's perspective it appears as though you're doing something anyone could do. But the real work of teaching isn't about *us* at all—it's about the students, about their long-term good, and about what that means for the world we all inhabit. The aim of our work isn't the top of some mountain or the right to say "I climbed that"; it's the long-term flourishing of young people, and thereby society. The Everest climber, faced with the toughest part of the climb in the Death Zone, has to look inside herself to find purpose in the endeavor; the teacher, in the throes of Survival Mode, needs only look at her students. What long-term good can come from our efforts this year, even when they seem fruitless? All *kinds* of good.

Consider the story of Matt de la Peña, decorated young adult and children's author. Growing up, Matt's identity wasn't rooted in writing—far from it. But something weird happened to Matt during his junior year in Ms. Blizzard's class. When everyone else was taking the exam, Ms. Blizzard told Matt that she had given him an "A" for the exam and that all she wanted him to do during the exam period was to write whatever he wanted. Afterward, Ms. Blizzard spoke to him once all the students had left, and she told him that she had given him this exercise because he was a great writer and she wanted to see what he'd produce given nothing but time and space. At the time, Matt thought his teacher was weird. It actually wasn't until three years later that Matt thought back on the experience, connected it with the college writing classes he was taking, and started to think of himself as a writer. Numerous bestsellers later, Matt still credits Ms. Blizzard for a key moment in his journey.

There are more classroom stories like this than there are stars in the sky, and that's the incredible thing about this job. Research has taught us a lot about teaching, but we still have *no real idea* if today we will say or do something to this kid or that one that has a positive effect some years down the road. There's no question that our work *might* help a kid flourish long-term; there are only questions of who and how and whether we'll ever know.

Yes, our work is more challenging than the Everest climbers'—but it's also so much more meaningful.

Each of the preceding six chapters is worthy of book-length treatment on its own; more important, the components of the *These 6 Things* bull's-eye are worthy of career-long study. I'm convinced of that. Despite the turbulent times of intense change we live in, I don't see how there will come a point in my career when it's not going to be handy having developed expertise in the cultivation of beliefs-based student motivation. When will I no longer need to bring to bear on my classes what I've learned about knowledge building? When will earnest and amicable argument become useless in the pursuit of the flourishing life? Will reading, writing, speaking, and listening become obsolete like Microsoft Windows 98 did? I don't think so.

What I know I've *not* created for you in the pages before this one is a perfect book on the aspects of learning that lead to long-term flourishing. I haven't. I don't have the wisdom or the expertise or the experience or the time in the literature that a master work on these topics would require. But I am confident that I've painted some lines on the path up to Everest for you; I'm sure that this book, should you take its bent toward both more learning for your students *and* less stress upon you, can make you a better, saner teacher.

Before we close, I'd like to end with some practical recommendations.

Pick a Project

When I lead workshops on this material, I like to save an hour or so at the end for teachers to actually move forward with a particular project in one of the areas of the bull's-eye. I think of teaching as a series of projects that we take on to push forward our practice and ensure that we're getting better every year. If you decide, like many teachers have, to try Pop-Up Debates in your classroom, that's a project. Commit to giving it enough time to get the hang of it—half a year or so, with seven to ten Pop-Up Debates—and while you're working on that project, keep the other areas of your practice stable. This project-based approach to professional development, when contained inside one of the six things treated in this book, helps faculty members move forward with professional interests while simultaneously aiming at the same bull's-eye as the rest of the school. You might have a project focused on reading, and mine might be on beliefs, but we're both working on a fixed set of things.

This project approach often helps us see the parts of our practice that are unsustainable. If the day-to-day is so time-consuming for us that we can't conceive of how we might add an exploratory project, then we're probably doing too much. In that case, I encourage you to take on a project of reduction. What can be satisficed? Where are your grading practices out of whack? (Chapter 6 can help with those things.)

But, of course, there are some teachers reading this book who can't possibly reduce—they've been given six preps, or they are micromanaged by their administrators, or something equally life-draining is taking place. In that case, I hope their administrators can read the next section.

Commit to This, and Nothing Else, for a Long Time

If you're a leader who truly wants your school to get better at writing throughout the school day, then this is something you've got to commit to, not for a month or a year, but for *years*. If you want knowledge building to happen more systematically and successfully, that's a years-long project. A benefit of the bull's-eye is that it provides a good place from which to launch enduring work at the whole-school or whole-system level. It's specific enough to keep us in the right sandboxes, but it's broad enough to challenge the highest and lowest performers in a school building.

If I had to place myself on a spectrum of performance in using this framework, I'd say that I'm somewhere in the middle. And that's not false humility—it's just me looking at how well I facilitate Pop-Up Debates, how far up the Pyramid of Writing priorities I am, and to what degree all of my students tomorrow will be believing the five Key Beliefs I need them to believe in my room.

But the better I get at the six areas of practice—and the better your teachers get—the better off I'll be and the better off my students will be. Indeed, along the way I don't need to freak out at all; I can just ask myself, on the hard days, *Am I working toward these six things*? If I am, then I'm guiding my students and myself up Everest.

I'm on the right path.

And I'm okay.

A Gift for You

First, I really appreciate your reading the whole book. Thank you. I know there are plenty of other things you could've done instead. In teaching, there always is. As a sign of my gratitude for the time and attention you've given my book, I want to give something to you.

For a set of videos that dive deeper into this book's material, just head to davestuartjr.com/t6t-gift.

I love teaching, and I plan to write for teachers for as long as I'm in the classroom. I hope we can continue the conversation about how to do better, saner work, and I hope you'll be in touch with any breakthroughs in your own classroom.

Acknowledgments

Without the people in this first paragraph, the life from which I write isn't possible, so I need to thank them first. Thank you to Jesus Christ, to whom I owe everything. May my work be an echo of Your excellence. Second, thank you to Crystal, whose sacrifices for the work I do far exceed my own. She earns no awards, and she receives no emails from thankful readers. And yet, her life's work is much more impressive than mine: Haddie, Laura, Marlena, and Dean. I love you, Crystal. (And I love you, kids! Your dad admires you so much.)

The staff and students of Cedar Springs give me far more daily inspiration, encouragement, and support than I deserve. Thank you all for your grace toward me and investment in me. I can still remember how dumb I felt around all of you when I first started—not much has changed! Anne and Ron, you are courageous leaders. Steve Seward, thank you for your mentorship. I'm also thankful for the staff of Thornapple-Kellogg Public Schools, who gave me a wonderful education growing up. The key beliefs were planted in me everywhere in that district.

Nearly six years ago, I decided that I wanted to write a book for teachers, so I started reading about how to do that, and I discovered that it was next to hopeless without some audience of my own. I didn't have one of those, so I started a blog called *Teaching the Core*. Initially, my goal was to help people (including me) who were struggling to wrap their heads around the Common Core and the freaking out that seemed to attend it. Little did I know, starting out, how much of a blessing it would be to write for earnest, like-hearted colleagues around the country and the world. It is for good reason that I've dedicated this book to them. Thank you.

I've talked through the material in this book at nearly one hundred different speaking events in almost half of the states in the United States over the past five years, so there are countless people whose in-person attention and questions and pushback have made this book better. I wish I knew all of their names, but the best I can do is thank them as a group. Here's a hearty thanks to folks who spent time with me in the following places, starting back in 2013: Allendale, MI; Harrah, OK; Lebanon, MO; Peterborough, NH; Royal Oak, MI; Grand Rapids, MI; Louisville, KY; Oak Brook Terrace, IL; Cleveland, OH; Independence, CA; Bishop, CA; Turlock, CA; Hartsburg, IL; Dublin, OH; New Lothrop, MI; Dearborn, MI; Sacramento, CA; Attica, NY; Eastern Illinois University in Charleston, IL; Rowan University in Glassboro, NJ; Parma, MI; Las Vegas, NV; St. Louis, MO; Mobile,

AL; Vancouver, WA; Bethel, WA; Plainwell, MI; Minneapolis, MN; Centralia, IL; Columbus, OH; Oshkosh, WI; Chicago, IL; Flint, MI; Desert Sands, CA; Round Rock, TX; Berwyn South, IL; Dubuque, IA; Grafton, MI; Austin, TX; DeSoto, MS; Atlanta, GA; Raleigh, NC; Cincinnati, OH; Murfreesboro, TN; Weston, MO; Turtle Lake, WI; Houston, TX; Beavercreek City, OH; Denver, CO; Palatine, IL; Normal, IL; Wausau, WI; Madison, WI; and Hailey, ID. (I'm still waiting for that invite to Hawaii . . .)

The first time I ever led professional development for teachers, it was because I was required to by a Lake Michigan Writing Project (LMWP) Invitational Summer Institute (ISI). That ISI was so formative for me. It was Lindsay Ellis, director of the LMWP, who told me, "You are not writing for publication. You are writing because it is a spiritual practice." I hold to that. Thank you also to Susan Mowers and Kari Reynolds, who co-led our institute with Lindsay that summer. This book grew from the practice of regular writing.

Finally, I've got an amazing publisher. Thanks most of all to the work that Lisa Luedeke did in cultivating me into a Corwin author. I've got a long way to go before I feel like I belong with such a strong publishing company, but I sure am honored to be a part. Two authors, in particular, helped me decide on Corwin Literacy: ReLeah Cossett Lent and Jim Burke. Corwin found great reviewers for my initial manuscript, too: I'm indebted to the exhaustive feedback of Eddie Johns, Erica Beaton, Gerard Dawson, Lydia Bowden, Jennifer Wheat Townsend, and Marsha Voigt. Tori Bachman was a godsend at just the right time, and she and I shared a special experience: mine was her first book at Corwin Literacy, too. The main difference between Tori and me is that I'm a rookie, and she's a pro—there are many times when she talked me out of insanity. This book is so much sharper (and I am much saner) because of her. Thank you! A special thank you, as well, to the many people at Corwin Literacy who worked to put this book in teachers' hands: Diana Breti, Gail Buschman, Wendy Jo Dymond, Laureen Gleason, Brian Grimm, Julie Nemer, Amy Schroller, Maria Sosnowski, Maura Sullivan, and Sharon Wu.

For the introduction, I owe a debt of gratitude to Edmund Hillary and Tenzing Norgay, whose iconic achievement provides me with a metaphor I use all the time. Mike Schmoker's comments on a later draft of the chapter made it sharper and more focused. Tori Bachman came up with "Everest Island," a term I like a lot. The following people contributed Everest sentences in response to my query, but due to unexpected constraints I wasn't able to include them: Luke Wilcox, Lisa Vahey, Chris Vander Ark, Dana Schmaling, Jane Tawel, Eddie Johns, Leslie Lucas,

Jenna Bragas, Sarah Garcia, Jennifer Baker, Heather Quinn, Kim Rensch, Janelle Miles, Celia Duran, Trisch Vessar, Todd Finley, Liz Coman, and Diane LaGrone.

For the key beliefs chapter, I've got to go back years ago to when my colleague Steve Vree pointed me to a Paul Tough article in the *New York Times*. Tough's writing got me thinking (and writing, and speaking) about character, and it also eventually pointed me toward Camille Farrington et. al.'s (2012) seminal *Teaching Adolescents to Become Learners*, where four of the five key beliefs are found. (Camille was also helpful when I emailed with questions.) Lisa Luedeke sent me a copy of Fisher, Frey, and Hattie's (2016b) *Visible Learning for Literacy*, and that book mentioned teacher credibility in a way that turned the light bulb on for me. Penny Kittle gave feedback on a section that featured her work, and she gave me the permission I unconsciously needed to remove that section. I'd still want my kids in your classes, Penny.

Character Lab, an organization that seeks to bridge the gap between character research and teacher practice, is owed a special thank you for this chapter. My colleague Tanya Ramm forwarded me a Character Lab grant opportunity several years ago, and that grant gave me the chance to learn about research at a workshop led by Angela Duckworth. Even better, it put me in close touch for a year with the brilliant Michelle McNamara, whose friendship has made me a lot smarter. Character Lab's annual Educator Summit also connected me with Chris Hulleman, Theresa Hulleman, and Meg Foran, three people who directly improved the Build Connections portion of this chapter. Ethan Kross and Matt Kraft were two other researchers I corresponded with while writing this chapter—thank you.

Finally, Brian Davidson of the Intrinsic Institute in Olathe, KS, gave me sage advice one summer over beer and BBQ, telling me that I should *not* use the label "non-cognitive factors" for this part of the bull's-eye. That was really good advice, Brian.

For the knowledge chapter, *Make It Stick* (Brown, Roediger, & McDaniel, 2014) was a critical read for me several years ago, and I wouldn't have read it were it not for the recommendations of Jenn Gonzalez, of CultofPedagogy.com, and Erica Beaton, of EricaLeeBeaton.com. Also, my principal Anne Kostus was nice enough to buy me a copy. Bill Strickland of East Grand Rapids taught me to balance knowledge and skill at an AP Summer Institute. Daniel Willingham's articles on knowledge are a treasure trove of the internet—everyone needs to visit Dan's website. Mike Schmoker's thoughts on reducing standards gave me permission I needed, years ago, to focus. The LMWP introduced me to the idea of "burning questions," which planted the seed in my mind for what would eventually become BQYs.

For the argument chapter, Jerry Graff and Cathy Birkenstein have become good friends, and their work continues to guide me. Lindsay Ellis gave me a last minute insight when we met in St. Louis; her writing on pragma-dialectics helped me clarify "earnest and amicable arguments," and Erica Beaton helped me land on the word *amicable*. Les Lynn is the debate-infused pedagogy genius over at *Argument-Centered Education*—I am not worthy to mention the word *debate* in his presence. Mike Schmoker and Jerry Graff wrote an article for *Ed Leadership* years ago that prompted me to host my first in-class debate—from there, eventually, grew Pop-Up Debates, Paraphrase Plus, and so on. Shelley Alvarez, friend and colleague, was instrumental in helping me relocate the Caulkins epigraph.

For the reading chapter, reviewer Lydia Bowden of Georgia gave withering feedback that ultimately made the chapter much, much better. I want Lydia to review all my books now. Thank you, too, to the several hundred people who have taken my online professional development course "Teaching With Articles"—their conversations in the course have made me smarter.

For the writing chapter, I've got to start by nodding again to the LMWP, where I learned to teach writing by practicing writing. That logic has stuck somewhere deep inside me. Perini, Dewing, and Silver's (2012) "writing to learn" concept in *The Core Six* has been seminal for me. The science teachers at Flint Powers Catholic High School let me participate in a seriously inspirational meeting where they demonstrated how writing throughout the school day can be a lot better and saner than it tends to be. Finally, Jim Burke, an ever-faithful friend and mentor, coached me through writing parts of the book like this one that I did not feel "ready" for.

For the speaking chapter, just Erik Palmer. Nobody writes books on teaching speaking like that guy. Actually, almost nobody writes books on teaching speaking at all. That's a problem that Erik made me aware of and that Erik is helping to fix. Thank you.

A few final notes: Barrett Brooks coached me to do this book. Thank you for your friendship, Barrett, which has kept me superglued to *why* I write. Rachael Farwell faithfully proofreads for all the moronic errors I make as a writer. Thank you, Rachael, for making my work look better than it does when I'm done with it. And finally, thank you to my parents, who believe in me and spend a lot of time loving on my children, which makes it more possible for me to write and travel. I love you guys.

References and Recommended Readings

Achebe, C. (1958). *Things fall apart*. New York, NY: Random House.

Adler, M., & Van Doren, C. (1940). *How to read a book: The classic guide to intelligent reading*. New York, NY: Simon & Schuster.

Adriaanse, M. A., Oettingen, G., Gollwitzer, P. M., Hennes, E. P., de Ridder, D. T. D., & de Wit, J. B. F. (2010). When planning is not enough: Fighting unhealthy snacking habits by mental contrasting with implementation intentions. *European Journal of Psychology, 40*, 1277–1293. doi:10.1002/ejssp.703

Agrawal, S., & Hastings, M. (2015). Lack of teacher engagement linked to 2.3 million missed work days. *Gallup*. Retrieved from http://www.gallup.com/poll/180455/lack-teacher-engagement-linked-million-missed-workdays.aspx

Amicable. (2018). *Oxford Dictionaries*. Retrieved from https://en.oxforddictionaries.com/definition/amicable

Arthur, J. & Case-Halferty, A. (2008). Review of Graff and Birkenstein, They Say/I Say. *Composition Forum*. Retrieved from http://compositionforum.com/issue/18/they-say-i-say-review.php

Barker, E. (2015). A Navy SEAL explains 8 secrets to grit and resilience. *Barking Up the Wrong Tree*. Retrieved from http://www.bakadesuyo.com/2015/01/grit/

Beaton, E. L. (2015). Five steps to memorizing the "big picture" of US history. *EricaLeeBeaton.com*. Retrieved from http://www.ericaleebeaton.com/five-steps-to-memorizing-the-big-picture-of-us-history/

Beaton, E. L. (2016). I've been thinking a lot lately about Savannah. *EricaLeeBeaton.com*. Retrieved from http://www.ericaleebeaton.com/ive-been-thinking-a-lot-lately-about-savannah/

Beers, K., & Probst, R. (2013). *Notice and note: Strategies for close reading*. Portsmouth, NH: Heinemann.

Bjork, R. A., & Koriat, A. (2005). Illusions of competence in monitoring one's knowledge during study. *National Center for Biotechnology Information, 31*, 187–194. doi:10.1037/0278-7393.31.2.187

Blad, E. (2016). Mindset a key factor in student success. *Education Week, 35*(37). Retrieved from https://www.edweek.org/ew/articles/2016/08/03/mindset-a-key-factor-in-student-success.html

Blad, E. (2017). The unexpected reason some students procrastinate. *Education Week*. Retrieved from http://blogs.edweek.org/edweek/rulesforengagement/2017/08/why_students_procrastinate-self-handicapping.html

Brennan, E. (2017, March 20). *No imposters among this Sweet 16*. Retrieved from http://www.espn.com/mens-college-basketball/story/_/id/18956871/no-mistakes-sweet-16-2017-ncaa-tournament

Briceno, E. (2012). *The power of belief: Mindset and success* [Video]. Retrieved from https://www.youtube.com/watch?v=pN34FNbOKXc

Britton, J. (1983). Writing and the story of the world. In B. M. Kroll & C. G. Wells (Eds.), *Explorations in the development of writing: Theory, research, and practice* (pp. 3–30). New York, NY: Wiley.

Brown, P., Roediger III, H., & McDaniel, M. (2014). *Make it stick: The science of successful learning.* Boston, MA: Bellknap Press.

Brunner, J. (1960). *The process of education.* Cambridge, MA: The President and Fellows of Harvard College.

Bryson, B. (2003). *A short history of nearly everything.* New York, NY: Broadway Books.

Burke, J. (2003). *Writing reminders: Tools, tips, and techniques.* Portsmouth, NH: Heinemann.

Burke, J. (2018). *The 6 academic writing assignments: Designing the user's journey.* Portsmouth, NH: Heinemann.

Burke, J., & Gilmore, B. (2015). *Academic moves for college and career readiness, grades 6–12: 15 must-have skills every student needs to achieve.* Thousand Oaks, CA: Corwin.

Cain, S. (2013). *Quiet: The power of introverts in a world that can't stop talking.* New York, NY: Broadway Paperbacks.

Cain, S., Mone, G., & Moroz, E. (2017). *Quiet power: The secret strengths of introverted kids.* New York, NY: Puffin Books.

Calkins, L., Ehrenworth, M., & Taranto, A. (2013). *The research-based argument essay: Argument, grade 4, unit 4.* Portsmouth, NH: Heinemann.

Carey, B. (2015). *How we learn: The surprising truth about when, where, and why it happens.* New York, NY: Random House.

Carty, J., & Wooden, J. (2005). *Coach Wooden's pyramid of success.* Grand Rapids, MI: Revell.

Cepeda, E. (2012). The writing's on the wall in lack of writing proficiency. *Bakersfield .com.* Retrieved from http://www.bakersfield.com/opinion/esther-cepeda-the-writing-s-on-the-wall-in-lack/article_86397b49-0fac-56a3-beeb-c3c38a836414.html

Character Lab. (n.d.). Social/emotional intelligence. *Character Lab.* Retrieved from https://characterlab.org/tools/social-emotional-intelligence

Clear, J. (2015). *Surprising power of small habits* [Video]. Retrieved from http://jamesclear.com/keynote-speaker

Cole, B. (2003). David McCullough interview: The title always comes last. *National Endowment for the Humanities.* Retrieved from https://www.neh.gov/about/awards/jefferson-lecture/david-mccullough-interview

The College Board. (2004). *Writing: A ticket to work . . . or a ticket out.* New York, NY: Author.

The College Board. (2017a). *AP world history course and exam description.* New York, NY: Author. Retrieved from https://secure-media.collegeboard.org/digitalServices/pdf/ap/ap-world-history-course-and-exam-description.pdf

The College Board. (2017b). *Rubrics for AP histories.* New York, NY: Author. Retrieved from https://apcentral.collegeboard.org/pdf/rubrics-ap-histories.pdf

Collins, J. (2001). *Good to great: Why some companies make the leap and others don't.* New York, NY: HarperCollins.

Conley, D. T. (2007). The challenge of college readiness. *Educational Leadership, 64,* 23–29. Retrieved from http://www.ascd.org/ASCD/pdf/journals/ed_lead/el200704_conley.pdf

Conley, D. T. (2012). A complete definition of college and career readiness. *Educational Policy Improvement Center.* Retrieved from http://www.avid.org/dl/eve_natcon/nc12_four_keys_handout2.pdf

Conley, D. T. (2014). *Getting ready for college, careers, and the Common Core: What every educator needs to know.* San Francisco, CA: Jossey-Bass.

Conley, D. T. (2015). *Renaming noncognitive skills to emphasize success.* Retrieved October 04, 2016, from http://blogs.edweek.org/edweek/learning_deeply/2015/08/whats_in_a_name _redux_how_about_success_skills.html

Core Knowledge Foundation. (2013). *Core knowledge sequence: Content and skill guidelines for grades K–8.* Charlottesville, VA: Author. Retrieved from https://3o83ip44005z3mk17t31679f-wpengine.netdna-ssl.com/wp-content/uploads/2016/09/CKFSequence_Rev.pdf

Coyle, D. (2012). *The little book of talent: 52 tips for improving your skills.* New York, NY: Bantam Books.

Cunningham, A. E., & Stanovich, K. E. (1998). What reading does for the mind. *American Federation of Teachers.* Retrieved from https://www.aft.org/sites/default/files/periodicals/cunningham.pdf

Daniels, H., & Steineke, N. (2014). *Teaching the social skills of academic interaction: Step-by-step lessons for respect, responsibility, and results.* Thousand Oaks, CA: Corwin.

Dominguez, C., McMillan, G., Vidulich, M., & Vogel, E. (1994). Situation awareness: Papers and annotated bibliography [Abstract]. *Defense Technical Information Center.* (Accession No. ADA248752).

Duckworth, A. (2016). *Grit: The power of passion and perseverance.* New York, NY: Scribner.

Duckworth, A. L., Grant, H., Loew, B., Oettingen, C., & Gollwitzer, P. M. (2011). Self-regulation strategies improve self-discipline in adolescents: Benefits of mental contrasting and implementation intentions. *Education Psychology, 31,* 17–26. https://dx.doi.org/10.1080/01443410.2010.506003

Dweck, C. S. (2007). *Mindset: The new psychology of success.* New York, NY: Ballantine Books.

Earnest. (2018). *Oxford Dictionaries.* Retrieved from https://en.oxforddictionaries.com/definition/earnest

Easton, J. Q., Johnson, E., & Sartain, L. (2017). *The predictive power of ninth-grade GPA.* Chicago, IL: University of Chicago Consortium on School Research.

Ehrlich, S. B., Farrington, C. A., Heath, R. D., & Nagaoka, J. (2015). *Foundations for young adult success: A developmental framework.* Retrieved from http://www.wallacefoundation.org/knowledge-center/Documents/Foundations-for-Young-Adult-Success.pdf

EL Education. (2015). *Dr. Camille Farrington keynote EL Education National Conference 2015* [Video]. Retrieved from https://vimeo.com/144690888

Ellis, L. M. (2015). A critique of the ubiquity of the Toulmin model in argumentative writing instruction in the U.S.A. In F. van Eemeren & B. Garssen (Eds.), *Scrutinizing argumentation in practice* (pp. 201–213). doi:10.1075/aic.9.11ell

Ericsson, A., & Pool, R. (2016). *Peak: Secrets from the new science of expertise.* New York, NY: Houghton Mifflin Harcourt.

Farrington, C. A., Roderick, M., Allensworth, E., Nagaoka, J., Keyes, T. S., Johnson, D. W., & Beechum, N. O. (2012). *Teaching adolescents to become learners. The role of noncognitive factors in shaping school performance: A critical literature review.* Chicago, IL: University of Chicago Consortium on Chicago School Research.

Fisher, D., & Frey, N. (2013) *Rigorous reading: Five access points for comprehending complex texts.* Thousand Oaks, CA: Corwin.

Fisher, D., & Frey, N. (2015). *Text-dependent questions*: Pathways to close and critical reading, grades 6–12. Thousand Oaks, CA: Corwin.

Fisher, D., Frey, N., & Hattie, J. (2016a). Surface, deep, and transfer? Considering the role of content literacy instructional strategies. *Wiley Online Library, 60*(5), 567–575. doi:10.1002/jaal.576

Fisher, D., Frey, N., & Hattie, J. (2016b). *Visible learning for literacy, grades K–12: Implementing the practices that work best to accelerate student learning.* Thousand Oaks, CA: Corwin.

Fletcher, J. (2015). *Teaching arguments: Rhetorical comprehension, critique, and response.* Portland, ME: Stenhouse.

Fredricksen, J., Smith, M., & Wilhelm, J. (2012). *Oh, yeah?!: Putting argument to work both in school and out.* Portsmouth, NH: Heinemann.

Fulkerson, R. (1996). *Teaching the argument in writing.* Urbana, IL: National Council of Teachers.

Gallagher, K. (2004). *Deeper reading: Comprehending challenging texts, 4–12.* Portland, ME: Stenhouse.

Gallagher, K. (2009). *Readicide: How schools are killing reading and what you can do about it.* Portland, ME: Stenhouse.

Gallagher, K. (2011). *Write like this: Teaching real-world writing through modeling and mentor texts.* Portland, ME: Stenhouse.

Gallagher, K. (2015). *In the best interest of students: Staying true to what works in the ELA classroom.* Portland, ME: Stenhouse.

Gallo, C. (2015). *Talk like TED: The 9 public-speaking secrets of the world's top minds.* New York, NY: St. Martin's Griffin.

Gewertz, C. (2017). Who gets hurt when high school diplomas are not created equal? *Education Week.* Retrieved from http://blogs.edweek.org/edweek/high_school_and_beyond/2017/08/who_gets_hurt_when_high_school_diplomas_are_not_created_equal.html

Gladwell, M. (2008). *Outliers: The story of success.* New York, NY: Little, Brown and Company.

Glover, M., & Keene, E. O. (2015). *The teacher you want to be: Essays about children, learning, and teaching.* Portsmouth, NH: Heinemann.

Godin, S. (2013). People like us do things like this. *Seth's Blog*. Retrieved from http://sethgodin.typepad.com/seths_blog/2013/07/people-like-us-do-stuff-like-this.html

Gordon, B. (2017). *No more fake reading: Merging the classics with independent reading to create joyful, lifelong readers*. Thousand Oaks, CA: Corwin.

Graff, G. (2001). Hidden intellectualism. *Pedagogy, 1*(1), 21–36. Retrieved from https://muse.jhu.edu/article/26320

Graff, G. (2003). *Clueless in academe: How schooling obscures the life of the mind*. New Haven, CT: Yale University Press.

Graff, G. (2009, January 13). "It's time to end 'courseocentrism.'" Retrieved from https://www.insidehighered.com/views/2009/01/13/its-time-end-courseocentrism

Graff, G., & Birkenstein, C. (2014). *They say, I say: The moves that matter in academic writing*. New York, NY: W. W. Norton & Company.

Graff, G., & Birkenstein, C. (2017). *They say, I say: The moves that matter in academic writing*. Paper presented at the invitation of the Chippewa River Writing Project, Mount Pleasant, MI.

Graham, S., & Hebert, M. (2010). *Writing to read: Evidence for how writing can improve reading. A Carnegie Corporation Time to Act Report*. Washington, DC: Alliance for Excellent Education.

Graham, S., & Perin, D. (2007). *Writing next: Effective strategies to improve writing of adolescents in middle and high schools. A report to the Carnegie Corporation of New York*. Washington, DC: Alliance for Excellent Education. Retrieved from https://www.carnegie.org/media/filer_public/3c/f5/3cf58727-34f4-4140-a014-723a00ac56f7/ccny_report_2007_writing.pdf

Gray, P. (2010). The decline of play and rise in children's mental disorders: There's a reason kids are more anxious and depressed than ever. *Psychology Today*. Retrieved from https://www.psychologytoday.com/blog/freedom-learn/201001/the-decline-play-and-rise-in-childrens-mental-disorders

Gross-Loh, C. (2016). How praise became a consolation prize. *The Atlantic*. Retrieved from https://www.theatlantic.com/education/archive/2016/12/how-praise-became-a-consolation-prize/510845/

Halvorson, H. G. (2012). *Nine things successful people do differently*. Boston, MA: Harvard Business Review Press.

Hamm, T. (2008). The difference between a job and a career. *The Simple Dollar*. Retrieved from http://www.thesimpledollar.com/the-difference-between-a-job-and-a-career/

Harris, A., & Harris, B. (2008). *Do hard things: A Teenage rebellion against low expectations*. Colorado Springs, CO: Multnomah Books.

Hattie, J. (2012). *Visible learning for teachers: Maximizing impact on learning*. New York, NY: Routledge.

Heckman, J. J., Humphries, J. E., & Kautz, T. (2014). *The myth of achievement tests: The GED and the role of character in American life*. Chicago, IL: University of Chicago Press.

Hendrick, C. (2016). Why schools shouldn't teach critical thinking. *The Week*. Retrieved from http://theweek.com/articles/665551/why-schools-shouldnt-teach-critical-thinking

Hirsch, E. D., Kett, J. F., & Trefil, J. (2002). *The new dictionary of cultural literacy: What every American needs to know.* New York, NY: Houghton Mifflin.

Hirsch Jr., E. D. (2006a). Building knowledge: The case for bringing content into the language arts block and for a knowledge-rich curriculum core for all children. *American Federation of Teachers.* Retrieved from https://www.aft.org/periodical/american-educator/spring-2006/building-knowledge

Hirsch Jr., E. D. (2006b). *The knowledge deficit: Closing the shocking education gap for American children.* New York, NY: Houghton Mifflin.

Hirsch Jr., E. D. (2016). *Why knowledge matters: Rescuing our children from failed educational theories.* Cambridge, MA: Harvard Education Press.

Housel, M. (2014). The peculiar habits of successful people. *USA Today.* Retrieved from https://www.usatoday.com/story/money/personalfinance/2014/08/24/peculiar-habits-of-successful-people/14447531/

Hulleman, C. (2015). I could be changing the world right now, but instead I'm solving for X: Finding value in classwork and why it matters. *Medium.* Retrieved from https://medium.com/@chris.hulleman/i-could-be-changing-the-world-right-now-but-instead-i-m-solving-for-x-599b7ce7e4a3

Hulleman, C. S., & Harackiewicz, J. M. (2009). Promoting interest and performance in high school science classes. *Science, 326,* 1410. doi:10.1126/science.1177067

Irvin, J. L. (2017). The role of content knowledge in reading comprehension. *The Exchange, 29*(2), 2–4. Retrieved from http://www.secondaryreadinginterestgroup.com/uploads/5/9/5/5/59552319/the_exchange_spr2017.pdf

Johnston, H. (2012). *The spiral curriculum.* Tampa, FL: Education Partnerships.

Kidd, D. C., & Castano, E. (2013). Reading literary fiction improves theory of mind. *Science, 342*(6156), 377–380. doi:10.1126/science.1239918

Killian, S. (2017). Teacher credibility: Why it matters and how to build it. *The Australian Society for Evidence-Based Teaching.* Retrieved from http://www.evidencebasedteaching.org.au/teacher-credibility/

Kittle, P. (2008). *Write beside them: Risk, voice, and clarity in high school writing.* Portsmouth, NH: Heinemann.

Kittle, P. (2010, March 15). *Why students don't read what is assigned in class* [Video]. Retrieved from https://www.youtube.com/watch?v=gokm9RUr4ME

Kittle, P. (2013). *Book love: Developing depth, stamina, and passion in adolescent readers.* Portsmouth, NH: Heinemann.

Kraft, M. A., & Rogers, T. (2014). The underutilized potential of teacher-to-parent communication: Evidence from a field experiment. *Harvard Kennedy School.* Retrieved from https://scholar.harvard.edu/files/mkraft/files/kraft_rogers_teacher-parent_communication_hks_working_paper.pdf

Lemov, D. (2014). *Teach like a champion 2.0: 62 Techniques that put students on the path to college.* San Francisco, CA: Jossey-Bass.

Lent, R. C. (2015). *This is disciplinary literacy: Reading, writing, thinking, and doing, content area by content area.* Thousand Oaks, CA: Corwin.

Lesesne, T. (2010). *Reading ladders: Leading students from where they are to where we'd like them to be.* Portsmouth, NH: Heinemann.

Levitin, D. J. (2015). *The organized mind: Thinking straight in the age of information overload.* New York, NY: Plume.

Lyman, F. (1981). *The responsive classroom discussion: The inclusion of ALL students.* College Park: University of Maryland.

Lynn, L. (2017a) Claims and counter-claims for use with the refutation two-chance activity. *Argument-Centered Education.* Retrieved from http://argumentcenterededucation .com/2017/02/15/claims-and-counter-claims-for-use-with-the-refutation-two-chance-activity/

Lynn, L. (2017b). Shaping arguments and the superhero square-off: Batman vs. Superman. *Argument-Centered Education.* Retrieved from http://argumentcenterededucation .com/shaping-arguments-and-the-superhero-square-off-batman-vs-spiderman/

Marzano, R. J. (2003). *What works in schools: Translating research into action.* Alexandria, VA: ASCD.

Marzano, R. J. (2009). The art and science of teaching: Six steps to better vocabulary instruction. *Educational Leadership, 67,* 83–84. Retrieved from http://www.ascd .org/publications/educational-leadership/sept09/vol67/num01/Six-Steps-to-Better-Vocabulary-Instruction.aspx

McGrew, S., Ortega, T., Breakstone, J., & Wineburg, S. (2017). The challenge that's bigger than fake news: Civic reasoning in a social media environment. *American Federation of Teachers.* Retrieved from https://www.aft.org/ae/fall2017/ mcgrew_ortega_breakstone_wineburg

McKeown, G. (2014). *Essentialism: The disciplined pursuit of less.* New York, NY: Crown Business.

Merton, R. K. (1968). The Matthew effect in science: The reward and communication systems of science are considered. *Science, 159*(3810), 56–63. Retrieved from http:// www.garfield.library.upenn.edu/merton/matthew1.pdf

Miller, J. (2006). *Cross-x: The amazing true story of how the most unlikely team from the most unlikely of places overcame staggering obstacles at home and at school to challenge the debate community on race, power, and education.* New York, NY: Farrar, Straus and Giroux.

Mindset Kit. (2015). Praise the process, not the person. *The Project for Education Research that Scales.* Retrieved from https://www.mindsetkit.org/topics/praise-process-not-person

NACE Staff. (2016). The attributes employers seek on a candidate's resume. *National Association of Colleges and Employers.* Retrieved from http://www.naceweb.org/talent-acquisition/candidate-selection/the-attributes-employers-seek-on-a-candidates-resume/

National Academy of Sciences. (2012). *A framework for K–12 science education.* Retrieved from http://www.nextgenscience.org/next-generation-science-standards

National Center for Education Statistics. (2008). *Fast facts: Graduation rates.* Retrieved October 8, 2016, from https://nces.ed.gov/fastfacts/display.asp?id=40

National Center for Education Statistics (2012). *The nation's report card: Writing 2011* (NCES 2012–470). Washington, DC: Institute of Education Sciences, U.S. Department of Education. Retrieved from https://nces.ed.gov/nationsreportcard/pdf/main2011/2012470.pdf

National Commission on Writing for America's Families, Schools, and Colleges. (2004). *Writing: A ticket to work . . . or a ticket out.* New York, NY: College Entrance Examination Board.

National Governors Association Center for Best Practices & Council of Chief State School Officers. (2010a). *Common core state standards for mathematics.* Washington, DC: Author.

National Governors Association Center for Best Practices & Council of Chief State School Officers. (2010b). *Common core state standards in English language arts and literacy.* Washington, DC: Author.

Oakley, B. (2014). *A mind for numbers: How to excel at math and science (even if you flunked algebra).* New York, NY: Penguin Group.

Oatley, K. (2011). *Such stuff as dreams: The psychology of fiction.* Hoboken, NJ: Wiley.

Oettingen, G. (2014). *Rethinking positive thinking: Inside the new science of motivation.* New York, NY: Penguin Random House.

Oettingen, G., Mayer, D., Sevincer, A. T., Stephens, E. J., Pak, H., & Hagenah, M. (2009). Mental contrasting and goal commitment: The mediating role of energization. *Personality and Social Psychology Bulletin, 35,* 608–622. doi:10.1177/0146167208330856

Oyserman, D. (2015). *Pathways to success through identity-based motivation.* New York, NY: Oxford University Press.

Palmer, E. (2011). *Well spoken: Teaching speaking to all students.* Portland, ME: Stenhouse.

Palmer, E. (2014). The forgotten language arts: Addressing listening & speaking. *Voices From the Middle, 22*(1), 70–73.

Palmer, E. (2016). *Good thinking: Teaching argument, persuasion, and reasoning.* Portland, ME: Stenhouse.

Palmer, E. (2017). *Own any occasion: Mastering the art of speaking and presenting.* Alexandria, VA: Association for Talent Development.

Palmer, E. (n.d.). *Effective communication with Erik Palmer* [Video]. Retrieved from https://my.hrw.com/content/hmof/language_arts/hmhcollections/resources/common/videoPlayer/index.html

Perini, M., Dewing, R., & Silver, H. (2012). *The core six: Essential strategies for achieving excellence with the Common Core.* Alexandria, VA: ASCD.

Pfeffer, J., & Sutton, R. (2000). *The knowing-doing gap: How smart companies turn knowledge into action.* Boston, MA: Harvard Business School Press.

Pink, D. H. (2009). *Drive: The surprising truth about what motivates us.* New York, NY: Riverhead Books.

Robb, L. (2014). *Vocabulary is comprehension: Getting to the root of text complexity.* Thousand Oaks, CA: Corwin.

Rotherham, A. J., & Willingham, D. (2009). 21st century skills: The challenges ahead. *ASCD, 67,* 16–21. Retrieved from http://www.ascd.org/publications/educational-leadership/sept09/vol67/num01/21st-Century-Skills@-The-Challenges-Ahead.aspx

Sacks, A. (2014). *Whole novels for the whole class: A student-centered approach*. San Francisco, CA: Jossey-Bass.

Schmoker, M. (1999). *Results: The key to continuous school improvement* (2nd ed.). Alexandria, VA: ASCD.

Schmoker, M. (2006). *Results now: How we can achieve unprecedented improvements in teaching and learning*. Alexandria, VA: ASCD.

Schmoker, M. (2011). *Focus: Elevating the essentials to radically improve student learning*. Alexandria, VA: ASCD.

Schmoker, M. (n.d.). Write more, grade less. *Mike Schmoker*. Retrieved from http://mike schmoker.com/write-more.html

Schroeder, A. (2009). *The snowball: Warren Buffett and the business of life*. New York, NY: Bantam Books.

Scutti, S. (2017). Yes, sitting too long can kill you, even if you exercise. *CNN.com*. Retrieved from https://www.cnn.com/2017/09/11/health/sitting-increases-risk-of-death-study/index.html

Seligman, M. (2012). *Flourish: A visionary new understanding of happiness and well-being*. New York, NY: Free Press.

Sparks, S. (2018). For teenagers, praising "effort" may not promote a growth mindset. *Education Week*. Retrieved from http://blogs.edweek.org/edweek/inside-school-research/2018/03/praising_effort_teenagers_growth_mindset.html

Stanford Graduate School of Business. (2012, May 10). *Encouraging a sense of belonging* [Video]. Retrieved from https://www.youtube.com/watch?v=—9xzUxOxpU

Stark, D. (2017). *Mechanics instruction that sticks: Using simple warm-ups to improve student writing*. Cedar Springs, MI: Dave Stuart Consulting.

Stuart Jr., D. (2014). *A non-freaked-out guide to teaching the common core: Using the 32 literacy anchor standards to develop college- and career-ready students*. San Francisco, CA: Jossey-Bass.

Stuart Jr., D. (2016). How long do you spend grading articles of the week? *DaveStuartJr .com*. Retrieved from http://www.davestuartjr.com/grading-articles-of-the-week/

Tough, P. (2013). *How children succeed: Grit, curiosity, and the hidden power of character*. New York, NY: Houghton Mifflin Harcourt.

Tough, P. (2016). *Helping children succeed: What works and why*. New York, NY: Houghton Mifflin Harcourt.

Toulmin, S. E. (1958). *The uses of argument*. New York, NY: Cambridge University Press.

Tucker, M. (2017). Getting social and emotional learning right. *Education Week*. Retrieved from http://blogs.edweek.org/edweek/top_performers/2017/07/getting_social_and_emotional_learning_right.html

Turkle, S. (2015). *Reclaiming conversation: The power of talk in a digital age*. New York, NY: Penguin Random House.

U.S. Citizenship and Immigration Services. (Jan 2017). *Civics (history and government) questions for the naturalization test*. Retrieved from https://www.uscis.gov/sites/default/files/USCIS/Office%20of%20Citizenship/Citizenship%20Resource%20Center%20Site/Publications/100q.pdf

U.S. Department of Education, National Center for Education Statistics. (2014). *Teacher attrition and mobility: Results from the 2012–13 Teacher Follow-Up Survey* (NCES 2014-077). Retrieved from http://nces.ed.gov/pubs2014/2014077.pdf

Visible Learning Partnership. (2017). 250+ Influences on student achievement. *Visible Learning Plus*. Retrieved from http://visiblelearningplus.com/sites/default/files/250%20Influences%20Final.pdf

Vygotsky, L. (1978). *Mind in society: The development of higher psychological processes.* Cambridge, MA: Harvard University Press.

Walker, T. D. (2016). The ticking clock of teacher burnout. *The Atlantic.* Retrieved from https://www.theatlantic.com/education/archive/2016/09/the-ticking-clock-of-us-teacher-burnout/502253/

Walton, G. (2012). *Encouraging a sense of belonging* [Video]. Retrieved from https://www.youtube.com/watch?v=--9xzUxOxpU

Wilcox, L. (2017). Top 5 strategies for motivating students. *LukeWilcox.org.* Retrieved from www.lukewilcox.org/blog/2017/6/6/top-5-strategies-for-motivating-students

Will, M. (2017). Educators are more stressed at work than average people, survey finds. *Education Week Teacher.* Retrieved from http://blogs.edweek.org/teachers/teaching_now/2017/10/educator_stress_aft_bat.html

Williams, J. M., & McEnerney, L. (n.d.). *Writing in college: A short guide to college writing.* Retrieved from https://writing-program.uchicago.edu/undergrads/wic1highschool

Willingham, D. T. (2002). Inflexible knowledge: The first step to expertise. *American Educator.* Retrieved from http://www.math.uri.edu/~eaton/HowDoWeLearn.pdf

Willingham, D. T. (2006a). Knowledge in the classroom. *American Federation of Teachers.* Retrieved from https://www.aft.org/periodical/american-educator/spring-2006/knowledge-classroom

Willingham, D. T. (2006b). The usefulness of brief instruction in reading comprehension strategies. *American Federation of Teachers.* Retrieved from https://www.aft.org/sites/default/files/periodicals/CogSci.pdf

Willingham, D. T. (2007). Critical thinking: Why is it so hard to teach? *American Educator,* 8–19. Retrieved from http://www.aft.org/sites/default/files/periodicals/Crit_Thinking.pdf

Willingham, D. T. (2009). Reading is not a skill—and why this is a problem for the Draft National Standards. *The Washington Post.* Retrieved from http://voices.washingtonpost.com/answer-sheet/daniel-willingham/willingham-reading-is-not-a-sk.html

Willingham, D. T. (2010). Have technology and multitasking rewired how students learn? *American Educator, 34,* 23–28. Retrieved from http://files.eric.ed.gov/fulltext/EJ889151.pdf

Willingham, D. T. (2017). You still need your brain. *The New York Times.* Retrieved from https://www.nytimes.com/2017/05/19/opinion/sunday/you-still-need-your-brain.html?mcubz=2

Wineburg, S., McGrew, S., Breakstone, J., & Ortega, T. (2016). Evaluating information: The cornerstone of civic online reasoning. *Stanford Digital Repository.* Retrieved from https://purl.stanford.edu/fv751yt5934

Wirt, J., Choy, S., Rooney, P., Provasnik, S., Sen, A., & Tobin, R. (2004). *The condition of education 2004* (NCES 2004-077). Washington, DC: U.S. Department of Education, National Center for Education Statistics. Retrieved from http://nces.ed.gov/pubs2004/2004077.pdf

Index

Note: Figures are indicated by *f* after the page number.

Sacrifice, 8

Sankey, Patty, 100

Satisfice, 164, 190–191, 192

Scaffolding, 50–51

Schmoker, Mike, 10, 147,
    166–167, 206

Schroeder, Alice, 48

SEALS, 56–57, 188–189

Seating charts, 43, 211–212

Self-efficacy. *See* Efficacy Belief

Self-reflection, 62 Stress, 9–10, 9f, 167

Seligman, Marty, 6–7

Seminal works, 16

Sen, A., 138

Sentence templates, 176–177

Short answer quizzes, 89, 90f

Shortest paths, 34

Signposting, 120–121, 121f

Silo speaking, 117

Silver, H., 172

Simon, Herbert, 164

Situational awareness, 70

Skull and crossbones lists,
    178–180, 179f

Social anxiety, 203–206,
    218–221, 227

Social skills, 139, 225

Societal flourishing, 7

Spaced practice, 93–97, 96f

Speaking/listening
    overview, 14–15, 14f
    Conversation Challenge for, 209f,
        212–216
    documentation prohibiting
        speaking, 204
    increasing amount of, 208–218,
        209f, 211f
    knowledge building and, 216
    need for, 205–207
    Pop-Up Debates for, 209f, 216–221
    professional development about, 229
    reflection and, 226–228
    resources for, 222

responsive instruction and,
    223–226, 223f
    Think-Pair-Share for, 208–212, 209f,
        211f, 218–219

Speaking tics, 216

Spiraling of content, 95

Standards, 107

Stark, Doug, 88

Steineke, N., 43, 210

Stereotype threats, 41

Stopwatch use, 194–196, 195f

Storytelling, 35, 38

Stress, 9–10, 9f, 167
    See also Social anxiety

Stuart, Dean Lewis, 21, 77–78, 78f

Survival Mode, 9f, 10

Sweet spots, 50–51

"Take a stand," 149–150

*Teaching Adolescents to Become
    Learners* (Farrington et al.), 27

Teaching Arguments (Fletcher), 129

Teach Like a Champion
    (Lemov), 34, 46

"Template for authentic
    literacy," 147

Templates, 147, 176–177

Testing effect, 85

Texting, 206

They Say, I Say method,
    124–125, 125f

Think-Pair-Share, 208–212,
    209f, 211f, 218–219

"Three Key Questions," 151

Toasts, 217–218

Tobin, R., 138

Tone of voice, 46

Topic immersion, 81, 84–85, 86f

Tracking of arguments,
    122–124, 123f
    See also Argument

Transition years, 40–41

Truth, 30

A SAGE Publishing Company

CORWIN HAS ONE MISSION: to enhance education through intentional professional learning.

We build long-term relationships with our authors, educators, clients, and associations who partner with us to develop and continuously improve the best evidence-based practices that establish and support lifelong learning.

CORWIN LITERACY

Douglas Fisher, Nancy Frey, John Hattie, and Marisol Thayre

High-impact strategies to use for all you teach—all in one place. Deliver sustained, comprehensive literacy experiences to Grades K–12 students each day.

Nancy Frey and Douglas Fisher

Nancy Frey and Douglas Fisher articulate an instructional plan for close reading so clearly, and so squarely built on research, that it's the only resource a teacher will need.

ReLeah Cossett Lent

This Is Disciplinary Literacy helps content-area teachers put into action the key literacies of their specialties—taking students from superficial understanding to deep content expertise.

Michael W. Smith and Jon-Philip Imbrenda

Forming effective arguments is essential to students' success in academics and life. This book's engaging lessons offer an innovative approach to teaching this critical transferable skill.

Nancy Akhavan

With 75 tasks on beautiful full-color pages, this book offers a literacy instruction plan that ensures students benefit from independent effort and engagement.

Douglas Fisher, Nancy Frey, Russell J. Quaglia, Dominique Smith, and Lisa L. Lande

Learn how focusing on relationships, clarity, and challenge can put you in control of managing your classroom's success, one motivated student at a time.

BECAUSE ALL TEACHERS ARE LEADERS

Nancy Frey, John Hattie, and Douglas Fisher

Imagine students who understand their educational goals and monitor their progress. This illuminating book focuses on self-assessment as a springboard for markedly higher levels of student achievement.

M. Colleen Cruz

By flipping the traditional "reading first, writing second" sequence, this innovative book lets you make the most of the writing-to-reading connection via more than 50 carefully matched paired lessons.

Berit Gordon

Discover how to transform your classroom into a vibrant reading environment. This groundbreaking book combines the benefits of classic literature with the motivational power of choice reading.

Patty McGee

Patty McGee helps you transform student writers by showing you what to do to build tone, trust, motivation, and choice into your daily lessons, conferences, and revision suggestions.

Leslie Blauman

Teaching Evidence-Based Writing: Fiction and *Nonfiction* help you educate students on how to do their best analytical writing about fiction and nonfiction. Whether annotating a text or writing a paragraph, an essay, or response on a test, your students will know how to support their thinking.

Gravity Goldberg and Renee Houser

With *What Do I Teach Readers Tomorrow? Fiction* and *Nonfiction*, discover how to move your readers forward with in-class, actionable formative assessment in just minutes a day with a proven 4-step process and lots of next-step resources.

800-233-9936

CORWIN
A SAGE Publishing Company